# THE GREEK
# HISTORIANS

# CIVILIZATION AND SOCIETY

Studies in Social, Economic, and Cultural History

**General Editor**

Theodore K. Rabb, Princeton University

**Consulting Editors**

Thomas W. Africa, State University of New York, Binghamton
David J. Herlihy, University of Wisconsin, Madison
David S. Landes, Harvard University
Henry Rosovsky, Harvard University
Stanley J. Stein, Princeton University
Stephan A. Thernstrom, University of Calfornia, Los Angeles

# THE GREEK HISTORIANS

TRUESDELL S. BROWN

University of California,
Los Angeles

D. C. HEATH AND COMPANY
Lexington, Massachusetts Toronto London

Published simultaneously in Canada.

Printed in the United States of America.

International Standard Book Number: 0-669-83881-0

Library of Congress Catalog Card Number: 72-13903

*To my very dear sister,*
*Margery Chandler*

# PREFACE

The reader should be warned that this is not intended to be a complete account of the Greek historians, but rather an attempt to indicate some of the important changes that took place in the writing of history from the old logographers down to the period of Roman supremacy. Greek historians with considerable talents continue to appear after the Roman conquest, but the spirit in which they wrote puts them in a different category from the men discussed in this volume. The old *historiē* was singularly bold and uncompromising, its practitioners wrote to please themselves without any worry about reprisals. This became increasingly difficult in later Hellenistic times when the monarch as the patron of the arts began to make his presence felt, but it becomes virtually impossible under Roman rule, not because of outright censorship but because contemporary political history as written by Thucydides no longer had any meaning. All the issues had been, or seemed to have been settled. The pursuit of antiquarian researches remained as a reputable but relatively tame intellectual exercise. The scholars who engaged in these researches might be men of great intellectual capacity—Posidonius for example—but they were not free men in the old tradition. The Greek, to be sure, never quite lost his sense of superiority. Critobulus, who lived at the time Constantinople fell to the Turks, wrote a history of the conqueror, Mohammed II, with the clear implication that his deeds would not be remembered unless they were celebrated in Greek! Therefore the Greek historical tradition never died out, but the loss of political freedom had a profound effect in modifying its tendencies. That is why I stop where I do.

Even within the chronological limits set there are historians well worth consideration who have been omitted or referred to only incidentally. To have included them all in the space available, would have been to fail to do justice to any.

I have tried to cite those to whom I am specifically indebted, in the notes, but some may have been forgotten inadvertently. My gratitude to those under whom I once studied—living and dead—is warmly felt even when it is not expressed.

# CONTENTS

# ILLUSTRATIONS

## PLATES

## MAPS

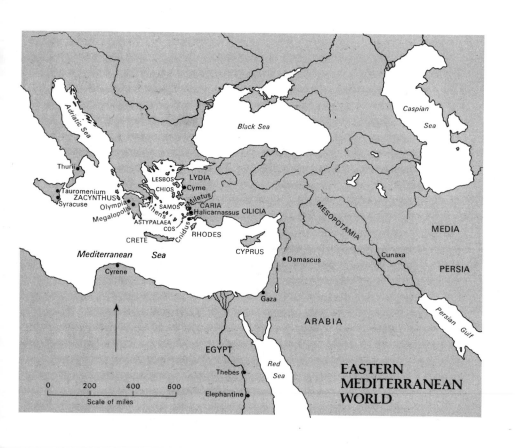

Adriatic Sea

Black Sea

Caspian Sea

Thurii

Tauromenium
Syracuse

ZACYNTHUS
Olympia
Megalopolis

LESBOS
CHIOS
Athens
SAMOS
ASTYPALAEA
COS
CRETE
Cnidus
RHODES

LYDIA
Cyme
Miletus
CARIA
Halicarnassus CILICIA

MESOPOTAMIA

MEDIA

Mediterranean    Sea

CYPRUS

Damascus

Cunaxa

PERSIA

Cyrene

Gaza

ARABIA

Persian Gulf

0    200    400    600

Scale of miles

EGYPT

Red Sea

Thebes

Elephantine

**EASTERN
MEDITERRANEAN
WORLD**

Had the ancient Greek historical writings come down to us intact, not only would our knowledge of classical antiquity be greatly enriched, but the present emphasis on certain periods and places would undoubtedly be modified. The extent of our loss may be guessed when we look at the collection of fragments of Greek historical works made by Professor Felix Jacoby. At the time of his death he had completed only three of the six sections into which he divided the texts, yet the number of historians had already reached eight hundred and fifty-six![1] In addition to the writers known to us in this incomplete fashion there must have been many others who have disappeared without leaving a trace. Confronted with such a statistic, our grandfathers might have argued that what we have lost was probably so badly written that it did not deserve to survive. But the most readable works, particularly the most readable histories, are not necessarily the best guides to the periods they depict. Furthermore, in antiquity, much more than in modern times, a book needed to be read in order not to disappear. The number of copies of any book, by our own standards, was very small, so that when a book was neglected for several generations it might be impossible to find an exemplar later on, when interest in the author had revived. This was shown in the Hellenistic period when librarians, with royal endowments behind them, were bidding against one another for rare books. Incidentally, their predicament helps to explain the appearance of many of the forgeries that still grace our shelves, works attributed to famous writers like Xenophon or Aristotle or Demosthenes, but actually written by an unknown.[2]

# THE PREHISTORIANS

The beginnings of Greek historical writing, however, take us back into a much earlier, less bookish era, when the question naturally arises as to what it was that made the Greeks curious about the past. We must remember that they were not the first people to write history: the Egyptians, the Babylonians, the Hittites, and the Assyrians all preceded them—to say nothing about the Chinese and perhaps other far eastern peoples—while the Jews were writing at least as early as the Greeks.

The problem of Greek origins has been unnecessarily confused by recent archaeological discoveries in Crete and the Aegean area. It is now thought that Greek was being written some five hundred years before the date that used to be accepted. Although no inscription in a Greek alphabet has been found earlier than 700 B.C., it has been convincingly argued that the writing Sir Arthur Evans labeled as Linear B was used to write Greek or—to satisfy the most doubting of Thomases—a tongue closely related to classical Greek.[3] Linear B is not an alphabetic script but a syllabary, and all that we have left was written on clay tablets not long before 1200 B.C. However, these precious documents were not intended for posterity, in fact their survival is the result of a series of tragic accidents: the fires that destroyed the palaces in which the records were kept also baked the raw clay tablets and made them virtually indestructible. The contents of these tablets, insofar as scholars have been able to agree about them, are not literary texts but inventories—perhaps tax records. They served the needs of the governmental bureaucracy of the palace states in Crete and on the Greek mainland. When the palace governments fell records of this kind were no longer required, so that the clerks who kept them found other employment and all knowledge of the script died when they did. This means that despite the very considerable influence exerted by the older civilizations of the Near East both upon Minoan and Mycenaean societies, for reasons unknown to us that influence stopped short of the introduction of writing for general use. Therefore, the tradition of the Near East for the writing of history had not made its way into Greek-speaking areas before the Phoenician alphabet was adopted, because until that time the Greeks themselves cannot accurately be described as literate.

Confusion still remains about when the alphabet was adopted, but for our purposes it is sufficient to know that the earliest Greek literature to be put in writing was epic poetry, with lyric poetry and literary prose coming some time afterwards.[4] Although the early prose writers (logographers) have often been spoken of with some contempt as mere compilers, in contrast with historians like Herodotus and Thucydides, this is not merely unfair but misleading. The paucity of the scattered references that are all that remain from these literary innovators undoubtedly presents a distorted impression of what they wrote, but it is worth the effort to try to give them some measure of justice.

At the outset it will be helpful to consider how the Greeks felt about poetry, and particularly epic poetry. The *Iliad* and the

*Odyssey* were so popular that at all periods in Greek history when a writer refers simply to "the poet," he means Homer. This is as though in our own day the author of the *Beowulf* or the *Song of Roland* enjoyed a similar distinction. The regard in which the Greek epic was held explains the great influence it had on other forms of literature, including history. In the sixth century B.C. the moralist Xenophanes was so much disturbed by what he thought of as the evil effects of such poetry, that he attacked Homer vehemently. Nearly two hundred years later we find another moralist, Plato, still worried over the bad influence of Homer on the younger generation. Nor was the great poet without his defenders, for as late as the time of Augustus we discover Strabo, who is quite a reputable authority, seething with indignation over criticisms of Homer as—of all things—a geographer.[5] The popularity of the heroic epic led to its prolongation in a series of later epics known to us only in a fragmentary way, but apparently the Greek literary critics never regarded them as belonging on the same level with the Homeric poems. One of these late epic poets, named Panyassis, will be mentioned again in the chapter on Herodotus.

Homer was not the only early poet to have an influence on later prose literature; there was also Hesiod, whose two most important poems were the *Theogony* and the *Works and Days,* both of which survive.[6] Hesiod attempts to do systematically what was only touched on incidentally in the heroic epic, that is to account for the existence of the world as we know it, from the origins of the gods themselves on down through the various ages of man to the present bleak Age of Iron. And Hesiod also must have had an appreciative following, for we find Plato denouncing him for his story of Cronus and Uranus—which Plato finds unfit for the ears of children. What is interesting and also characteristic of Greek thought is that Homer and Hesiod are never treated as purely fictional writers.[7] Thucydides, the very model of a critical historian, attempts to reconstruct the Trojan War from Homer,[8] and even Plato is not ready to say that Hesiod's tale about Cronus is untrue, only that it is improper. For a Greek, the mythological past was a part of history, differing from the more recent past only in that some exaggeration had crept in and marvelous details had been added. However, Nestor and Agamemnon, Heracles and Perseus were real people who acted from the same motives that affect men in historic times. In view of the fact that the heroic tales were regarded as dealing with real people, a knotty problem for the Greek prehistorians was that of sorting out a plethora of such tales, assigning each hero to a particular time and place. This meant working out a chronology for the entire mythical period. The language of myth is seldom precise in providing vital statistics, so that in their efforts to achieve some measure of consistency early scholars tended to group the heroes into generations, with perhaps three such generations to one hundred years.[9] Equally necessary was the establishment of genealogies, for Greek noble families everywhere claimed descent from one or more of these heroes. So varied were the stories told in different parts of the world about heroes who, like Heracles, enjoyed universal popularity, that great ingenuity was required to reconcile the obvious contradictions. One useful device was that of positing two or more heroes of the same name, but living at different times, for this enabled the investigator to avoid chronological absurdities. While this loophole was discovered by the prehistorian, it proved valuable to the historian too. Timaeus, for example, the celebrated third century historian, makes use of it to reconcile contradictory reports about the Spartan lawgiver Lycurgus, by suggesting that there were two men named Lycurgus who lived in Sparta at different times, and that one of them became so famous that he was credited not only with what he had done himself, but also with the deeds of his namesake![10] In a period like the present when "prosopography" has come into such favor with classical historians,[11] it is pleasant to reflect that this was also the approach of the Greek prehistorian: the marital ties of Greek heroes—sometimes it must be feared rather artificial ones—were used to link the generations together and to explain the alliances or the enmities of individuals or groups. But the single most important result of this sustained effort to establish a corpus of Greek mythology was that it taught scholars how to use literary evidence. Principles of criticism were developed that could be applied later to documents of a more reliable kind about the more recent past. When that happened it was time for the historian to make his appearance. Despite the persuasive arguments in Jacoby's *Atthis*[12] there remains some lingering doubt as to whether the first history written in Greek was a general history or a local one. Jacoby took up the cudgels reluctantly in order to challenge the contention of Wilamowitz, his own teacher, that historical writing in Athens arose from a chronicle kept by priestly officials called the *exegetae*. In this Jacoby was completely successful, and also he has made it seem probable that local chronicles were not written anywhere else until after the publication of Herodotus' work. He puts his thesis very clearly as follows:

*Any exact examination of the names, the time, and the purposes of the local historians shows the form to be related to the development of Great History and to the progress which this class of literature had made during the fifth century from Hekataios to Herodotos and Hellanikos, and from these authors to Thukydides and his successors in the fourth century: the relation is that of effect to cause. The species of the local chronicles came up because each individual city endeavoured to secure in*

*Greek history a place for herself, which Great Historiography did not assign to her. [He adds that] historical consciousness (in the narrower sense of the word) is not older than historical literature; and it is primarily directed to the history of the whole Hellenic people.*[13]

Jacoby goes on to say that local history was the last of the five main forms of history to appear, the other four being: genealogies and periegeses (both represented by Hecataeus), ethnographies, and chronographies and general Greek histories (or Hellenica). He finds Herodotus to be the earliest to write such a general history.

But Jacoby's approach is altogether too schematic. As von Fritz recently pointed out, the term local history is misleading when limited, as Jacoby limits it, to local chronicles. Yet some early local histories, like that of Ion of Chios, for example, were definitely not chronicles. Jacoby has merely shown that, at least in Athens, a local chronicle did not develop as the result of keeping official records.[14] Another weakness in this theory is that one of the chief motivations suggested by Jacoby for the writing of local history antedates what he calls "Great Historiography." A city might well be more upset over an unsatisfactory role in the Trojan War of the epic than in the Persian War of Herodotus.[15] Moreover, it is not accurate to speak of Herodotus' work as merely a Greek history. For him, as perhaps for no other Greek writer, the term *history* meant an inquiry into the past of all men, Greeks and barbarians alike. Jacoby has oversimplified the account of Greek historiography by concentrating his attention on an assumed main line of development: Hecataeus–Herodotus–Thucydides.[16] This is misleading, in that Herodotus certainly and Hecataeus probably each represents a high point in certain aspects of historiography. But now let us turn to another side of the story, the relationship between the Greek historians and the early Greek philosophers.

One of these philosophers, Anaximander of Miletus, is said to have written the first scientific work in Greek prose, and to have been sixty-four years of age at the time of the fifty-eighth Olympiad (or 547/546 B.C.). He died not long afterwards.[17] In the later tradition he is held to have been the pupil of Thales and the teacher of Anaximenes, a fate that might have been predicted for a philosopher who was thought to have lived in Miletus at a later date than Thales and before Anaximenes! For that is how the history of philosophy was written by lesser men in an unimaginative period. It is too bad that so little remains of the work of this daring thinker who not only theorized about the origins of the universe and about how life arose on our planet, but who also drew the first map of the world known to have been made by a Greek. The famous scholar Eratosthenes, writing in the third century B.C., evidently regarded Anaximander as the founder of scientific geography, for he refers to him and his younger contemporary Hecataeus of Miletus as the first geographers after Homer.[18] Historians would dearly love to recover the text of Anaximander's work, along with a copy of his map of the world. We are told that he thought of the earth as shaped like a rather squat cylinder (sometimes compared with the drum of a Doric column), with mankind living on one of the flat circular ends.[19] He was also credited with trying to explain both solar and lunar eclipses and with calculating the relative size of the earth and other heavenly bodies along with an estimate of the distances separating them.[20] The Babylonians had long concerned themselves with such matters and they had also tried their hands at producing a world map.[21] This is one area in which Greek obligations are clear and unmistakable. But Anaximander went beyond this. He also concerned himself with changes in the surface of the earth, with how land could emerge from water at the mouths of large rivers, and with the progressive desiccation of the earth.[22] Details need not be insisted on; what matters is that Anaximander attempts to explain our world without reference to divine agency. As was inevitable at the beginning of this scientific revolution, the natural causes stressed by Anaximander and his immediate successors act almost as arbitrarily as the gods on Olympus; but the first great step had been taken, that of basing speculation about the world on observation rather than tradition. This new attitude could not fail to have its effects also on the writing of history.

But let us not oversimplify this aspect of the origins of Greek historiography, for the Homeric poems were quite sophisticated in their religious tone. Zeus is no Old Testament god, he is in fact all too human. Nor can the behavior of Athena or Hera or Poseidon be put on a higher plane than that of the heroes who occasionally defied them. And of course that is why Xenophanes and Plato are so angry with Homer. But even in the Homeric poems themselves we hear echoes of higher criticism. In the beginning of the *Odyssey* Zeus is represented as haranguing his fellow gods on the subject of mankind. Men always blame the gods for anything that happens to them, without realizing that the responsibility is their own. As an example he cites Aegisthus who, despite being warned in advance by divine messenger to give up his murderous plan, went ahead with it anyway and must therefore be punished. Clearly, for the poet who wrote these lines there is a moral law which transcends the law of Zeus, and one by which the gods themselves are capable of being judged. Zeus feels the need to defend his actions—not so Yahweh! Therefore one effect of the epic on the future historian—and we will see this in Herodotus—is to impel him to find moral justification for the course of events; and that is not the same thing as attributing the results to the irresponsible actions of an angry deity.

And now it is time to consider the prose writers who may be thought of as the immediate predecessors of Herodotus. The most important of these is probably Hecataeus of Miletus. The following notice has been preserved by the author of a tenth century Byzantine lexicon called the *Suda*:[23]

*Hecataeus of Miletus, the son of Hegesander, lived under Darius, who succeeded Cambyses on the [Persian] throne. He was a historian, and contemporary with Dionysius of Miletus who flourished at the time of the sixty-fifth Olympiad [220–216 B.C.]. Herodotus, who lived later, borrowed from him. . . . Hecataeus was the first man to write a prose history.*[24]

This dating of Hecataeus is confirmed by Herodotus, who refers to him as the one man who advised his fellow citizens against precipitating the Ionian Revolt. Hecataeus must have been a person of considerable standing to have been consulted at such an important moment, but whether this was because of his reputation as a geographer with an expert's knowledge of the enemy's country, or because he belonged to the Milesian nobility is difficult to determine.[25] We are told by Diodorus Siculus that Hecataeus was one of the envoys sent to meet with the Persian satrap Artaphernes after the war, and this is likely enough.[26] His original opposition to the war would have made him acceptable to the Persians. We also learn that Hecataeus was a great traveler, and it is certain, from a passage in Herodotus, that his travels took him at least as far as Egyptian Thebes.[27] This generally favorable account of him may be supplemented by a statement made about him by a contemporary, the philosopher Heraclitus, to the effect that knowing a great many things is not enough to teach a man common sense, otherwise it would have had that effect on Pythagoras, Xenophanes, and Hecataeus.[28] But Heraclitus despised almost everyone, including Homer and the entire medical profession, so that his condemnation of Hecataeus amounts to a grudging recognition of his high reputation.[29]

Two works, under a variety of titles, are attributed to Hecataeus: one a geographical treatise in two books, the other a work on the genealogies of heroes in four books. Of these two the geography is much more frequently cited, chiefly because lexicographers like Stephanus of Byzantium found it very useful as a source of information on old place names. In the fifth century it was probably the standard geography, only to be superseded by the ever popular fourth century B.C. *Periplus* falsely attributed to Scylax, which we still possess, and by other works, most of which we do not.[30] That it did not disappear much earlier than it did may be explained by the zeal of the Hellenistic librarians. Thanks to them copies of the work were made and Dionysius of Halicarnassus found it available to him in Rome at the time of Augustus.[31] One half of the treatise was rescued from oblivion by Eratosthenes of Cyrene while serving as Chief Librarian in Alexandria, if we accept Jacoby's attractive but far from conclusive argument.[32] However that may be, the original treatise was written before the use of titles, a fact that explains the various ways in which it is cited by later writers.[33] We may conveniently call it the *Periegesis*, which comes to be a fairly general term for a descriptive geography. Although Hecataeus was the first Greek to write such a geography, he cannot possibly have obtained all his information from personal observation and Anaximander's map alone. Partly, no doubt like Anaximander himself, Hecataeus will have learned a great deal from the ship captains of Miletus. Throughout the sixth century, and even earlier, her merchants had sailed to the western Mediterranean, while the Black Sea and its appendages became an open book as the result of the scores of colonies she established there. As the leading Ionian city she had friends (and enemies) all the way to Sicily and Magna Graecia; but Hecataeus is likely to have talked to seamen from other Ionian cities as well, some of whom had even sailed beyond the Straits of Gibraltar. It is known that Colaeus, a sea captain from the island of Samos, was blown through the Straits and out into the Atlantic, and that he then reached Tartessus, in about 630 B.C. Later the Phocaeans established regular trading relations with the Spanish coast. These sea captains, however, while they had picked up much information about distant places, were primarily interested in profit. Colaeus, for example, who is said to have brought back enormous wealth from his Atlantic voyage, may not have cared to give away his secrets by providing anyone with an accurate account of his discoveries.[34] Then, too, piracy was flourishing, so that it might even be dangerous to tell all one knew.[35]

More recently, the Persians had conquered Lydia (546 B.C.) and forced the Asiatic Greeks to pay them tribute. Darius I, Hecataeus' contemporary, at one time controlled Cyrene and also Egypt on the African continent, as well as Asia all the way to India. He it was who built, or rather completed, the canal begun by Egyptian Necho connecting the Red Sea with the Nile.[36] Darius also led an expedition against the Scythians and extended Persian rule over Thrace and Macedonia. This same energetic monarch found time to overhaul the whole administrative structure of the Persian empire, including the institution of an efficient system of tax collection. This meant that the quality of public records of all kinds improved, and they became a very important source for any historian or geographer who had access to them. Did Hecataeus learn to speak Persian? Few Greeks did, Themistocles was one of the few, but even in Alexander's day it was regarded as remarkable that Peucestas, the Macedonian governor of Persis, should have learned the language of the people over whom he ruled.[37] Herodotus, who like Hecataeus was an Asiatic Greek, is very proud at having picked up a few Persian words.[38]

The references to the northern regions in the fragments of Hecataeus have been used to prove that he wrote his geographical work after Darius' Scythian expedition.[39] This may be true in the sense that the expedition must have aroused interest in that remote area, and would therefore have influenced Hecataeus to include all he could find on the north. However, he need not have depended on Persian sources. A contemporary of Croesus and Cyrus, a Greek named Aristeas of Proconnesus had made a journey into the far north, which he described in a poem called *The Arimaspeians*, known to Aeschylus and to Herodotus and surely known to Hecataeus as well. But the unsatisfactory fragments from Hecataeus that deal with the north do not tell us much about how he obtained his information.[40]

The most famous exploration carried out for Darius was in quite a different direction. For it was under his orders that Scylax of Caryanda sailed all the way down the Indus to the Indian Ocean, and then westward beyond Arabia and into the Red Sea, the entire voyage being completed in less than thirty months. Now Scylax wrote an account of his adventures in Greek, and there is no reason why Hecataeus should not have read it. The form of the *Periplus*, primarily an account of a coasting voyage, is thought to have influenced the organization of Hecataeus' *Periegesis*.[41]

Hecataeus, perhaps following Anaximander, conceived of the inhabited world (the oecumene) as consisting of three parts: Europe, Asia, and Libya. Europe stretched all the way from east to west above both Asia and Libya to the south. His procedure seems to have been to start with the Straits of Gibraltar on the European side, then to follow the coastline eastward. Rivers would be indicated, and then some account given of the inland areas continuing up the river valleys as far away as any data was obtainable, making use of hearsay reports when there was no alternative.[42] Hecataeus also included a map with his work, and he must have tried to add details not known to Anaximander, and also to correct any errors in Anaximander's map which he discovered through his own observation, or through the reports of others. Agathemerus, undoubtedly echoing Eratosthenes here, says that the improvements Hecataeus made in the older map were nothing short of amazing.[43] Today maps are taken for granted, so that it is easy to forget how difficult a task it was for the early geographers to represent the

THE WORLD ACCORDING TO HECATAEUS
Hecataeus in turn depended on the map of Anaximander. Note particularly the
Caspian and the Nile.

outlines of a body of land or the meanderings of a river on a small
flat surface. Methods had not yet been found for determining the
position of a given point on the earth's surface by astronomic
observation,[44] so that distances between places had to be estimated
by travelers' reports of the number of days it took to go from one
place to the other, a particularly unsatisfactory method for determining distances by sea, where unseen currents and varying winds
had so much effect. Hecataeus' text also included some descriptive
details about the customs of the people in a particular region, their
dress, the products of the country and the wild life that was to
be found there. Such details might be obtained from travelers, and
there is every reason for Hecataeus to have included them. The
evidence is particularly compelling for Egypt, and it is certain that
Herodotus borrowed from him.[45]

Incidentally, Hecataeus set the fashion for some time to come
by describing the lands around the Mediterranean in a clockwise

direction beginning with the Straits of Gibraltar,[46] for we find the same procedure followed in the popular fourth century *Periplus* attributed to Scylax, and also by Strabo in the Augustan Age. Of course neither Hecataeus nor Pseudo-Scylax was describing an actual coasting voyage—no one ship having sailed the whole way around the Mediterranean—but each was constructing a general account from many separate reports. A continuous voyage was sometimes made around a lesser body of water, the Black Sea, for example, or the Sea of Azov, and then the results might be written up as a periplus. If the vessel, for perfectly practical reasons, happened to sail in a counterclockwise direction, later geographers could become quite confused in trying to combine clockwise and counterclockwise reports.[47] This in fact did happen to reports about the Black Sea. The task of writing the first descriptive geography of the world presented other problems as well. What ought to be done with the islands? Should they be treated separately, or should each be attached to the account of the nearest coastal area? The bulk of the fragments of Hecataeus reach us by way of Stephanus of Byzantium, and they are too cryptic to enable us to reconstruct the plan of his work in any detail. To complicate matters still further there is another Hecataeus, probably from Abdera, who wrote early in the Hellenistic period. His history was extremely popular and it is often referred to by later writers. Since the two namesakes also overlapped in their subject matter and since each was frequently cited simply as "Hecataeus," separating the two has not been easy.[48]

The other work by Hecataeus of Miletus, the *Genealogies* (also cited as the *Histories* or the *Heroölogy*), is regarded by Jacoby as having been written later than the *Periegesis,* but his reasons are not compelling. He argues that the *Genealogies* has gone a step beyond the *Periegesis* in rationalizing Greek myths, for example the story of Heracles.[49] But Hecataeus obviously approaches the subject from a different viewpoint in the two works, regardless of which one he wrote first. In the *Periegesis* he was interested in identifying a particular town when he mentioned that it was connected with a story about Heracles, rather than in discussing the authenticity of the story itself. Even today someone may point out the spot where George Washington is said to have stood when he threw a dollar across the Potomac, without necessarily believing that he did so. Legends, like real events, have a recognized geographical setting. But in the *Genealogies* the author is attempting to separate the Heracles of history from the Heracles of legend, not realizing— as in fact the Greeks never fully realized—that this is an impossible task. We may count ourselves fortunate that the introductory lines of the *Genealogies* survive just as Hecataeus wrote them.[50] They may be translated as follows:

*These are the words of Hecataeus of Miletus. In what follows I write what I believe to be the truth, for what the Greeks have to say strikes me as being both inconsistent and ridiculous.*

This has a Hesiodic ring to it which suggests to Pearson that, like Hesiod, Hecataeus merely promises to give a single (therefore not inconsistent) version of the Greek legends, rather than to call attention to any particularly original research on the part of the author. At the most, the tone of the introduction betrays a certain aristocratic pride.[51] But surely more than that can be expected from a Milesian writer in the period when that city was the intellectual capital of Greece. Hecataeus deserves a leading place in the development of historical method. The tests he applied to the mythological period were later used by Herodotus in dealing with the more recent past, and finally applied with even more rigor to the contemporary scene by Thucydides. Hecataeus evidently operates on the natural but dangerous assumption that human beings are motivated in much the same way in all periods of history, a view which was modified by later historians to allow for differences brought about by the physical environment in which people lived, or the form of government they enjoyed.[52] The arrangement of events in a fixed chronological order, which Hecataeus must have worked out before he could construct his narrative of heroic times, must have been his greatest problem. He also devoted much time to the study of etymologies, on the assumption that somehow the name of a place must contain some clue to its history. But Hecataeus' overriding achievement both in his geographical work and in the *Genealogies* is that he saw the need for applying logic to data of any kind in order to arrive at a pattern. Later writers might work from more data and better data, thus necessitating a more complex pattern to include the new evidence, but their method is still the method of Hecataeus, an attempt to account for what goes on in the world of men and in the natural world in terms of cause and effect. And here the original debt is to the early Greek philosophers.

Many other more or less shadowy figures are known to us from this early period,[53] but I will content myself here with discussing only two of them as especially useful for understanding Herodotus: those two are Xanthus the Lydian and Hellanicus of Lesbos. Xanthus, who will be considered first, is an interesting early example of the cultural interchange between Greek and barbarian. We sense but cannot clearly document the obligations of the Greek philosophers to their Babylonian and Egyptian trail-breakers; but Xanthus represents the opposite side of the coin, for he was deeply influenced by the Greeks. There is the usual notice about him in the *Suda*,[54] which I translate:

*Xanthus the son of Candaules a Lydian from Sardis, and a historian,*

*was born [or lived?] at the time of the fall of Sardis. He [wrote] a*
Lydiaca *in four books. . . .*

Remembering that Cyrus took Sardis in 546 B.C., we are startled to read in Strabo that he also described a drought that occurred in the reign of Artaxerxes, who came to the throne in 426 B.C.![55] However, our chief authority on the logographers, Dionysius of Halicarnassus, puts Xanthus among the writers in the period just before Thucydides and the Peloponnesian War.[56] Modern scholars have tried to reconcile these statements in various ways, but even when we get around this particular dilemma other difficulties remain. The historian Ephorus, a reputable and very popular writer of the fourth century B.C., tells us that Xanthus lived before Herodotus, and that it was his work that impelled Herodotus to write. Then we have a disturbing notice which Athenaeus (who lived during the Roman empire) repeats from Artemon (second century B.C.) to the effect that the *Lydiaca* was really the work of a Hellenistic writer named Dionysius Scytobrachion.[57] Jacoby tries to save the situation by suggesting that Dionysius brought out a new edition with a forged preface.[58]

Although I think Xanthus deserves better treatment than he has usually received this is not the place for more than a summary discussion.[59] The date that really counts is Xanthus' own reference to Artaxerxes, and this is quite compatible with his having written before Herodotus, particularly if his work was issued in installments. There is a possibility, then, that Herodotus read him, and Pearson has discussed this carefully in his book on the *Early Ionian Historians* without finding it possible to reach any definite conclusion.[60] The name Xanthus is Greek, but Candaules his father has a Lydian name, identical with that of a famous Lydian king in Herodotus. Later we find the name Candaules in Caria, perhaps the result of a migration after the fall of Sardis. The *Lydiaca* probably contained more information on customs, geographic features, and religious beliefs than it did about political history: it was essentially an ethnographic treatise like the lost *Persica* of Dionysius of Miletus. He apparently had a particular interest in natural phenomena, such as the strange area in Asia Minor called *Katakekaumene* because of its scorched look, and he also noted the appearance of shells and other marine objects far inland. Sometimes his explanation might be called "scientific," while at others he finds corroborative evidence for an angry god with a thunderbolt.[61] This does not mean that he was unaffected by the new rationalism. Herodotus, too, wavers between one type of explanation and the other. Like Hecataeus and most early rationalists Xanthus was concerned with etymological explanations.[62] Of particular interest are the Lydian historian's references to the Trojans and his use of the fall of Troy as a fixed point in his chronology. For here we see how influential the Greek epic could be on a non-Greek tradition.[63]

Although Xanthus is credited with two other works (which may or may not have been his), we are interested here only in the *Lydiaca*. In concluding, it would be appropriate to comment on his literary talents; but the direct evidence for judgment is most unsatisfactory. It is known that Nicolaus of Damascus made extensive use of the *Lydiaca* and we have some rather long excerpts from the relevant parts of Nicolaus' History, but it also is probable that Nicolaus made use of a bowdlerized version of the *Lydiaca,* which means that some unknown writer, who combined genuine passages from Xanthus with late and worthless materials, stood between Nicolaus and Xanthus. Therefore it would certainly be unfair to blame the ineptitude of Nicolaus' watered down account on the Lydian historian, although we recognize the link between the two works.[64] Someone may eventually find a way to separate the impurities from the fine gold, but even before that happens we may safely assume that Xanthus wrote with a certain charm. Otherwise Dionysius of Halicarnassus, essentially a judge of style, would not praise him as he does.[65]

Hellanicus of Lesbos, our last pre-Herodotean historian, was also the most prolific writer of his time. The *Suda* has this to say:

*Hellanicus of Mitylene, the son of Andromenes, [was] a historian. There are those who say he was the son of Aristomenes, while still others call him Scamon's son, inferring that from the fact that his own son bore the same name. Hellanicus spent some time, together with Herodotus, at the court of Amyntas, the Macedonian king who was contemporary with Sophocles and Euripides. Hellanicus came after Hecataeus of Miletus and was born at the time of the Persian War or shortly before. He lived in the reign of Perdiccas and died in Perperene across from Lesbos. He wrote a great deal, some of it in prose and some in verse.*[66]

I have quoted this in full as a good example of why the *Suda* (often extremely important to us) has to be carefully interpreted. At best it may reflect scholarship in the Hellenistic age when every effort was made to obtain reliable information on the lives of eminent men of letters. No such interest can be detected in the fifth century, and the early writers themselves carefully avoided making autobiographical statements unless such a statement was needed to support the argument. A writer might say that he had seen something with his own eyes, or he might tell us that he had obtained a certain piece of information by talking with someone in a particular place; but he would not go beyond that. The Hellenistic scholars, therefore, had their work cut out for them, but often it was not too late to pick up some of the facts through local tradition about the great man. The real difficulty was that where no tradition had survived it might be invented to the greater glory of the city concerned! In the present biography there are obvious errors. It is quite possible that Hellanicus lived in Macedonia for a time, but not under King Amyntas.[67] Nor do we need to believe Herodotus was there at all. It was inevitable that two near contemporaries of great reputation should later be brought into touch with one another, precisely what happened later on to Alexander the Great and Diogenes the Cynic. But the statement that Hellanicus was buried in Perperene is much more likely to rest on genuine tradition, if only because of the insignificance of the town. There is no way of deciding what his father's name was unless we surmise, as the *Suda* author suggests, that Hellanicus called his son Scamon (also a writer) in honor of the grandfather. But of course it is also possible that given the existence of two writers from Lesbos of unknown antecedents, some compiler decided they were father and son. The *Suda* reference to Sophocles and Euripides, though cryptic, can mean only one thing, the year 456 B.C., a favorite synchronism (though not necessarily correct) when it was held that Aeschylus died, Sophocles "flourished" (that is when he was forty years old), and Euripides produced his first play.[68]

It would be tedious for the reader to go over every detail in the modern discussion of Hellanicus' dates, but one or two points may be mentioned in order to illustrate the kind of problems that arise. It has been argued that the reason for dating Hellanicus "at the time of the Persian War" (meaning 480 B.C.) is because of a punning association between the meaning of his name in Greek ("Hellenic victory"?) with the Battle of Salamis. But obviously the *Suda* biographer shows some misgivings when he adds, "or shortly before."[69] A further text used in dating this eminent historian is a passage from Dionysius of Halicarnassus, already referred to above in connection with Xanthus, for Dionysius puts Hellanicus in the same group of historians to which Xanthus belongs, those who wrote shortly before the time of Thucydides.[70] Another passage may also be mentioned, and that comes from the *Macrobioi*, a work falsely attributed to Lucian, on the subject of men who lived to a ripe old age. It is reassuring to note how many of these fortunate persons were historians. Hellanicus makes his appearance among the eighty-five year olds.[71] But the best evidence comes from a fragment of Hellanicus, where he refers to the desperate measures taken in Athens to find oarsmen for the Battle of Arginusae, for this means that Hellanicus was still writing after that date (406 B.C.).[72]

This result proves to be valuable. The fragment must surely come from Hellanicus' *Atthis* (or Chronicle of Athens), and that makes it pretty certain that he carried the story down to the end of the war in 404 B.C. And this in turn means that he wrote the *Atthis* after Herodotus wrote his History, and that while he could and did make use of Herodotus, Herodotus was in no way dependent on him, though both writers could and did make use of Hecataeus.[73] The chief reason Hellanicus has been thought of as belonging to Herodotus' generation rather than to that of Thucydides is very likely that he continued to write in the old literary Ionian style.[74]

We may fairly include Hellanicus among the sophists. Without relinquishing his citizenship in Lesbos (Mytilene?) he must have visited most of the important Greek cities, not so much to gather information as to impart it. As Jacoby notes, Eratosthenes speaks of Hecataeus as a man who traveled widely, while in contrast he speaks of Hellanicus as a man of great erudition.[75] In other words Hellanicus got his information from books, and he makes no original contribution either to geography or to ethnography, though he did work up a great variety of subjects on which he lectured as a traveling sophist on the Greek mainland and perhaps in the Greek west as well. Some of this material was then published, and must have enjoyed a considerable vogue. What we have left are only fragments, along with the titles assigned to Hellanicus' writings by later scholars. The list of titles is so formidable that it is easy to see why the *Suda* biographer contents himself with saying: "He wrote a great deal, some of it in prose and some in verse."

Hellanicus' most important claim to fame is that he tried to work out the chronology of the twilight zone between the everyday world and the age of heroes. While others had been satisfied with bringing some kind of order into the mythological period from the beginnings on down to, let us say, the Return of the Heraclidae, Hellanicus aimed at a total picture which would carry the story of Hesiod's *Theogony* without a break into modern times.[76] He also made use of such materials as he could find without subjecting them to critical study. That is, he accepted the traditions represented by official lists such as those of the Spartan kings, the Argive priestesses, and the Athenian archons without seriously troubling himself as to their authenticity. None of these lists was dated in an absolute sense, for there was no common system to which they could be referred. Hellanicus, therefore, worked back into the mythological period, for which he had already established his own chronology, and then attempted to attach names on the lists referred to above to one or more of the early heroes. In this way he tied the lists in with the period of myth, while by the same token he brought them into a time relationship with one another. All that remained to be done to complete the scaffold for a universal chronology was to link the lists together with the modern period, a comparatively easy task, though there would still be rough spots.

Greeks did not all begin the year at the same time, nor did they have the same number of days in a calendar year, therefore no system of dating had any chance of general acceptance. Theoretically, however, it was possible, and the attempt of the historian from Lesbos showed the great advantages of having a common measuring rod for all past history.[77]

Hellanicus' own interests were centered in mythological times rather than in the modern period, if we are to judge by the titles of his lost works. For example the *Deucalionea*, the *Phoronis*, and the *Atlantis* each dealt with a particular figure in mythology, tracing the deeds of his descendants as well. Other works, such as the *Lesbiaca*, the *Aeolica*, the *Troica*, and even the *Aegyptiaca* describe the legendary history of a particular region. There is no reason to believe Hellanicus traveled to Egypt, or even that if he did so the *Aegyptiaca* represented original research on his part.[78]

As an example of Hellanicus' methods, one of the longer passages that has come down to us is translated below. Its provenance is not certain, though Jacoby's second thought, that it comes from the *Atthis*, has much to recommend it. This is the way it goes:

*According to Hellanicus, Codrus was descended from Deucalion, for Hellen was the son of Deucalion and Pyrrha—or as others say of Zeus and Pyrrha—and Xuthus, Aeolus, Dorus and Xenopatra were the children of Hellen and Ortheis. Salmoneus, in turn, was the son of Aeolus and Peneius' daughter Iphis. Salmoneus and Alcidice had a daughter Tyro, who became the mother of Neleus by Poseidon. Periclymenus was the son of Neleus and Chloris, while Borus was born to Periclymenus and Pisidice. Penthilus was the son of Borus and Lysidice, while to Penthilus and Anchirrhoe Andropompus was born. Andropompus became the father of Melanthus by Henioche, and she was the daughter of Armenius, who was the son of Xeuxippus the son of Eumelus who, in turn, was the son of Admetus. Now when the Heraclidae marched out from Messene against him Melanthus withdrew to Athens, and it was there that his son Codrus was born. (2) Later on a dispute arose between the Boeotians and the Athenians over the possession of Oenoe and Panactum, or as some say over Melaenae. The Boeotians suggested that the two kings fight it out for the disputed territory in single combat. Xanthius, the Boeotian king accepted this proposal, but King Thymoetes of Athens refused on his own account, but he promised to give up his throne to anyone who was willing to fight in his place. In return for the kingship, to be given both to him and to his descendants, Melanthus accepted the challenge and armed himself for battle. As he came out and drew near his opponent, Melanthus called to him: "Xanthius, you ought to have come to meet me alone, as we agreed, not with a companion!" When Xanthius turned around to see whether anyone was following him, Melanthus struck him down and that is how he became the king of Athens. The Athenians voted to establish a festival which was called the Apatenoria at first and later the Apaturia, because of the deceit [apatē] which had been used.*[79]

In this passage we see how Hellanicus worked out a pedigree for King Codrus that went all the way back to the common ancestor of all Greece, Hellen, and to Deucalion and Pyrrha, the survivors of the Flood. But he also associates Codrus' father Melanthus with contemporary Athenian history. One of the reasons for the breakdown of the Peace of Nicias (421 B.C.) and the resumption of the Peloponnesian War was the behavior of Thebes when required to return the border territory of Panactum to Athens,[80] a circumstance of which Hellanicus was aware at the time he wrote. The punning explanation of the Apaturia is characteristic of other early Greek writers, and continues throughout the classical period. Otherwise the commentator on Plato to whom we owe this fragment of Hellanicus would probably not have copied it down.

In leaving Hellanicus let us not fail to give him his due.[81] He had a broad conception of the unity of human history which was to bear fruit in the Hellenistic age with the adoption of a universal chronology, at least by some historians. The best-known chronologist of that period was Eratosthenes, and he, unlike Hellanicus, was careful to distinguish between different ages in the history of man in terms of whether the events described are credible or incredible. Yet even Eratosthenes, for all his skepticism, did include the mythological period in his chronology, because he too was impressed by the unity of the human experience. Hellanicus was essentially a compromiser, not a scholar. Plausibility was what he sought rather than the truth for its own sake, and it may be that that great early relativist Protagoras influenced his thinking. But he was a witty and persuasive man, and he was certainly read and used by Thucydides, whose attack on him is confined to the *Atthis,* clearly not the work that made his reputation. It is not at all fair to blame him for not writing like Herodotus; there is surely honor enough for both men.

### Notes to Chapter One

1. The title of Jacoby's work is *Die Fragmente der griechischen Historiker* (hereafter cited as *FGrH*), the first volume of which appeared in 1923, and the last in 1958. He completed the texts for the following sections:

   I History of the Legendary Past (Genealogy and Mythography)
   II Universal History and Contemporary History (Chronography)
   III Histories of Peoples and Cities (Ethnography and Chronicles)

   Although the text is complete through no. 856, the commentary stops with no. 607 (the work is to be completed by H. Bloch and others). Altogether there are sixteen volumes, seven of text and nine of commentary (including a special volume called *Atthis*), which can best be consulted through the author index at the end of the second volume of iii C. Still indispensable is the older collection by C. and T. Müller and others, *Fragmenta Historicorum Graecorum* (hereafter cited as *FHG*), which was published by Didot in Paris in five volumes (1841–1870). This includes a Latin translation, a commentary, and detailed indices.

2. Not all the works falsely attributed to famous authors were forgeries in the strict sense. For example, the essay on The Athenian Constitution attributed to Xenophon was actually written before his time, and probably brought out anonymously. It was clearly to the advantage of anyone who got hold of such a manuscript at a later date to represent it as the work of Xenophon, if he intended to sell it; and that may well be what happened.

3. There is already a vast literature on the decipherment of Linear B and its consequences. For a provocative statement of the problem see Leonard R. Palmer, *Mycenaeans and Minoans* (London, 1961), chap. 2 (though this book itself has become controversial); T. B. L. Webster, *From Mycenae to Homer,* 2nd ed. (New York, 1964), Introduction and Addenda; also see the appropriate sections of the new edition of Volumes I and II of the *Cambridge Ancient History* (hereafter cited as *CAH*) most of which has already appeared in separate fascicles.

4. Not everyone agrees with this interpretation. N. G. L. Hammond, *History of Greece to 322 B.C.,* 1st ed. (Oxford, 1959), 93, believes that Linear B survived in a modified form, but admits that we have no examples, "from the period *c.* 1050–700, *presumably because perishable materials were used.*" This is a transparently weak argument, but it contains a useful implication. The Greeks probably did use the Phoenician alphabet for business purposes before they began carving inscriptions on stone, so that 700 B.C. is too late a date for the adoption of the alphabet. But the use of writing for literary purposes in Greek means that symbols must have been adapted to represent the vowels (unnecessary in Phoenician or Hebrew). Anyone who takes the trouble to transcribe a few lines from the *Iliad,* leaving out the vowels, will see that for himself. Someday we will know more about this whole question of Greek literacy, perhaps by further study of the other syllabary used to write Greek, that of Cyprus.

5. On Xenophanes' views about Homer (and Hesiod) see W. K. C. Guthrie, *A History of Greek Philosophy* (London, 1962), I, 370 f.; for Plato see the *Republic,* bk. iii; for Strabo consult the index of his *Geography,* s.v. Homer, but see esp. i. 2. 3–20.

6. For a translation (and text) of these poems see the Loeb Library edition of H. G. Evelyn White with additions by D. L. Page as revised in 1936.

7. See Pl. *Rep.* 377 e.

8. Thuc. i. 9–11.

9. Part of the work of sorting out the legends was done by the later Hesiodic writers, such as the unknown author of the *Catalogue of Women,* of which only fragments remain. But something of what they accomplished can be seen when we examine the *Bibliotheca* falsely attributed to the learned Apollodorus of Athens (see Lionel Pearson, *Early Ionian Historians,* Oxford, 1939, 160—though Pearson is speaking particularly about Hellanicus who completed the task). For the relationship between Greek mythology and historiography see W. Schmid, in Schmid and Stählin, *Geschichte der griechischen Literatur* I, 1[7], (Munich, 1929), 685 f.; and also Kurt von Fritz, *Die griechische Geschichtsschreibung* (Berlin, 1967), I:69 ff. (Text cited hereafter as *GG* I, Anmerkungen cited hereafter as *GG* IA.)

10. For Timaeus' statement see *FGrH* no. 566, fr. 127. For the duplication of Heracles see *The Oxford Classical Dictionary,* 2nd ed. (Oxford, 1970)—hereafter cited as *OCD*[2]—s.v. Heracles; also see H. J. Rose, *Handbook of Greek Mythology,* 5th ed. (London, 1953), 166 f.

11. The term is really untranslatable. The Roman *imagines* or portrait masks of their ancestors are called πρόσωπα by Polybius in a famous passage (vi. 53. 5). "Prosopography" is a modern tool which uses biographical data to interpret history. Statistics may be selected for various purposes. For example, a list of every Athenian known to us from literary or documentary sources (J. Kirchner,

*Prosopographia Attica,* 2 vols., Berlin, 1901–1903); or a list of everyone who had or was presumed to have had anything to do with Alexander the Great (H. Berve, *Das Alexanderreich auf prosopographischer Grundlage,* Munich, 1926); or a documented list of Greek mercenaries in Hellenistic times (M. Launey, *Recherches sur les Armées hellénistiques* (Paris, 1950), II, 1111–1271).

12. Felix Jacoby, *Atthis: The Local Chronicles of Ancient Athens* (Oxford, 1949).

13. Jacoby, *Atthis* 201. See also pp. 184–185.

14. See von Fritz, *GG* I, 96 f.; IA, 74, n. 80.

15. Clisthenes the tyrant of Sicyon forbade the Homeric rhapsodes to perform in Sicyon, because he was on bad terms with Argos (Hdt. v. 67). Sparta made political propaganda out of the reverence for the epic tradition when she "discovered" the bones of Orestes in Tegea and had them carried off to Sparta (Hdt. i. 67–68). For discussion see A. Andrewes, *The Greek Tyrants* (London, 1956), 58–59; G. L. Huxley, *Early Sparta* (London, 1962), 67–69; H. Berve, *Die Tyrannis bei den Griechen* (Munich, 1967), Vol. 1, 27 f.

16. See Jacoby, *Atthis,* 68—where Hellanicus also is given a place, though a lesser one; also his "Hekataios" (3), in Pauly-Wissowa, *Real-Encyclopädie* (Stuttgart, 1893—)—hereafter cited as *PW*—vii. 2737. For Hecataeus' influence on Herodotus, see *PW* viii. 2676–2686; and on Thucydides-Herodotus, see "Herodotos," (7) *PW* vii, supp. II, 484–486. However, Jacoby, more than anyone else, has set these matters in proper perspective, leaving the materials at hand with which later scholarship can make refinements in detail (see Arnaldo Momigliano, in his Inaugural Lecture on, "George Grote and the Study of Greek History," at University College London, 1952, 19).

17. The ancient texts on Anaximander will be found in H. Diels, *Die Fragmente der Vorsokratiker,* 8th ed. by W. Kranz (Berlin, 1956), vol. 1—hereafter Diels, *Vorsokr.*[8]—no. 12. For his dates see ibid., 12 A. 1; for his priority in science, ibid., A. 7. For a recent discussion of his achievements see G. S. Kirk and J. E. Raven, *The Presocratic Philosophers* (Cambridge, 1960), chap. 3 (the Greek texts there are given with a translation); and Guthrie, *Hist. Gk. Phil.,* I, 72–115.

18. For Eratosthenes' statement see Diels, *Vorsokr.*[8] 12 A. 6 = Strabo i. 1. 11. For Anaximander's views on the development of living things, see Diels, *Vorsokr.*[8] 12 A. 10, 11, 30; and Kirk-Raven, *Presocratic Philosophers,* 141. On Anaximander as a geographer, see J. O. Thomson, *History of Ancient Geography* (London, 1948), 47, 96–97.

19. Diels, *Vorsokr.*[8] 12 A. 10, 11, 25; see also Guthrie, *Hist. Gk. Phil.,* I. 98; and Kirk-Raven, *Presocratic Philosophers,* 134.

20. See Diels, *Vorsokr.*[8] 12 A. 18–22; and Guthrie, *Hist. Gk. Phil.,* I. 96 f.

21. For a brief appraisal of Babylonian astronomy with useful references to the literature, see H. E. Sigerist, *A History of Medicine* (New York, Galaxy Books, 1967), I, 392 ff. On the earliest maps, including Babylonia, see Thomson, *Hist. Anc. Geog.,* 37–39.

22. See Guthrie, *Hist. Gk. Phil.,* I. 92; and esp. Kirk-Raven, *Presocratic Philosophers,* 139–140. Whether he also thought of rivers as bringing silt down from the interior and in this way pushing the coastline farther out, is not clear.

23. Until 1937 the work was attributed to an otherwise unknown Suidas, but now we know that ἡ Σοῦδα is the title although we still have no idea who wrote it. The best edition is that of Ada Adler *Suidae Lexicon,* in five volumes, (Leipzig, 1928–1938). The arrangement is not strictly alphabetical, but the sequence of letters is given at the beginning of each volume, and a series of indices in volume 5 make it very convenient to use.

24. The *Suda,* s.vv. Ἑκαταῖος, Ἡγησάνδρου, Μιλήσιος.

25. On his advice, see Hdt. v. 36. If they insisted on war he advised seizing the treasures from Apollo's temple at Branchidae and then using the proceeds to build an invincible fleet—a curious anticipation of Themistocles. For Hecataeus' noble birth see Hdt. ii. 143.

26. See Diod. Sic. x. 25. 4 (the Loeb editor, C. H. Oldfather, probably following Jacoby, regards this as the invention of Ephorus). Jacoby assumes that Ephorus merely added this as an embellishment to what Herodotus has to say about Artaphernes after the war (Hdt. vi. 42–43), and that Ephorus did *not* supplement

Herodotus here, as he sometimes did, by referring to a *Persica* (*FGrH* I a, commenting on Hecataeus T 7). But why not? L. Pearson in *Early Ionian Historians* (Oxford, 1939), 27, suggests that the story of the embassy may be true; W. Spoerri appears to accept it—"Hekataios" (3), *Kl. Pauly* 1967, II, col. 977; but von Fritz rejects it—*GG* IA, 34–35, n. 12.

27. Viz. Hdt. ii. 143. Agathemerus (*Geog. inf.* I. 1 = *FGrH* (Hecataeus) 1. T 12a), no doubt echoing Eratosthenes calls him an ἀνὴρ πολυπλανής. For discussion see von Fritz, *GG* IA, 47, n. 69.

28. See Hec. T 21 (Diels, *Vorsokr.*[8] 22 B. 40) = D.L. ix. 1. 1.

29. He said that Homer should have been banned from all competitions and soundly beaten (Diels *Vorsokr.*[8] 22 B. 42), while he thought doctors deserved no pay because they were just as dangerous as the ailments they professed to cure (ibid., 58). See further Guthrie, *Hist. Gk. Phil.*, I, 413 f.

30. See Jacoby, "Hekataios" (3), in *PW* vii. 2700. 36 ff. The Pseudo-Scylax *Periplus* is confined to the Mediterranean and Black Sea areas, and probably came out in the mid fourth century B.C. See Thomson, *Hist. Anc. Geog.*, 88. W. W. Hyde rather wildly suggests a work by a namesake of the earlier Scylax (*Ancient Greek Mariners*, New York, 1947, 115 ff). Herodotus, for all his criticism of the Ionians, probably followed Hecataeus' map and his descriptive geography pretty closely.

31. In a well-known passage (*De Thucyd.* 5 = *FGrH* 1. T 17a) Dionysius lists and dates a number of logographers, including Hecataeus, and goes on to say that their works still survived (see *Amer. Hist. Rev.* 1954, 59:834, for translation and discussion).

32. See his article "Hekataios" (3), in *PW* vii. 2672 f. Briefly, Jacoby credits Eratosthenes with seeing that an *Asia*, cataloged at Alexandria under a certain Nesiotes (real name or "islander"?) belonged with the *Europe* already cataloged under Hecataeus. Originally the geography consisted of two papyrus rolls, the first of which (*Europe*) would have contained the author's name. When they became separated the authorship of *Asia* was no longer clear, and for some reason came to be attributed to a Nesiotes. Did the Alexandrian library acquire them as two works? Or did Callimachus make the error in cataloging? Arguments based on the separation of papyrus rolls are tempting, because that is just the sort of thing that must sometimes have occurred. But was it *this* time? Also we are still in the dark about Nesiotes, real man or figment.

33. Viz. as Εὐρώπη for Ἀσίη for the separate parts, and as Περιήγησις or Περίοδος γῆς for the whole. Περίοδος γῆς also means "map," and of course Hecataeus did bring out a map of his own. See von Fritz, *GG* I, 50 f.

34. On the period of these early voyages see Thomson, *Hist. Anc. Geog.*, 44–56; E. H. Bunbury, *A History of Ancient Geography* (New York: Dover reprint, 1959), I, 91–119; and von Fritz, *GG* I, 25–33.

35. On this subject in general see J. A. Ormerod, *Piracy in the Ancient World* (Chicago, Argonaut reprint, 1967). He suggests that Colaeus himself may have been at least a part-time pirate, p. 101 n. 1.

36. See A. T. Olmstead, *History of the Persian Empire* (Chicago, 1948), 145 f.; and Sir Alan Gardiner, *Egypt of the Pharaohs* (London: Galaxy, 1966), 357.

37. Alexander, with rare good judgment, apparently chose Peucestas as his governor because of his interest in Persian customs rather than for having saved his life. See Arr. *Anab.* vii. 30. 2.

38. See, for example, Hdt. ix. 110. But he wrongly maintained that all Persian names end in "s" (i. 139).

39. Jacoby says, for example, that Darius' "Unternehmungen" were important for Hecataeus' knowledge of Thrace and the Scythians ("Hekataios" (3), in *PW* vii. 2707. 49 ff).

40. On this subject see now J. D. P. Bolton, *Aristeas of Proconnesus* (Oxford, 1962), who provides us with a general discussion, a better text of the fragments, and a commentary with up-to-date references to the literature. See also von Fritz, *GG* IA, Index, for further discussion. The main point is that Hecataeus may be presumed to have been familiar with Aristeas' work.

41. See Jacoby, "Hekataios" (3), *PW* vii. 2700.

42. See *PW* viii. 2699; and Pearson, *Early Ion. Hist.*, 30 ff. Von Fritz (*GG* I, 53 ff.)

goes farther than Jacoby in freeing Hecataeus' *Periegesis* from the limitations of a periplus, and suggests that modern editors have grouped the fragments in such a way as to support a preconceived view.

43. See *FGrH* 1. T 12a: διηκρίβωσεν ὥστε θαυμασθῆναι τὸ πρᾶγμα.

44. What was needed was a geometric scheme for dividing up the surface of the earth into sections, plus a method for pinpointing the places that were known within each section. Von Fritz argues that Hecataeus made a beginning, but that Eudoxus of Cnidus was the first to attack the problem systematically, with Eratosthenes working out what came to be the most sophisticated solution (*GG* I, 62–65). Hecataeus was still limited by Anaximander's conception of a flat circular earth's surface.

45. Porphyry, who lived during the later Roman empire, accuses Herodotus of copying from Hecataeus in Book II, with a few alterations (*FGrH* 1. T 22). However, it must be remembered that while Herodotus wrote an entire book (or papyrus roll) on Egypt, Hecataeus had only one book for all of Asia and Africa. There was not nearly enough of Hecataeus, even if Herodotus transcribed the whole, to fill up his account of Egypt in Book II.

46. Cf. Jacoby, "Hekataios" (3), *PW* vii. 1691; Pearson, *Early Ion. Hist.*, 30; von Fritz, *GG* I, 53–54; Bunbury, *Hist. Anc. Geog.* I, 137 and n. 8. Jacoby is more insistent both on the close relationship in form between the *Periegesis* and earlier accounts of voyages (e.g., Scylax) than von Fritz, but both find traces of a clockwise direction, as does Pearson who, however, thinks of Hecataeus as essentially a writer of popular science (*Early Ion. Hist.*, esp. 18). Bunbury regards the order in which Hecataeus described the lands around the Mediterranean as unimportant, but tentatively rejects the clockwise theory.

47. For the Black Sea, Pseudo-Scylax proceeds in a counterclockwise direction, while Arrian and Menippus go "to the right"—i.e., clockwise. See A. Diller, *The Tradition of the Minor Greek Geographers*, American Philological Association publication, 1952, 102.

48. On the other Hecataeus see *FGrH* no. 264. For an extreme view, claiming most of what is usually attributed to the later Hecataeus for Hecataeus of Miletus, see F. Dornseiff, *Echtheitsfragen antik-griechischer Lit.* 1939, 52 ff. Jacoby changes his mind. See *FGrH* i a, Addenda on F 195 and FF 370–373.

49. On Heracles see *FGrH* 1. F 26, and Jacoby's commentary. Strangely, Jacoby prints the fragments of what he regards as the later work (the *Genealogies*) first.

50. See *FGrH* 1. F 1. For a perceptive discussion of the Preface see G. De Sanctis, *Studi di Storia della Storiografia Greca* (Florence, 1951), 3 ff.

51. *Early Ion. Hist.*, 98. Jacoby finds Pearson's statement "incomprehensible" (*FGrH* i a. 535. 35 ff.)

52. Both factors are emphasized by the author of *Airs, Waters Places* (attributed to Hippocrates, see Loeb ed. of Hippocrates, vol. I, esp. c. 16).

53. Including Pherecydes of Athens and Acusilaus of Argos. For a treatment of the writers mentioned by Dionysius of Halicarnassus in the passage already cited (*De Thucyd.* 5), see von Fritz, *GG* I, chap. 4.

54. S. vv. Ξάνθος Κανδαύλου. The fragments will be found in *FGrH.* no. 765—unfortunately without a commentary.

55. See *FGrH* 765. F 12 = Strabo i. 3. 4.

56. See Dion. Hal. *Thuc.* 5.

57. See *FGrH* 765. T 5.

58. See *FGrH* I a. 510. 28 ff. (commenting on no. 32, T 6). Other suggestions are that somehow the date for the end of the *Lydiaca*, i.e., the fall of Lydia to Persia in 546 B.C., was wrongly taken as the date when the author was born. Another view is that Xanthus was born when Sardis was captured by the Ionians (498 B.C.). See Müller, *FHG* i. xx–xxiii. Pearson rightly prefers Ephorus' testimony to that of Artemon, and also cites the favorable opinion of the *Lydiaca* held by Dionysius of Halicarnassus (*Ant. Rom.* I. 28), see *Early Ion. Hist.*, 109–137.

59. For a recent and unsympathetic study of Xanthus see von Fritz, *GG* I, 88–91; IA, 348–377. Pearson is more favorable (*Early Ion. Hist.*, 109–137).

60. Pearson, *Early Ion. Hist.*, 123–125.

61. On the *Katakekaumene* see *FGrH* 765. F 13a–b; on the shells, F 12. See von Fritz' interpretation, *GG* I, 89.
62. He explains "Mysians," for example, as derived from the Lydian word for a beech tree—there being many beech trees in the Mt. Olympus area of Mysia (*FGrH* 765. F 15).
63. See *FGrH* 765. FF 14, 21. The best example of all, naturally, was Rome.
64. For a discussion of the relationship between Xanthus and Nicolaus see now von Fritz, *GG* IA, 348 ff. While he points out the difficulties in reaching Xanthus through Nicolaus, he still makes a qualitative judgment on Xanthus which goes beyond the evidence.
65. See Dion. Hal. *Ant. Rom.* i. 28.
66. *Suda* s.vv. Ἑλλάνικος Μιτυληναῖος. For testimony and fragments see *FGrH* no. 4 (supplemented under nos. 323a, 601a, 608a, 645a, and 687a).
67. No King Amyntas fits the period. See K. J. Beloch, *Griechische Geschichte* (Berlin and Leipzig, 1923) III, 2², 62 for the list of Macedonian kings.
68. For discussion see Jacoby, "Hellanikos" (7), *PW* viii. 106; von Fritz, *GG* I, chap. 6, and esp. IA, 221, n. 1.
69. See Müller, *FHG* i. xxiv–xxv; Jacoby, *FGrH* i a (commenting on 4. T 6).
70. Dion. Hal. *Thuc.* 5.
71. *FGrH* 4. T 8 = [Lucian] *Macrob.* 22. The *Macrobioi* was written after Lucian's day, perhaps in 212 or 213 A.D. See Christ-Schmid-Stählin, *Geschichte der griechischen Litteratur*, II, 2⁶, 738–739.
72. See *FGrH* 323a. F 25 (= 4. F 171). Hellanicus alludes to a measure sponsored by Antigenes (i.e. the archon for 407/406 B.C.) freeing certain Athenian slaves and registering them as Plataeans. For the dating of this measure and the evidence for a *terminus post quem* for the *Atthis* see *FGrH* iii b, supp. I, 54–55.
73. See Jacoby, "Hellanikos" (7), *PW* viii. 109.
74. See von Fritz, *GG* I, 479.
75. See his "Hellanikos" (7), *PW* viii. 106. 39–42.
76. See esp. *FGrH* iii b, supp. I, 9.
77. I may have given Hellanicus more credit than he deserves. Von Fritz, e.g., denies that Hellanicus was trying to use the priestesses of Argos as the basis for a general chronology (*GG* I, 481), but he also recognizes that there is room for considerable latitude in our estimate of this prehistorian (*GG* IA, 224 f., nn. 10–13).
78. See Jacoby, "Hellanikos" (7), *PW* viii. 130. C. Müller had argued, chiefly on the basis of a passage in Photius (*Bibl.* 161. 104a. 11 = *FGrH* 4. T 29) that this was a spurious work, perhaps written by a later Hellanicus (*FHG* i. xxx–xxxi). Pearson accepts it as genuine (*Early Ion. Hist.*, 201), as does R. Henry in the Budé edition of Photius *Bibl.*, (Paris, 1960), II, 126, n. 2).
79. *FGrH* 4. F 125, where Jacoby prints the passage under the caption "Descendants of Aeolus: Argonautica (Deucalionea)"; and *FGrH* 323a. F 23, where it appears under the *Atthis*.
80. Under great pressure from Sparta, Thebes restored Panactum, but not without first completely destroying the buildings—a procedure which incensed the Athenians (Thuc. V. 39–40).
81. Even Jacoby, who sets such store by Hellanicus, speaks of him as "a notable scholar and historian *even if not a great writer,* as Herodotus and Thukydides were." (*Atthis* 68). Yet Hellanicus' treatment of the royal duel suggests he could tell a story, and with humor. He may have influenced Ephorus a century later. See below, Chapter 5, n. 38.

The two greatest historians of Greece, like her two most famous philosophers, flourished in successive generations; and, like Plato and Aristotle, Herodotus and Thucydides came, willy-nilly, to stand for two contrasting points of view to later practitioners of their craft. Unlike Aristotle, Thucydides did not sit at the feet of his predecessor. But he was certainly familiar with his work, for he pays him the compliment of sketching in the period between where Herodotus left off and his own History began, remarking that Hellanicus' account was not reliable.[1] And this is an important piece of evidence to keep in mind at the very outset, for without it there might be some temptation to say that Herodotus owes his reputation to the accident of survival, while Hellanicus—and others like him—might stand as high if only we had their entire work instead of unsatisfactory fragments. Thucydides' judgment, made while the logographers were still being read, outweighs a host of critics like Plutarch and Porphyry who lived in Roman times.

Although, unlike Thucydides, Herodotus enjoyed instant success,[2] the popularity of his History did not help to preserve for us the facts of his life. In Alexandrian times when scholars interested themselves in such matters an effort was made to remedy this deficiency, but we no longer know the name of the biographer who worked up a *Life* of the Father of History, for the biography has disappeared. However, some conclusions can be drawn from the evidence we still possess. The manuscripts of Herodotus' History that we have today all begin with the phrase "What follows sets forth the results of the investigations of Herodotus of Halicarnassus". And Aristotle, quoting perhaps from memory, uses the same phrase, except that instead of "Herodotus of Halicarnassus," he writes, "Herodotus of Thurii."[3] Which is correct? Did Herodotus come from Thurii, or from Halicarnassus? The terms are not mutually exclusive, because Thurii was founded by

# HERODOTUS

Pericles in 444 B.C., and nothing need have prevented a citizen of Halicarnassus from taking part in the colonization of Thurii. However, it is important for us to know whether Herodotus appeared as a Thurian or as a Halicarnassian in the *editio princeps*. The claim of Thurii was persistent. Plutarch mentions both, adding that Herodotus did go out to Thurii to live;[4] while Julian the Apostate, deep in the fourth century A.D., obviously has Herodotus in mind when he alludes to "the Thurian historian."[5] But still another possibility suggests itself as the result of a puzzling statement attributed to Duris of Samos, a historian who was writing early in the third century B.C. He is cited by the compiler of the *Suda*, a tenth century lexicographer. The statement from the *Suda*, as emended, reads as follows:[6]

*Panyasis the son of Polyarchus of Halicarnassus: a soothsayer and an epic poet, who revived the epic when it had become extinguished. Duris makes him the son of Diocles and a Samian, just as he does with Herodotus the Thurian.*[7]

For detailed consideration of this and the other bits of evidence which cannot be enumerated here the reader is referred chiefly to Felix Jacoby and Ph.-E. Legrand.[8] It now seems probable that in the *editio princeps* Herodotus referred to himself as a Thurian.[9] The relative insignificance of Thurii and the importance of Halicarnassus in Hellenistic times make it unlikely that any writer in that period would have called Herodotus a Thurian if he had referred to himself as a Halicarnassian in the History. The scholar who decided he had been born in Halicarnassus must also have lived after Duris, otherwise Duris would not have been able to claim Herodotus for Samos. So long as Herodotus was known as a Thurian there was still the question of his original citizenship; once he had been assigned to Halicarnassus there was no longer room for a Samian attribution. But was the unknown biographer right when he decided on Halicarnassus? We can never be sure, although the name of Herodotus of Halicarnassus can still be read on the base of a statue which once stood in the library of Pergamum built under Eumenes II (197–159 B.C.). This suggests that our unknown biographer came after Duris and far enough ahead of Eumenes II to establish what came to be the prevailing tradition about Herodotus. The references to Halicarnassus in the History, though of considerable interest,[10] would not have enabled the Hellenistic biographer to refute Duris, because Samos is treated in even greater detail.[11] Therefore, it appears likely that the biographer may have been influenced by the alleged relationship between our historian and the epic poet Panyassis, for the tradition that Panyassis came from Halicarnassus is unchallenged in antiquity— except by Duris. Duris claimed Herodotus for Samos and that would logically have led him to claim Panyassis as well, assuming that their relationship was generally believed at the time he wrote. If it was, we are carried back into the late fourth or at least the early third century B.C., when it was still possible for a genuine oral tradition to have survived.[12] With this background, we are now ready to examine the strange article on Herodotus in the *Suda*, which begins as follows:

*Herodotus, a Halicarnassian the son of Lyxus and Dryo, from a prominent family, also had a brother named Theodorus. He was forced to emigrate to Samos by Lygdamis, who became the third tyrant of Halicarnassus after Artemisia: for Pisindelis was the son of Artemisia and Lygdamis was the son of Pisindelis. While in Samos he learned the Ionian dialect and wrote a History in nine books. . . . Returning to Halicarnassus he drove out the tyrant, but later, finding himself an object of resentment to his fellow citizens, he went out as a volunteer to Thurii, which was being colonized by Athens. There he died and was buried in the market place. Some say he died in Pella.*

This passage is far from satisfactory. There are minor discrepancies between Herodotus' pedigree as given here and that which appears in the *Suda* article on Panyassis, but they need not detain us.[13] More important, is what is meant by saying that Herodotus came from a "prominent family" (τῶν ἐπιφανῶν). Was the historian a member of the nobility? Jacoby thinks he was.[14] Legrand, on the other hand, argues that Herodotus' family was of mixed Greek and Carian ancestry, a fact he uses to explain certain *obiter dicta* in the History.[15] Legrand may well be right, but the fact that no one named Panyassis or Lyxus appears in the list of priests on a Halicarnassian inscription proves nothing.[16] The statement that Herodotus learned Ionian in Samos is, on the face of it, an attempt at a much later date to explain how a citizen of Dorian Halicarnassus happened to write in Ionian Greek. But this was the literary language of the period, so much so that an official state document preserved for us on stone from Herodotus' time was written in Ionian.[17] Equally unacceptable is the idea that the History was written in Samos, that Herodotus was buried in the Thurian market place, or that he died in Pella. We can accept his exile in Samos and his hostility to Lygdamis, but there is a strong possibility that Herodotus' role in overthrowing Lygdamis may be exaggerated. National heroes seldom go into exile because they are disliked by the citizens they liberate.

Granted that Herodotus was born in Halicarnassus, when did that auspicious event take place? Some scholar, probably Apollodorus, worked out the date as 484 B.C.[18] But this is transparently an inference based on the foundation of Thurii in 444 B.C. as the only established date for Herodotus, who was therefore assumed to have "flourished," that is to have been forty years old, at that time.[19] Dionysius of Halicarnassus says that Herodotus was born a little before the Persian War,[20] which amounts to the same thing. Obviously this is not a satisfactory way to obtain a date, but we have no method for improving on it, and 484 B.C. fits in reasonably well with the circumstances under which the History was written, allowing for a possible error of not more than ten years either way. The exact date of his death is also unknown, to us as it was to the ancients. Dionysius of Halicarnassus adds that Herodotus lived on until the Peloponnesian War.[21] Beloch contents himself with noting two passages in the History which refer to events as late as 430 B.C., and suggests that Herodotus probably finished writing not long afterwards.[22] Legrand rightly points out that this does not tell us when the historian died, merely when he stopped adding on to his History.[23] Arguments based on Herodotus' failure to revise his text after this or that event prove not what Herodotus would have done, but only what the critic would have done had he been in Herodotus' shoes. Jacoby tries very hard to show that Herodotus died sometime after 430 and before 424, though his argument is really a circular one. He holds the view (not generally shared) that Herodotus never finished his History, and "therefore we venture to place his death at the same time as that at which the work breaks off."[24] If the theory of the unfinished History is unsound, then so is the 424 date.

We may now summarize what it is reasonable to believe about Herodotus. He was born sometime between 494 and 474 in Hali-carnassus as a member of a prominent family, which included his father Lyxus and the epic poet Panyassis. Politically at odds with the tyrant Lygdamis, a Persian satellite, he and his family were forced into exile, finding asylum in the island of Samos. Later he returned and may have played a part in driving out Lygdamis (more fortunate than his relative Panyassis who was killed), an event that probably came before 454 B.C. when Halicarnassus appears on the Athenian tribute lists.[25] Later, for reasons unknown, Herodotus became unpopular with his fellow citizens and went into exile once more. In 444 B.C. he took part in the colonization of Thurii.[26] He ceased to work on his History in 430 B.C. or very soon thereafter and died at an indeterminate date. The original edition of the complete History refers to him as a Thurian.

Before dealing with the composition of the History and how Herodotus came to write it, we may consider the question of his travels—places that he tells us he visited and places that we are quite sure he must have visited to obtain the kind of information we find in his work. For convenience, but without implying that the order followed was that followed by Herodotus, we will begin by discussing Egypt and Cyrene, second the non-Greek parts of

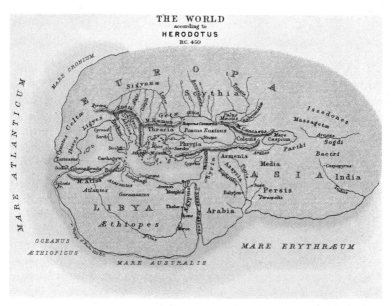

THE WORLD
according to
HERODOTUS
B.C. 450

(*The Granger Collection*)

THE WORLD ACCORDING TO HERODOTUS
Much here is conjectural, especially the African "hump" at Carthage. Still, there is real improvement in detail over Hecataeus.

Asia, third the Black Sea area, and finally Greece itself along with the West. For the Greek cities of Asia Minor and the islands nearby no discussion will be necessary: Herodotus knew them better than any other region, either through personal observation or an abundance of reliable informants.

There can be no doubt that Herodotus went to Egypt, that he saw the pyramids and Memphis, that he traveled south as far as Elephantine and the First Cataract of the Nile, for he tells us so. In a justly celebrated monograph Camille Sourdille demonstrates that Herodotus spent less than four months in Egypt all told, landing in the western Delta at Canopus after the end of July and leaving Pelusium, the eastern boundary of Egypt, before December first.[27] Sourdille works out a plausible itinerary which includes a glimpse of Naucratis on the way to Memphis by canal; a side trip from Memphis to Heliopolis and back; a voyage up river from Memphis to Thebes, where Herodotus stopped off; the return trip downstream (this time going by Bubastis); and finally his departure by way of the eastern Delta, where he saw both Papremis and Pelusium.[28] Scholars have usually accepted these results as to the duration of Herodotus' visit,[29] but there is no agreement as to the year itself. Discussion centers around Papremis, where Herodotus tells us he confirmed his views on the relative strength of Persian and Egyptian skulls.[30] The battle to which he alludes was fought in 459 (or 460), and was won by the Egyptians under their rebel leader Amyrtaeus against the Persians. Since Herodotus found Egypt firmly under Persian rule, and also since he was a Greek, the chances are that he could not have visited Egypt safely until after the much discussed Peace of Callias, that is after about 449 B.C.[31] But how long after? Beloch suggests that it was probably before he went to Thurii, but offers no proof.[32] The suggestion made by Sourdille and others that Herodotus came to Egypt from Cyrene is attractive, but as Jacoby shows, incapable of proof;[33] but he does argue convincingly that Herodotus must have visited Cyrene at some time, because he could not have obtained all his information from the mother city, the island of Thera.[34] He is unlikely to have gone by sea from Egypt to Cyrene direct, because the ocean current there is quite strong, and flows from west to east;[35] but of course he need not have gone to Cyrene and Egypt as part of the same voyage. However that may be, the historian's direct acquaintance with north Africa does not extend west of Cyrene, and much of his information about the interior of Africa was probably obtained in Cyrene.[36]

Turning next to the non-Greek parts of Asia, we know that Herodotus made a special trip to Tyre to see the temple of Heracles. He refers to a city named Cadytis, in Palestine in such a way as to make it quite certain he was there; and for once it is permissible to speculate.[37] What would be more natural than to continue on to Palestine after leaving Egypt at Pelusium? Cadytis, once hopefully identified with Jerusalem, is now thought to have been Gaza.[38] It is likely, therefore, that he traveled all along the coast of Syria-Palestine. He also visited ancient Babylon,[39] though Legrand warns us that it is not easy to separate what Herodotus saw from what he read in the works of others.[40] He notes the existence of certain sculptures that could be seen from the road leading up from Ephesus to Sardes, but while he attributes these monuments to the Egyptian conqueror Sesostris, they are thought now to have been Hittite carvings.[41] At least this indicates he went to Sardes. So far as we can judge, Herodotus probably went no further into the interior than Babylon. His description of the Royal Road, unsatisfactory in many details, suggests that he did not.[42]

The Black Sea region was of special interest to the historian, who has a great deal to tell us about the Scythians who lived north of the Black Sea, and something about the Colchians, who lived on its southeastern shores. He almost certainly visited Olbia, probably the place where he met his Scythian informant, Tymnes;[43] if Jacoby is right in thinking he started out from Byzantium,[44] then he probably knew the whole west coast as well as a part of the north. As to what lies beyond the Black Sea, westward and in the north, we are told expressly that he had seen the Vale of Tempe;[45]

and it is generally thought he traveled through a part of Mace-donia.[46] But it is worth noting that Herodotus' northern journey (or journeys) was not taken in preparation for his History. Other-wise he would have followed a different route, leaving out much of what he actually saw and concentrating on the invasion route of Xerxes and the territory covered by Darius in his ill-fated Scyth-ian expedition.[47]

Finally, Herodotus traveled extensively in Greece. The con-siderable time that he spent in Athens can be inferred from the very intimate knowledge of Athens and her past shown throughout his History, but it is well illustrated by two curious statements in the *Moralia*. Citing Diyllus as his authority, Plutarch tells us that Herodotus received a gift of ten talents from the Athenians, as proposed in a decree introduced by Anytus.[48] Now Diyllus is a reputable historian who lived in the fourth century and on into the third, and who wrote a continuation to the ever-popular History of Ephorus. Therefore we can accept the decree as genuine, though the sum of ten talents must be an error.[49] In another passage, Plutarch tells us that when Sophocles was fifty-five years old he wrote a poem to Herodotus,[50] but this testimony has been variously interpreted. The Herodotus in question may or may not have been the historian. If he was the historian then we have an approximate date for his close friendship with Sophocles, because Sophocles was born sometime between 500 and 494 B.C.[51] Legrand, with his usual good sense, avoids drawing any conclusions as to whether or not the historian and the dramatist knew one another.[52] What is im-portant is that everyone recognizes that Herodotus lived in Athens for a considerable period of time. It was only to be expected that later writers would have provided him with suitable friends, and certain passages in the Plays suggest that Sophocles had read the History.[53] Similarly, because of his knowledge of Macedonia, par-ticularly of details favorable to the king, it has been assumed that Herodotus had met Alexander.[54] This may all be true, but we have no direct evidence one way or the other.

Presumably with Athens as his more or less permanent base, Herodotus visited many other places that were to be of importance to him as a historian. These surely included Sparta, whose version of Thermopylae in which a defeat becomes more memorable than any victory, is immortalized in the History; Delphi, where texts (revised?) of many of the oracles were available and where the gifts of Croesus and others had evidently been seen by the historian; Thebes, where he tells us he saw an inscription in the temple of Ismenian Apollo,[55] and a host of other cities such as Plataea, Argos, Megara, and Corinth which must have lain across his path. He refers quite incidentally to visiting Zacynthus,[56] which Jacoby rightly suggests was probably on his way out to Thurii.[57] In the

West, aside from Thurii, we have only scattered indications of his presence. Croton seems almost certain. Where else could he have obtained the story of the physician Democedes in such detail, a success story in which Democedes comes home and marries the daughter of the town celebrity, Milon the wrestler?[58] He tells us he went to Metapontum and Jacoby believes, while admitting he cannot prove it, that Herodotus had also been in Sicily.[59] His sketchy and inaccurate statements about northern Italy and the western Mediterranean preclude the possibility of a western voyage, even one as far as Massilia.

Such were the regions of the ancient world Herodotus knew through personal observation. As was pointed out earlier, his travels began before his intention to write about the Persian War had taken shape. The question that naturally arises is how and (if possible) when did Herodotus decide on the subject of his History? We may begin with his own statement in the Preface, the first sentence of which may be translated in this way:

*What follows sets forth the results of the investigations of Herodotus of Halicarnassus, undertaken in order that what men have done may not be forgotten through the passage of time, and so that the great and admirable deeds performed both by Greeks and by barbarians may not be without honor; and particularly, as to what it was that led them to make war on one another.*

And here we see history emerging from epic, yet still concerned like the *Iliad* with honor, great deeds, and warfare. The emphasis on war as the chief subject for the historian continues throughout classical times with few exceptions, and for this we must hold Herodotus responsible, but he also deserves credit for transcending the epic in his search for the cause or causes lying behind the events. The epic motivation, expressed in the clash of personalities and the will of the gods, is by no means forgotten and may often play a leading role, but for Herodotus this is not sufficient: the causes and effects that he sees in history are more complex. He looks beyond the statesmen and their actions to the institutions that produce them and to the environmental factors that limit their activities. However, the strength of the epic tradition is such that he dare not, probably does not even wish to break with it entirely. Unconsciously, perhaps, he tries to work the story out in such a way that the results can be interpreted equally well in religious or in rational terms. It will help to keep this ambivalence of Herodotus in mind as we turn now to the circumstances that led him to write his History.

No Asiatic Greek of Herodotus' generation who was also capable of reflection could escape the influence of the Ionian intellectual movement. We have every right to assume that Herodotus had read Anaximander and knew about his map; that he was also familiar with the writings of Heraclitus and of Xenophanes and the others who preceded him. Perhaps (as was suggested earlier) he had read Xanthus' *Lydiaca;* and he must have known both major works of Hecataeus, the *Genealogies* and the *Periegesis.* Yet none of his predecessors had written a history in the sense that Herodotus was to write the history of the Persian War. Therefore, it is natural to suppose that the future historian worked into his subject gradually, a supposition greatly strengthened by a careful examination of the text. What surprises the reader first, is the comparatively small part of the History which deals directly with the Persian War. In fact, it is not until Book VII that Xerxes finally decides to invade Greece. Yet earlier books are crowded with detailed information on the geography, the customs, and the past history, not only of Persia and the Greek cities with which she went to war, but of states that preceded Persia, such as Egypt, Babylonia, and Lydia— even remote lands such as western Africa, Ethiopia, and India. These famous digressions of Herodotus greatly enhance his reputation as a social historian and as a geographer. But it remains unlikely he would have devoted an entire book (Book II) to Egypt and her past had he started out with the idea of writing a History of the Persian War. Further, it has long been noted that certain parts of the History can easily be pulled out of their present context and stand alone as separate essays, lectures perhaps—*logoi* (λόγοι) as the Greeks might have called them. The assumption has not infrequently been made that Herodotus was in the habit of giving public lectures in various Greek cities where he was visiting, as one means of meeting his expenses. No doubt this would seem very natural to Greeks living in Roman days, particularly in the time of the Antonines, when lectures by visiting celebrities were even more popular, if that can be credited, than in our own day.[60] But we should not build too much on the one statement we have from an early and also a reliable source, Diyllus (see p. 31), that Herodotus was voted an enormous sum of money by the Athenian assembly.[61]

Herodotus may very well have worked up certain topics for oral presentation, but it will not do for us to think of him as simply combining a great number of lectures (or papers) he had given over the years into a new framework which converted them into a History of the Persian War. Jacoby, in my opinion, is quite right in stressing that at some time in his life, perhaps quite late, he became convinced of the importance of the Persian War as a crucial point in a struggle between East and West, and decided to write about it.[62] Naturally, he would use whatever materials he already had that could be made to contribute to his main subject. Had he started out to write about the Persian War he would have gone about it more directly, as Thucydides was to do in writing about the Peloponnesian War.

And once again, it is reasonable to believe that Herodotus began by collecting information for a prose work of a type already familiar to him. His references to Hecataeus, either directly—or, as is usual, indirectly ("the Ionians say" etc.)—show that while in Egypt Herodotus had in mind verifying or correcting the account of his predecessor who, in his turn, had gone out to test the conclusions of an earlier writer, Anaximander of Miletus.[63] But was Herodotus trying to write a *Periegesis* of his own, or was he interested in improving on the *Genealogies?* Was it the mythological past that interested him, or the geographical and ethnographical features of the world in which he lived? I do not believe there ought to be any doubt but that Herodotus' intellectual interest was in his own times, not the days of the Homeric heroes or the creation of the world, but the present. However, he wanted to understand it and the only way to understand it was to look back and determine, if at all possible, how it had come about. Two obvious topics for study were man's changing environment and man himself. The study of environment had been approached theoretically by the Ionian philosophers, and practically by Hecataeus and no doubt others. Some attention had also been paid to gathering data about the customs of people who lived in different parts of the world. But although philosophers had speculated on the cycle of changes through which the world had passed and was still passing, there had been no serious attempt to integrate man's activities in the past with the history of his environment.[64] Mythology, then, was the only source of knowledge about men in the past, though the myths had been rationalized to adapt them to modern taste. We have already seen that Hecataeus and Hellanicus both tried to work out a consistent chronology for the heroic age. Now Herodotus applied the critical methods they invented to more promising material, and in this way he became the first western historian. For he saw clearly enough, and was probably the first Greek to do so, the difference between the legendary past and the historic period. Two examples may be cited, the first of which comes towards the end of the Preface. Dismissing what he has just said about the earlier incidents in the struggle between East and West, Herodotus continues:

*Now that is what the Persians and the Phoenicians have to say, though I am not going to maintain that these things happened in this way or in some other way. But I do intend to point out the man whom I myself know was the first to do wrong against the Greeks.*[65]

The man he alludes to is Croesus, but this passage by itself might be interpreted merely as defining the first known act leading to the Persian War, rather than as separating history from pre-history. That is to say Croesus, by exacting tribute from the Greek cities and then failing to protect them from Persia, left them an easy prey to Cyrus, and then the Persian treatment of the con-quered Greeks along with their resentment of it led inevitably to Xerxes' invasion and Herodotus' war. However, there is another passage which cannot be explained away so easily. It has to do with the famous tyrant of Samos:

*Polycrates is the first Greek we know about who set out to rule the sea, unless perhaps Minos the Cnossian or someone else before him ruled the sea; but Polycrates was the first of the race of men. . . .*[66]

Polycrates, like Croesus, lived in the sixth century B.C. For Herodo-tus that is when history begins. What happened before that time interested him also, because it was necessary for understanding the historic period, but he recognized that the evidence about it was of a different kind and had to be handled differently.

One last factor may be alluded to because it contributed to Herodotus' development as a historian, and that is the circumstance that he spent his formative years as an exile. The Greek who remained at home would not easily acquire the wider perspective needed in a historian, nor would he, especially if he belonged to a prominent political family, have the leisure to carry out his inves-tigations. Exile among the Greeks was a recognized institution, each city-state having a number of its leading citizens in exile at any particular date, men always hoping some day to return and banish their political opponents. Such exiles did not need to leave Greece. They ordinarily settled down in another Greek city where of course there was no language barrier, but where they were prevented from taking any part in public life. Men in exile saw things in a different light, they were more apt to see Greece as a whole rather than merely the intense political and social life of a particular city. Herodotus, in Athens, might learn to weigh the position of Athens in the history of his own day better than an Athenian, however gifted, who had never lived away from home. There is the re-markable coincidence that all the major Greek historians wrote at least a part of their works in exile. Plutarch, in his essay *On Exile* points this out, citing Herodotus, Thucydides, Xenophon, Philistus, Timaeus, and Androtion;[67] but this list is far from complete. Among those omitted are Ephorus and Theopompus, the best known historians of the fourth century, and Polybius, the last great Greek historian, who lived in the second century B.C.

Returning to the History, let us see how Herodotus organized his material. The text we have is probably arranged as it was originally, except for the arbitrary division into nine books, which must have been made many years later.[68] Although this division may not always seem logical,[69] the convenience of uniformity in the way we cite passages in the text far outweighs the disadvantages. There is not space here to permit a detailed examination of the entire History, so I have decided to summarize the topics treated in one book by Herodotus, and for that purpose I have chosen the first book of all.

It has already been noted that Herodotus attaches particular importance to Croesus of Lydia, "the man whom I myself know was the first to do wrong to the Greeks" (ch. 5). But before telling us more about Croesus he gives us a summary of earlier Lydian history, explaining how Gyges, the first of Croesus' line, made himself king by murder most foul, and how Gyges' successors became involved more and more deeply with the Ionian Greeks. And then we come back to Croesus, whose history forms the main thread of the narrative for the next sixty-seven chapters (chs. 26–92). But Croesus' military conquest of the Asiatic mainland Greeks takes only one chapter, his treaty with the island Greeks is the concern of another chapter, and a third rounds this all off with a brief description of the extent of his dominions. Then come seventeen chapters (29–45) taken up entirely with Croesus' private life: the visit of Solon, and Croesus' contempt for him; followed by a long account of how the king was punished for his arrogance by the death of his favorite son and intended successor, Atys. At this point a new major figure enters the stage in the person of Cyrus of Persia. But we are told nothing here about Cyrus' rise to power, merely that he has taken over the Median kingdom and that Croesus was concerned about his growing strength. Should he not attack Cyrus before he becomes even stronger? He decides to consult the oracles, but first he will test them to learn which ones can be trusted. Delphi wins his confidence by passing the test, and is rewarded munificently with gifts before Croesus ventures to ask the god for advice. Among the questions he asks is whether to seek an ally in the war against Cyrus, to which Apollo replies that he will do well to ally with the strongest Greek state. Croesus decides to make an alliance with Sparta (46–56). This enables Herodotus to offer his explanation of why Sparta was selected rather than Athens, which serves to introduce a digression on early Athenian history including the tyranny of Pisistratus (57–64), followed by another digression on early Sparta (65–68). After concluding the alliance with Sparta, Croesus takes the initiative, and leads his forces into Cappadocia, where they fight a drawn battle against the Persians. Returning to Sardes he dismisses his troops for the winter (69–77). Cyrus, however, appears unexpectedly and lays siege to Sardes, and Croesus sends to his allies for help (78–81). Sparta is then engaged in a successful war with Argos which delays her preparations to help Croesus, with the result that no troops are sent until it is too late (82–83). There follows an account of the fall of Sardes, along with the capture of Croesus and Delphi's explanation of the oracles whose meaning Croesus had misunderstood (84–92). After a brief account of Lydian inventions (93–94), Herodotus turns to the Medes and tells us how they became the rulers of Asia under Cyaxares (95–106). The rest of Book I (107–216) centers around Cyrus of Persia. The story of Cyrus, all the way from the circumstances surrounding his birth to his conquest of the Medes reads like a fairy tale rather than a history, a tale with resemblances to the familiar story of Romulus and Remus and many others (107–130). Then the narrative is interrupted by a digression on Persian customs (130–140). The thirty-six chapters (141–176) that follow describe the conquest of the Asiatic Greeks by Cyrus' general, Harpagus, with occasional interruptions to explain Ionian and Dorian institutions and other matters. A short chapter brings us back to Cyrus, who has now decided to attack the "Assyrians" and their capital city of Babylon (177). But before this campaign gets under way Herodotus presents us with yet another excursus on the great cities of Babylon and Nineveh and their past history (178–187). The campaign of Cyrus and his capture of Babylon are then related (188–191). Cyrus is no longer a fairytale figure, he has become a ruthless conqueror subject to ungovernable fits of temper. Once more the narrative is interrupted for further details about Babylonian customs (192–200). The book closes with the account of Cyrus' last campaign, fought against an eastern nomadic people known as the Massagetae, in which Cyrus loses his life, but leaves the empire intact for his son Cambyses.

Herodotus has accomplished a great deal in this first book. The background both on the Greek side and on the barbarian side has been filled in, and the events of many centuries related in such a way as to prepare us for future conflict; Sparta has warned the Persians who in turn have ignored that warning. The surprising thing is how little of the book deals directly either with political or military history. This applies to the two kings whose lives are given in such detail, to Croesus and to Cyrus. For both, the interest lies rather in the kind of decisions they make, in their moral qualities, and in how they react to success or adversity. We have more a study of two men than a history of Lydia or Persia. The story of Croesus can well serve as an illustration of Herodotus' views about history. Croesus' downfall can be explained on purely religious grounds. When Gyges seized the throne after murdering Candaules, the Pythian oracle proclaimed that vengeance would overtake his fifth descendant on the throne. "But," says Herodotus, "the Lydians and their kings paid no attention to this pronouncement until it was fulfilled" (13). Therefore Croesus was always doomed, whatever he might do, because of the crimes of Gyges.

But there is more. An early king of Lydia named Meles had been told that if he carried a lion cub around the perimeter of the citadel of Sardes that citadel would be impregnable. He did so, except for one part which seemed too steep to permit any enemy to attack (84). And that, of course, is where the Persians breached the defenses. There is yet another aspect of Croesus' fate that has religious overtones. He disregarded Solon's warning that the gods are always jealous of men who become too prosperous (32), and his contemptuous treatment of the Athenian sage thereafter shows him to be guilty of *hybris*; as in the Old Testament pride is a deadly sin. We may round out Croesus' errors on the religious and moral side by mentioning his wishful interpretation of the three Delphic oracles on Persia (53; 55–56), and his misunderstanding of the warning that was given him about his son Atys (34).

However, Herodotus is not satisfied with this kind of an explanation—one reason we call him a historian. Croesus' mistakes in judgment, judgments without moral implication, are sufficient to bring about his destruction. First, before he sets out against Cyrus a Lydian named Sandanis advises him not to go, because this was a war in which the Lydians had nothing to gain and the Persians nothing to lose (71). Later, after the drawn battle, it was Croesus who committed the cardinal error of assuming that Cyrus would not dare invade Lydia (77); and it was Cyrus who, learning that Croesus had dismissed his troops, then decided to advance against Sardes (79). Further, while we are told that King Meles failed to have the lion cub carried past the steep side of the acropolis, we are also told that the Lydians failed to post a guard on that side. Herodotus evidently knows what he is doing: he cannot omit the supernatural trappings associated with the epic, for that would be considered a violation of literary good taste;[70] but he can provide a rational alternative. Nothing perhaps suggests his state of mind better than the reply of Delphi to Croesus' outraged wails that he had been betrayed. The priestess says, in effect, that even the god cannot alter what has been decreed by fate, but that Apollo had managed to provide Croesus with three more years on the throne than he was supposed to have had (91)! The historian makes no comment on this interpretation, the reader is free to believe it or not as he chooses. This compliment to the intelligence of the reader will not be found in Thucydides or, so far as I have observed, in any other major Greek historian.

Book II, on Egypt, illustrates the scope of Herodotus' intellectual interests. This, the longest of all his digressions, is loosely tied in with the main theme by a reference in the first chapter to Cambyses' intention of invading Egypt, a subject which is not resumed until the book following. The account of Egypt is important for our judgment of Herodotus because he was competing with

Hecataeus. How can we be sure that what we now read was not simply taken over from the famous Ionian logographer? Although Porphyry charges Herodotus with stealing a great deal of Book II from Hecataeus,[71] Porphyry was in the habit of accusing everyone, even Plato, of plagiarism, a fact which takes much of the sting out of his accusation.[72] Then too, it should be kept in mind that Herodotus' account of Egypt is much more detailed than that of Hecataeus; therefore he must have added a great deal of his own to the earlier work. The charge of plagiarism is also irrelevant. History was considered a part of belles-lettres, and all Greek historians appropriated material from earlier authors. The object was to make one's own account more readable and more accurate than any preceding work, pointing out the mistakes of earlier writers but not acknowledging literary obligations. There were no copyright laws. Ultimately the reader would decide which work would survive and which would lapse into obscurity. That is just what happened here: Herodotus continued to be read while Hecataeus dropped out of sight. Later, Ctesias of Cnidus wrote a History which was certainly meant to eclipse that of Herodotus, while still later Theopompus of Chios did something much worse—he abridged him.[73]

Herodotus is still capable of defending himself against his critics, both ancient and modern, so that there is no reason to repeat here what he says so much better himself. It will be useful, however, to illustrate the way he goes to work by one or two examples. A favorite subject for dispute throughout antiquity was the Nile river. Where does it come from? Why does it rise every year at such an odd time? What effects has it had on the life of the people? After citing other theories on the rise of the Nile, Herodotus proudly offers one of his own, which involves the startling assumption that the sun can be blown off course by a strong north wind! Yet this assumption is consistent with early speculation in Ionia.[74] Characteristically he cites other opinions as well as his own, the reader is once more presumed capable of making up his own mind. This habit of his sometimes preserves for us contemporary views that otherwise we would know nothing about. In discussing the source of the Nile, Herodotus gives us authentic details about an expedition which reached the land of the pygmies, although he draws the unwarranted conclusion that because crocodiles were seen in an African river which flows from west to east, that that river must be the upper Nile, whose course roughly parallels that of the Danube in Europe.[75] Once more, he is wrong, but he preserves the evidence which we need, and which would otherwise have disappeared. Most interesting of all are Herodotus' speculations about the effects of the Nile on Egypt. Using the little information he had, he attributes the creation of much (if not all) of

Egypt to the annual deposits of silt left by the Nile,[76] and concludes that a time will come when the river banks will be too high for the river to overflow them, with disastrous results for Egyptian farmers, who will find themselves worse off than the Greeks whom they commiserate.[77] But he also projects this theory about the formation of Egypt backwards into time, as we can see by his calculations on how long it would take the Nile to turn the Red Sea into another Egypt, if the river changed its present course (II. 11). And this calculation may help us to unravel the mystery of Herodotus' famous error in placing the Pyramid builders, who belong to the Old Kingdom, in a comparatively recent period. How could they have built the pyramids before that part of Egypt had become dry land?[78] What is most remarkable about all this is Herodotus' insistence on the relevance of scientific theory for the understanding of history. He was not, as is sometimes implied, first a geologist or a geographer and then later on a historian.[79] His earlier interests were not forgotten, merely enlarged.

Nevertheless, Herodotus did become a historian and he did write about a war. Something must be said about the way he wrote military history, beginning with his sources of information. To a large extent they must have been oral sources. In the course of his travels he asked many questions and carefully noted down the answers he received, but in Egypt and other non-Greek areas he was at the mercy of the interpreters and guides. His own linguistic abilities seem to have been mediocre, to judge by the occasional observations he makes—for example, that all Persian names end in "s." But on the war itself he will have been able to talk to some of the actual participants. However, his informants must all have been young at the time when Xerxes invaded Greece. None of them could have known at first hand what went on in the inner circles where policy matters were decided. Thus, ignorance, plus the glorification of the war which developed in subsequent decades, made them unsatisfactory witnesses. But the historian had to use what information he could get. Where possible Herodotus does introduce documentary material, and he could read inscriptions in public places in Athens and elsewhere. No doubt he also met Greeks who were men of influence, and they would be able to give him what had become the official view of military events, or at least the view of a particular faction. One or two examples will establish this point.

Although no battle in all Greek history has greater fascination than the Battle of Marathon, it is not my intention here to discuss once more the question of what happened to the Persian cavalry. What does have present relevance is the shield signal, a signal sent to the Persian fleet by would-be traitors in Athens.[80] Herodotus assures us that there is no truth in the rumor that the traitors within the walls were the Alcmaeonidae (VI. 121). Yet when we consider that Pericles was the virtual ruler of Athens in Herodotus' time, and that Pericles was also an Alcmaeonid, the political coloration becomes apparent. Similarly, the disgraceful circumstances of Miltiades' death as reported in the History (VI. 136) have a similar connotation because of the rivalry between Miltiades' son Cimon and Pericles. Finally, we may mention the alleged rascally conduct of Themistocles in pocketing most of the money offered by the desperate Euboeans in a vain attempt to persuade the Greek fleet not to abandon them (VIII. 5). But Themistocles, who set Athenian policy during the war, later fell out of favor and went into exile. What Herodotus heard about him in Athens, therefore, reflects the views of his political enemies.

The weakest point, perhaps, in Herodotus' account of the war is his use of figures. The land forces reviewed by Xerxes at Doriscus during the march to Greece are said to have amounted to 1,700,000, estimated roughly by marking off a circle around 10,000 men, then counting the number of times the circle was filled successively by the rest of the army (VII. 60)! In contrast the Greek numbers are microscopic, though not in themselves unreasonable. It appears probable that Herodotus has obtained some sort of listing of the total military forces available to the Persian king, while Greek figures represent the forces actually engaged. However that may be, the vast discrepancy in numbers between the two sides shows that Herodotus had little personal military experience or even an adequate understanding of actual combat, though he is worried about how supplies and particularly water, could be procured for such a vast number of men.[81] Leonidas and his Spartans at Thermopylae are in the old epic tradition of heroes. On the other hand Herodotus does give a creditable description of the terrain, so that modern investigators who visit the battlefields are often able to reconstruct what happened quite differently from Herodotus, and yet using his text.[82] Once more we learn to appreciate what a virtue it is in an ancient historian to give us all the evidence he has, even though his own interpretation may prove inacceptable.

Another aspect of Herodotus' History should not be neglected. He has a great interest in what was later to become a special branch of historical writing, the history of inventions (εὑρήματα). For example he tells us that Glaucus of Chios was the first to discover how to weld iron (I. 25); he describes the methods used by Egyptian embalmers (II. 86 ff.); he notes how the islanders on Zacynthus obtain pitch from their lakes (IV. 195); he concerns himself with the engineering problem of transporting an army across a large river (I. 75) or with irrigation projects (I. 84; II. 150).

And he was fascinated by two of Xerxes' constructions, the pontoon bridge over the Hellespont and the Athos canal.[83] His curiosity in this direction has no limits, ranging from the devices used to raise the stone blocks and put them in place on the Great Pyramid (II. 125) to the little carts fastened behind a certain breed of Arabian sheep to prevent their tails from dragging along the ground.[84] Herodotus is always delighted when confronted with evidence of human ingenuity.[85] But his admiration is not tinctured with aesthetic considerations. What he wants to know is: how big is it? How much did it cost? How were the purely physical difficulties surmounted? The paintings on the ceiling of the Sistine chapel would have intrigued him chiefly because of the mechanical ingenuity and the physical endurance displayed by Michelangelo.

And now we may go back once more, to the earlier question as to Herodotus' choice of a subject and also as to whether or not he finished his History. Legrand rightly calls attention to the vagueness of Herodotus' prefatory remarks, where he speaks of warfare between Greeks and barbarians without even specifying the Persian War;[86] instead he implies an unending struggle between Europe and Asia (East and West) in which the invasion of Xerxes was an episode. We have tried to show that Herodotus collected materials of various kinds over a long period of time, and that when he became more and more interested in the Persian War he tried to bring as much of this material as he could into the new plan for a History. J. L. Myres, on the other hand, believes Herodotus was a master craftsman whose work was carefully and elaborately constructed.[87] He has performed a most useful service in focusing our attention on the History as a great work of literature. The effects Herodotus achieves are not accidental; he planned it that way. However, Myres' own analysis of the text and the theory of "pedimental composition" which he attributes to the historian[88] need not be accepted. Herodotus' methods cannot so easily be reduced to a stylistic formula. He was a great writer, a sophisticated writer, but one who lived well ahead of the formulation of specific rules for prose composition such as those we associate particularly with an Isocrates. Did Herodotus finish his History? My own view is that he did, and like Myres' mine is primarily a literary judgment. Once Xerxes has been repulsed and the course has been set by Athens for the liberation of the Asiatic Greeks, continued fighting with the Persians could only be anticlimactic, blunting the impact of the History as a whole. The Peace of Callias, for example (if there was a Peace of Callias), was at best a recognition only of what had long been obvious to everyone concerned. The Persian threat no longer existed. But I may be wrong, this is a matter which every intelligent reader must decide for himself, and that is precisely what Herodotus would have expected him to do!

# Notes for Chapter Two

1. Thuc. i. 97. 2.
2. John H. Finley, Jr., *Thucydides* (Cambridge, Mass., 1942), 5, remarks ". . . he evidently had no fame in his own day." One of the reasons Finley gives for this is that Thucydides "died before completing the one work on which his fame rests." This might be used in reverse as an argument to show that Herodotus did complete his History.
3. Arist. *Rh.* iii. 9. 1.
4. See Plut. *De exil.* 3.
5. (Hercher, *Epistolog Graec.*, Julian Epist. 21 *init.*)
6. For the emendation see Jacoby, *FGrH* 76. F 64, and also his "Herodotos" (7) in *PW* suppl. II, 207 (henceforth simply "Herod." (7)).
7. *Suda, s.v.* Πανύασις, 248.
8. See "Herod." (7), also the commentary on 76. F 64 in *FGrH* ii C; Ph.-E. Legrand, *Hérodote, Introduction*, 2nd. ed. (Budé) 1955, 6 ff.; Heinrich Stein, *Herodotos*[7], (Berlin, 1962, reprint), I, iii ff.; W. W. How and J. Wells, *A Commentary on Herodotus*, 2 vols. (Oxford, 1912), I, 1 ff.; John L. Myres, *Herodotus, Father of History* (Oxford, 1953), 2 f.
9. Legrand has the courage of his convictions. In his edition of Herodotus we read at the very beginning: Ἡροδότου Θουρίου.
10. We meet the following Halicarnassians: Agasicles, an athlete who refused to dedicate his prize to Apollo as was usual (Hdt. i. 144); Xenagoras, who was rewarded for saving the life of a son of Darius (ix. 107); Phanes, a wily turncoat who deserted Amasis for Cambyses (iii. 4); and the famous Queen Artemisia, who rammed one of Xerxes' ships at Salamis to avoid being attacked by an Athenian vessel (viii. 87). All shady characters!
11. For a guide to the numerous references to Samos see Legrand, *Hérodote, Index Analytique*, 207. Herodotus' partiality for Samos is shown by his account of the Battle of Lade, which was lost because most of the Samian ships pulled out of the line. Herodotus mentions the eleven ships that remained, and describes a monument later erected to honor them in Samos (Hdt. vi. 14).
12. Jacoby suggests Demodamas of Miletus (or Halicarnassus) as the biographer who established Halicarnassus' claim to Herodotus. See *FGrH* iii B. 428, and the commentary on F 1; also "Herod." (7), 213. This is possible, but it does not leave very much time for Duris to advance his Samian claim before Demodamas demolished it; Jacoby gives ca. 300/280 B.C. for Demodamas, and also says that Duris was still alive for at least a few years after 281 B.C. (*FGrH* ii C. 115).
13. In the Panyassis article, Herodotus' brother Theodorus is not mentioned, and we are told that the historian's mother was either Lixes or Rhoio instead of Dryo. His father is called Lyxus.
14. See "Herod." (7), 219.
15. Legrand, *Hérod. Introd.*, 8 f. The key passage is ii. 143, where Herodotus says that, unlike Hecataeus, he did not recite his pedigree to the priests in Thebes. Why not? Was it because he thought Hecataeus was foolish to do so, or because he had none to recite?
16. Legrand, *Hérod. Introd.*, 8; W. Dittenberger, *Sylloge Inscriptionum Graecarum*[3] (1915–1924), 1020 (hereafter cited as *SIG*).
17. See M. N. Tod, *Greek Historical Inscriptions* (hereafter cited as Tod, *GHI*), 2nd. ed. (Oxford, 1946), vol. I, no. 25 and Tod's comments on the dialect, p. 39.
18. See "Herod." (7), 230.
19. Ibid. Jacoby argues that Apollodorus found no date for Herodotus in Eratosthenes, therefore was forced to resort to the "Akmemethode."
20. Dion. Hal. *Thuc.* 5: ὁ δ' Ἁλικαρνασσεὺς Ἡρόδοτος γενόμενος ὀλίγῳ πρότερον τῶν Περσικῶν. . . .
21. Ibid. . . . παρεκτείνας δὲ μέχρι τῶν Πελοποννησιακῶν. . . .
22. Karl Julius Beloch, *Griechische Geschichte* (Strassburg, 1916), II 2², 3 (henceforth Beloch, *Gr. Gesch.*).
23. Legrand, *Hérod. Introd.*, 21.
24. See "Herod." (7), 232.

25. See Tod, *GHI*, I, 38.

26. He need not have gone out the first year, but probably he did—the Athenian invitation could not have been extended indefinitely. Among other famous men connected with this enterprise were Protagoras, who drew up the laws (D.L. ix 50 = Diels *Die Fragmente der Vorsokratiker*, 8th and later ed., no. 80, A 1); Hippodamus, who laid out the city (for refs. see "Hippodamos" in *Kl. Pauly* 1967, II, 1161 f.); also Kathleen Freeman, *Greek City-States*, (Norton Library, 1963), 29 f.); and the philosopher Empedocles (D.L. viii. 51), who, like Herodotus, was assumed to have "flourished" at that time (see Kirk-Raven, *Presocratic Philosophers*, 320 f.).

27. Camille Sourdille, *La Durée et l'Étendue du Voyage d'Hérodote en Égypte* (Paris, 1910), 236 (summarizing his conclusions).

28. Ibid., 247 ff.

29. But not everyone agrees. It is odd to read the following in Aubrey de Sélincourt, *The World of Herodotus* (Boston and Toronto, 1962), 217: "Herodotus probably spent a couple of years over his tour of the Nile valley. . . ."

30. Hdt. III. 12.

31. This is not the place to discuss the Peace of Callias, whose authenticity has been denied and also vigorously defended. See H. Bengtson, *Griechische Geschichte*, 2nd. ed., Munich, 1960, 206.

32. Beloch, *Gr. Gesch.*, II 2², 2. For a recent discussion of the possibilities see Pierre Salmon, *La Politique Égyptienne d'Athènes* (Brussells, 1965), 213–216; also Jacoby, "Herod." (7), 265–267; Myres, *Herod.* 152 f.

33. "Herod." (7), 254.

34. "Herod." (7), 253.

35. Salmon, *op cit.*, 10.

36. The well-known account of the Nasamonians who reached the land of the pygmies (Hdt. II. 32) was told by Herodotus on the authority of "some Cyrenaeans." They in turn had heard about it from Etearchus the King of the Ammonians who, in his turn, heard it from Nasamonian visitors to the oracle. The natural inference is that Herodotus picked the story up in Cyrene. It is barely possible that he met the Cyrenaeans elsewhere, or that he borrowed the whole account from a written work. If so, it could hardly have been Hecataeus, who seems to have thought of the Nile in quite different terms.

37. For Tyre, see Hdt. ii. 44; for Cadytis see Hdt. iii. 5.

38. See How and Wells, *Commentary*, on Hdt. ii. 159 (echoing Stein's remarks on Hdt. iii. 5); see also Myres, *Herodotus*, 7.

39. A particular puzzle is Herodotus' description of the walls of Babylon, with their bronze doors, which Darius had already destroyed in part. Stein thinks enough was left for Herodotus to get a general impression of them, with the aid of local information. See his *Herodotos*, I, xlvi n. 2.

40. See Legrand, *Hérod. Hist.*, I, 114 f. ("Notice").

41. See Hdt. ii. 106, as well as Legrand, *Hérod. Hist.*, ii. 135 n. 2 (French side); and How and Wells. *Commentary*, on Hdt. ii. 106, 2.

42. See Myres, *Herodotus*, 6 ("If Herodotus went to Persia, it was not by the 'Royal Road'.")

43. Hdt. ii. 76.

44. "Herod." (7), 262.

45. Hdt. vii. 129.

46. See Legrand, *Hérod. Introd.*, 24; Jacoby, "Herod." (7), 259. But his knowledge was not extensive ("nicht umfangreich," ibid., 261).

47. Cf. Jacoby, "Herod." (7), 261; see also Kurt von Fritz, *Die griechische Geschichtsschreibung* (Berlin, 1967), I, 130 (hereafter *GG* I).

48. Plut. *Mor.* 862 (*De malignitate 26*).

49. See Jacoby, "Herod." (7), 226 f.

50. Plut. *Mor.* 785 B (*An seni sit ger. rep. 3*).

51. See Jacoby, "Herod." (7), 233.

52. See Legrand, *Hérod. Introd.*, 29; Jacoby is also cautious ("Herod." (7), 233 f.); not so Myres (*Herodotus* 12), who unequivocally supports the friendship idea and cites passages from the plays as evidence.

53. In *Herodotus* 12 n. 2, Myres cites *Oedipus Coloneus* 337, *Electra* 62, *Oedipus Tyran-*

*nus* 981, and *Philoctetes* 1207; Jacoby compares *Antigone* 904 ff. with Hdt. iii. 118–119 ("Herod." (7), 234); but see esp. Helen Bacon's guarded statement in *Barbarians in Greek Tragedy* (New Haven, 1961), 79: "Whether or not Sophocles knew Herodotus as a friend, or read his works, it is clear that he was interested in the same kinds of ethnological material, and learned about them, if not from Herodotus himself, then from some of Herodotus' masters or imitators."

54. See Jacoby ["Herod." (7), 255], who thinks it probable. The passages about Alexander in Herodotus may be the reason for the *Suda* statement that some thought Herodotus had died in Pella (quoted above p. 27).

55. Hdt. v. 59; see Jacoby, "Herod." (7), 272.

56. Hdt. iv. 195.

57. Jacoby, "Herod." (7), 274.

58. Hdt. iii. 129–137.

59. For Metapontum see Hdt. iv. 15; for Sicily, see Jacoby, "Herod." (7), 276.

60. See Samuel Dill, *Roman Society from Nero to Marcus Aurelius* (New York, Meridian reprint, 1956), 343 ff.; also C. W. Bowersock, *Greek Sophists in the Roman Empire* (New York 1969), *passim*.

61. See Jacoby, *FGrH* 73. F 3 = Plut. *Moral.* 862 (*De malignitate* 26). The sum mentioned is ten talents, the enormity of which can be illustrated through Herodotus' *History*. The physician Democedes of Croton, after a year in Aegina in which he surpassed all the local doctors, was voted one talent by the government; later Athens raised the amount to one talent and two thirds, while Polycrates the rich ruler of Samos raised the amount to a full two talents (Hdt. iii. 131). It is inconceivable that the Athenians should have voted five times this sum to a history professor, however eloquent!

62. See Jacoby, "Herod." (7), esp. 352–360.

63. See discussion of Hecataeus in the previous chapter; also my article, "Herodotus speculates about Egypt," *AJPhil.* 1965, 86, 65.

64. There are always exceptions. Anaximander did consider the question of environment. Early man was supposed to have been carried around inside a fish as long as the world was covered with water. See Kirk-Raven, *Presocratic Philosophers,* 141; W. K. C. Guthrie, *A History of Greek Philosophy,* (London, 1962), I, 103. But this is still prehistory.

65. Hdt. i. 5.

66. Hdt. iii. 122.

67. Plut. *De exilio,* 13 f.; see my article, *Amer. Hist. Rev.* 1954, 59, 829–843. At that time I had not noticed the Plutarch passage.

68. Various theories have been propounded about the order in which Herodotus brought out the nine books that now comprise his *History*. A view long held, and still influential wherever How and Wells' *Commentary* is used, is that Herodotus composed Books VII–IX first (*Commentary,* I, 14 f.); Jacoby has convinced most scholars that this is not so. For a judicious summary of the views held, see Myres, *Herodotus,* 26–31.

69. In the Budé edition of Herodotus, Legrand, while preserving the traditional nine books as the basis of his text, has attempted in the various "Notices" to provide the reader with a more logical division of the material. E.g. he treats Book II and the first 66 chapters of Book III as one division, which he entitles: "The Persians in Egypt; History of Cambyses; Polycrates of Samos."

70. The supernatural in Herodotus is also found quite late in the narrative, e.g., not long before Salamis (viii 65), though Legrand (*Hérodote VIII,* 66, n. 3) suggests this particular prodigy may have resulted from a hallucination. As to the good taste in not rejecting such stories see Arrian *Ind.* 31. 9, where the author rebukes Nearchus for going out of his way to disprove a local legend—and Arrian lived more than five hundred years later.

71. Cited in Euseb. *Praep. Evang.* x. 3. 16.

72. See ibid., x. 3. 24–25.

73. On Ctesias, see Jacoby, "Ktesias," *PW* xi. esp. 2042, where in speaking of the Ninus story preserved for us by Diodorus he says: "Es ist sicher kein Irrtum Diodors sondern einer von K's vielen verunglückten Versuchen, Herodot zu verbessern." Theopompus wrote an *Epitome of Herodotus* in two books accord-

ing to the *Suda* (s. vv. Θεόπομπος Χίος ῥήτωρ = *FGrH* 115. T 1), but to our great good fortune the original remains while Theopompus' abridgment has disappeared.

74. Anaximander, e.g., see Kirk-Raven, *Presocratic Philosophers*, 137, 138, and 155. This idea evidently appealed to Democritus and therefore to Epicurus, as it turns up in Lucretius' *De Rerum Natura* (v 635 f.). See Stein's note on Hdt. ii. 24, which is also picked up in How and Wells; but see now Guthrie, *Hist. of Gk. Phil.*, I, 308, n. 2.

75. Hdt. ii. 32–34. This kind of reasoning did not die out. When Alexander found crocodiles in the Indus he is said to have thought he had found the source of the Nile (Arr. *Anab.* vi. 1).

76. For further discussion and references see *AJPhil.* 1965, 86, 68 f.

77. See ibid., and Hdt. ii. 13.

78. See *AJPhil.*, 1965, 86:72 f. The difficulty is in explaining why, if it was too wet to build the pyramids in the Old Kingdom it was not also too wet to build Memphis. But Herodotus describes how Semiramis accomplished a similar feat for Babylon by building a mound above the waters (Hdt. i. 184). This convenient method might well have been combined by his undisciplined imagination with stories of the creation of Egypt, which began as a mound rising from the flood; see James B. Pritchard, *Ancient Near Eastern Texts*, 2nd. ed. (Princeton, 1955), 3 f. On Memphis see also von Fritz, *GG* I, 142; *GG* IA, 96, n. 55.

79. I find von Fritz a little arbitrary in separating the early from the later Herodotus, e.g., on Egypt (*GG* I, 142 f.), and also in his general discussion of Herodotus' development as a historian (*GG* I, 442–475). For Jacoby, presenting what was then a new theory of Herodotus' development, this was unavoidable. Now we can see that the real separation of history and science came later. Anaximander was interested in "history" as well as in geography, and so probably were Heraclitus (despite his obscurity), Empedocles, and others.

80. For a recent study of this incident which demonstrates the difficulties in reaching the Persian fleet by flashing a shield under any circumstances, and the impossibility of determining the time of day the signal was sent, see A. T. Hodge and L. A. Losada, *AJArch.* 1970, 74, 31–36—an article called to my attention by a graduate student, Mrs. Arlene Wolinski. My own feeling at the moment, is that the shield was raised (from the acropolis?) where it could be seen by ships waiting below, which then sped to the Persian fleet with the news that traitors were ready to admit them.

81. See his remarks on the hardships experienced by the Greeks along the invasion route who had to receive the army (Hdt. vii. 118 f.), and also his statement that most rivers were drunk dry by the Persian host (ibid., 127).

82. See, e.g., W. Kendrick Pritchett, *Studies in Ancient Greek Topography*, University of California, 1965–1969, pt. I, 71–121; pt. II, 1–23.

83. For this bridge see Hdt. vii. 36; for the canal see vii. 23–24. Herodotus also tells us of a canal begun by Necho (ii. 158) and completed by Darius (iv. 39) between the Nile and the Red Sea.

84. These sheep are now called Barbary sheep, and carts are still sometimes used, according to How and Wells, commenting on this passage.

85. And here Sophocles and he are one. The famous lines of the *Antigone*, 332 ff., beginning "Many a wonder lives and moves but the wonder of all is man" (Lewis Campbell trans.) would have delighted Herodotus.

86. See Legrand, *Hérodote Introd.*, 227–235.

87. See Myres, *Herodotus*, v–vi and chap. 4.

88. Ibid., esp. 81–86.

We are told that while still a boy Thucydides happened to be present on an occasion when Herodotus gave a public reading from his *History,* and that the future historian of the Peloponnesian War was so moved that he burst into tears. Herodotus is then said to have congratulated Thucydides' father on having a son with a natural gift for learning.[1] This anecdote must be of late manufacture because it presupposes Thucydides' fame as a historian, yet when Thucydides died there can have been a mere handful of friends who knew that an unfinished manuscript of the *History of the Peloponnesian War* was among his personal effects, let alone that this incomplete work would one day make his reputation for all future time. This story of Herodotus and Thucydides pleases us, as it pleased the ancients, because it is somehow appropriate that the two should have met, and that the Father of History should have recognized the talents of his future rival. But we must turn now from pious fiction to facts, beginning with what can be learned from the *History* itself. These are the important statements: (1) Thucydides, an Athenian, wrote a history of the war between Athens and the Peloponnesians, beginning when the war began—because he already expected it to be a great and very important war. (2) The historian was able to give a detailed description of the Great Plague because he had been sick himself, and because he had also been in a position to observe other sufferers. (3) Thucydides tells us his father's name was Olorus, that he himself held the leases to gold mines in Thrace, and finally that he was one of the Athenian *strategi* in 424 B.C. (4) The historian says that he lived through the entire twenty-seven years of the war down to the destruction of the walls of Athens, and that he spent the last twenty years of that time in exile, following an unsuccessful tour as general (*strategus*).[2]

These statements tell us a great deal: that Thucydides was a rich man who, for one

## THUCYDIDES

(*The Granger Collection*)

HORSEMEN JOINING THE PANATHENAIC
PROCESSION IN ATHENS
Thucydides may have seen these figures when they were first carved on the Parthenon frieze, while to Xenophon they were always a part of the acropolis as he knew it. Both historians belong to the upper class of Athenians that is depicted here.

year at least, was a member of the Board of Ten Generals, the highest elective office in Athens. Also we learn that he was exiled (rightly or wrongly) for failing to save Amphipolis from the Spartans.[3] This gave him twenty years to observe the war from the outside. As to the date of his birth, we are reasonably sure he was born no later than 454 B.C., to qualify for the generalship in 424,[4] and he must have lived beyond the age of fifty in order to have been alive when the walls of Athens were pulled down.

With perhaps little more than this to go on, the *Life* that has come down to us under the name of Marcellinus quite reasonably infers that Thucydides belongs to the same aristocratic family already made famous by Miltiades and Cimon. But Marcellinus does add one important bit of evidence, to the effect that the tomb of Thucydides in Athens was empty, because it was ornamented with an *ikrion*, one meaning for which is some part of a ship. The biographer adds that in Athens it was customary to place an *ikrion* on the cenotaph when a man had perished "by that sort of a misfortune."[5] Therefore it has been argued that Thucydides left Athens soon after he returned from exile, where finding life intolerable under the Thirty Tyrants he left once more. He must have died soon thereafter when the ship went down at sea.[6] But there are other reports, for example that he died in Thrace, that he died in Italy, or that he was murdered in Athens after his return from exile.[7] We do know there was a monument to Thucydides which was still there in the second century A.D., because Pausanias saw it.[8] The variety of stories about where and when he died serve only to illustrate the absence of reliable evidence.

Even more important for our understanding of Thucydides than these disputed biographical details are the questions raised by the so-called "second preface" of the *History*,[9] which has been used to support the following argument: Like everyone else the historian probably assumed the war had ended with the Peace of Nicias in 421 B.C. and therefore stopped collecting evidence. Only later did he come to realize that the struggle was not over, but that the whole twenty-seven years from 431 B.C. to the Fall of Athens represent a single war. With this in mind, therefore, he wrote a second preface and also made certain revisions in what he had already written to bring his work into harmony with this revised plan.[10] The problem is further complicated for us by the fact that the text of the *History* breaks off so abruptly in 411 B.C. Does this mean that Thucydides stopped at this point, or only that the rest of what he wrote (however extensive that may have been) was never published?[11] This also raises questions about his style. Book VIII lacks long speeches in direct discourse. In antiquity the historian Cratippus explained this as a deliberate change in style made by Thucydides,[12] while modern scholars have usually preferred to think that the historian had no time to put this part of his work into final shape.[13] There can be no final answers to such questions as these, but they must and will continue to be asked by all who read his *History* carefully, whether in Greek or in translation, for any competent translation also reflects the major problems.

Another difficulty lying across the path of anyone who studies Thucydides is the partisanship of almost everyone who has written about him, a partisanship which attempts mistakenly to defend him at all costs. For the Peloponnesian War not only is he virtually our only reliable source, but also, unlike Herodotus, the author almost never mentions other explanations than his own. That is to say he has excluded materials that would have permitted later historians to criticize his interpretation of events. This is a brilliant literary device. As we read along from one chapter to the next the story unfolds as reasonably and, as it were, as inevitably as fire burns and water flows downhill. Extraneous details are excluded with a rigor never achieved by any other major historian describing the events of his own lifetime. *The Peloponnesian War* is therefore first and foremost a work of art, a piece of literary prose destined to be read for itself alone, even by those with no serious historical interest in fifth century Greece. In that sense Thucydides is more than justified in calling his work a "possession for all time,"[14] though he cannot have foreseen the wider relevance of his assertion.

Much has been written about Thucydides' style, in antiquity as well as in modern times;[15] but here we are more interested in his conception of history. In discussing Herodotus most scholars recognize the need to explain how his subject developed from the sort of thing Hecataeus and the other early prose writers were doing into a history of the Persian War. Thucydides' method of paring down the narrative to the bone makes it much more difficult for us to detect any change of heart he may have gone through along the way. Perhaps, despite twenty years of exile, he saw no need to revise his earlier ideas as to the function of a historian. For undoubtedly there are men like that, Arnold Toynbee for example, for whom the factors behind the changing events on the historical scene, once analyzed need not be thought out again. David Hume's brilliant philosophical contribution was made early, and never abandoned. Are we to think of Thucydides as this kind of precocious genius? Professor H. D. Westlake, in a recent essay on "Irrelevant notes and minor excursuses in Thucydides" opens up a new line of approach that has interesting implications.[16] He shows that in the earlier books of the *Peloponnesian War* Thucydides displays a Herodotean curiosity about natural phenomena and an interest in antiquarianism that tends to disappear as he gets deeper into his subject. This means that Thucydides began writing while he was still under the influence of his predecessors, notably Herodotus, then gradually worked out a special conception of history which was his own. Thereafter he deliberately avoided putting in any details, however interesting in themselves, unless they bear directly on his main theme. This is an attractive suggestion, but it does not quite settle matters. The long digression on Harmodius and Aristogeiton, for example, comes quite late,[17] so that we are asked to allow Thucydides to follow the older tradition in major digressions, while avoiding it on principle in minor digressions.

Once we admit that Thucydides changed his mind about how history ought to be written, the door will be open again to discarded theories like those of Eduard Schwartz, who argued persuasively that Thucydides drastically revised his ideas after the war had ended, and perhaps that is a good thing.[18] Those who believe he did what he apparently set out to do—write a current account of the war as it occurred—will explain references to the end of the war, such as the "second preface," as later insertions. Others will argue that Thucydides kept notes throughout the war, working them up into the form in which we have it after the war was over. The possibilities are almost unlimited while the evidence is inconclusive. Any reader, having been apprised of the state of our information, is free to make up his own mind, with the assurance he will find scholarly support for his opinion.

It is remarkable that a historian who never finished what he set out to do should have won such great fame posthumously, one of the results of which is the report that at least three other authors wrote a continuation of his unfinished work, namely: Cratippus, Xenophon, and Theopompus. The last two will be discussed later in this volume, but here a word needs to be said about Cratippus, truly a misunderstood literary figure. He is said to have been contemporary with Thucydides. But this has been vehemently denied by some modern scholars, who even regard him as a fraudulent writer who lived in the Hellenistic period.[19] But his early date would probably not have been challenged under ordinary circumstances, supported as it is by the testimony of the famous literary critic Dionysius of Halicarnassus, and by Plutarch.[20] The trouble is that Cratippus, as was mentioned earlier, says that Thucydides deliberately modified his use of speeches in Book VIII, a practice Cratippus apparently followed.[21] The fact that there are no long speeches in direct discourse in Book VIII cannot be ignored,[22] but whether this was because Thucydides did not have time to put the book into finished form, or because he decided the narrative did not warrant such speeches in that particular book has no bearing on when Cratippus lived. He may well have continued Thucydides' book without having enjoyed the historian's confidence. It is worth noting that he goes beyond the twenty-seven years of which Thucydides speaks in the "second preface," and reaches the time of the restoration of Athens as a sea power under Conon.[23] Let us not dismiss Cratippus from the ranks of early fourth century historians merely because we dislike what he says about his famous predecessor!

And now it is high time to return to Book I, where Thucydides announces his intentions in a twenty-three chapter "first preface." He justifies his choice of a subject by its importance, not, as is so often stated, because the war was the biggest war in which Greeks had ever been engaged,[24] but because of its total impact. And in this he appears to have been remarkably prescient. In support of his contention that this was the most important, if not the largest war ever fought, he finds it necessary to digress for a moment on past wars with which it might be compared. This digression, sometimes referred to as the *Archaeologia*, reflects the advance of man from a primitive to a more sophisticated culture, rather than the traditional view of Homer or Hesiod, where the poet looks backward to a greater age than his own. Thucydides, like Herodotus, rationalizes the Trojan War. But, for him, the war dragged on because the Greeks of that day lacked the economic resources to bring it to an early end. While it lasted a long time it was not fought with the same intensity as the war he is about to describe. After the Trojan War came the period of colonization and the age of tyrannies, the latter finally being overthrown under the leadership of Sparta. In due course Athens won her famous victory at Marathon, to be followed ten years later by the defeat of Xerxes' forces in their sustained effort to conquer all of Greece. The numbers who fought in the Persian War are regarded by Thucydides as greater than in any other war (he makes no attempt as modern scholars do to criticize Herodotus' figures), but the duration was short. In fact, only two land and two naval battles were needed to bring about a decision (i. 23). The chances are very good that this introduction was written, if not at the very beginning, at least long before the end of the Peloponnesian War. Otherwise Thucydides would have pointed out how much longer it had lasted than the Trojan War. It is not unlikely he wrote it before the Peace of Nicias. Thucydides gives further reasons for his belief that the impending war would be a major one, pointing out that both sides had fought one another before and were therefore preparing for a long bitter struggle. He adds that the portents that preceded the outbreak of hostilities, such as earthquakes and an eclipse of the sun, were more notable than those recorded before other wars (i. 23). I find it hard not to take Thucydides at his word. He may, in his own mind, have had a rational explanation of these occurrences, but that does not mean he thought that their manifestation at this time was irrelevant to the terrible days ahead. The introduction ends as follows:

*The war began when the Athenians and the Peloponnesians broke the Thirty Years Peace which they had made after the capture of Euboea. In the first place I have recorded the reasons why they broke it, and the arguments that they used, so that no one will ever need to inquire as to how such a great war took place among the Greeks. But I am convinced that the most important reason (ἡ ἀληθεστάτη πρόφασις), even though it was the one least mentioned, was that fear of the growing power of Athens forced the Lacedaemonians to go to war. But the following were publicly proclaimed on both sides as their reasons for breaking the peace and going to war. . . .*

What follows describes the series of events that took place in two opposite corners of Greece, one on the Adriatic coast, the other on the northern shores of the Aegean Sea (i. 24–66). Although neither Athens' alliance with Corinth's onetime colony of Corcyra, nor Corinth's military support of another former colony, Potidaea (which rebelled from Athens), constituted a breach of the Thirty Years Peace, both incidents emphasized the will of Athens to continue enlarging her authority. This must in turn have increased Sparta's nervousness. The Corcyraean episode is particularly instructive for the student of Thucydides, for it gives us the first example of his use of paired speeches. He has already reminded us in the introduction that it was very difficult to remember accurately just what every speaker said, even when he had heard the speeches himself, or talked to someone who was there. Accordingly he will try to give what was appropriate for the occasion, without doing violence to the actual speech. As Finley remarks, "he has given himself a good deal of latitude";[25] the question is, how much? Herodotus, following the epic tradition, usually wrote speeches without seriously concerning himself with their authenticity; but Thucydides wished to be more accurate than that, the speeches are to represent the views of the speaker on an occasion on which he actually made a speech. The words are not intended to be exact, but they are intended to give us the substance of what was said. One noticeable feature of this first pair of speeches is that they are anonymous. Is this deliberate on Thucydides' part, or was he unable to learn the names of the Corcyraean and Corinthian speakers? I suspect it was intentional, like the anonymity that surrounds Athens' decision to assist Corcyra, though it is sufficiently obvious that Pericles was responsible. Why should the names be omitted? In general, this omission allows the historian greater freedom to express his own views; in particular, it helps to establish Thucydides' main point, that the real cause lies deeper than the Corcyraean affair. As speeches, they are good examples of the contemporary art of insincere rhetoric; they reflect the atmosphere of a debate, where each side attempts to score points at the expense of the other, rather than to engage in a serious discussion of the issues.[26] It may also be noted that the Athenians decide in favor of Corinth, but that at a later meeting of the assembly they reverse themselves, and accept the Corcyraean alliance (i. 44). They do so because a loophole has been found permitting them to join Corcyra without violating the Thirty Years Peace. Athens agreed to assist Corcyra militarily only if she were attacked. Although it was common knowledge that Corinth was gathering a large fleet, with Spartan approval, in order to punish Corcyra, the Athenian resolution blandly ignores this known fact. The Athenians appear attracted by the very ingenuity of the solution almost more than by any solid advantages they might obtain from it. This same legal correctness was adhered to by Athens in the naval engagement between Corinth and Corcyra: only when the Corcyraeans were in retreat did Athenian warships engage the enemy; and after the battle the Athenian commander refused to accept the surrender of a Corinthian ship because Athens and Corinth were not technically at war (i. 53). Militarily this was risky, but Thucydides makes no comment, either because he fails to see the risk or because in this particular instance no harm resulted.

The Potidaean affair, which follows, was stirred up by Perdiccas, King of Macedon, who had been alarmed by an alliance between Athens and his brother—and other Macedonian malcontents. Therefore he hoped to persuade Potidaea to rebel, thus leading to a war between Sparta and Athens. The immediate result was another encounter between Athens and Corinth, which found Athens attacking Potidaea and Corinth defending it. Under these circumstances the Spartans summoned a meeting of their assembly, at which anyone who might wish to do so was encouraged to bring complaints against the Athenians. The Spartans would then decide by a vote whether, in their opinion, war should be proclaimed. This procedure on Sparta's part is somewhat hypocritical in that the government had already promised the Potidaeans that if they were attacked, the Spartans would invade Attica (i. 58). But Thucydides' account of the proceedings is invaluable, because it gives us much-needed information on how the Peloponnesian Confederacy operated: that is the Spartans must first reach a decision independently, a decision which their allies, also meeting separately, might support or reject. On the present occasion we are given four speeches: the first by the Corinthians; then the Athenians; next King Archidamus of Sparta; and finally a speech by a Spartan ephor named Sthenelaidas.[27] And this time we have both anonymous and named speakers. The unnamed ones are probably farther from what was actually said than the others. The Corinthians, who held back until the other allies had already aired their grievances, sum up the whole case against Athens with an eloquence that still compels our admiration. But would an actual speaker have been quite as blunt in attacking the do-nothing policy of the Spartans—particularly when the Spartan government had already promised to act? It may be doubted. The Athenian speech is almost transparently a rhetorical exercise. We are told that an Athenian embassy that happened to be in Sparta on other business, asked for and received permission to address the assembly (i. 72). It should not have been difficult for the historian to find out who these envoys were, if he meant to present their actual arguments to his readers. More likely, the speech is meant to make us see the confident mood of the Athenians in this time of crisis and the kind of justification for their imperialistic policy which was then current.[28] But when it comes to Archidamus' speech we have every right to assume that it represents the king's own views. He was in favor of preparing for war at a time of their own choosing rather than rushing in prematurely, and he makes some fairly trenchant observations on the reluctance of Sparta's allies to furnish the troops and the money that are needed. His emphasis on the economic aspects of war is particularly interesting coming from a Spartan, and the whole tone of the speech is cautious. The brief angry words of Sthenelaidas outweigh the statesmanlike arguments of Archidamus, and also serve to remind us that normally the ephors had more to say about policy than the kings. In concluding this account of the meeting, Thucydides alludes once more to the most important reason of all (i. 23. 6), saying in effect that the Spartans were less influenced in their vote by the complaints of their allies than by fear of the increasing power of Athens.

The next thirty chapters (i. 89–118) are used by the author to summarize what happened between the Persian and the Peloponnesian wars, the Pentecontaëtia as it is called, bridging the gap between his own work and that of Herodotus. He tells us specifically that Hellanicus' *History of Athens* was inadequate (i. 97). This sketch of fifty years of history remains the best account that we have of the period, but it is far from satisfactory. Just enough details are introduced to indicate Thucydides' interpretation of the growing rift between Athens and Sparta, without giving enough evidence for us to make an independent judgment.

The remainder of Book I concludes all the preliminary steps before the actual beginning of hostilities. Sparta's allies met and voted for war, and last minute diplomatic negotiations were tried and failed. Pericles' importance is shown on both sides: the Spartans revive the story of the "curse of the Alcmaeonidae" as a way of urging that Pericles, an Alcmaeonid, be banished from Athens; and Pericles himself persuades the Athenians to reject all Spartan proposals out of hand.[29]

Book II contains the narrative of the first three years of the war. Thucydides' chronology is based on the solar year, which he divides into the summer and winter seasons, but he does not follow any general system of dating, such as the list of the Priestesses of Hera in Argos or the Athenian archon list.[30] He prefers to date by the year of the war itself, as when he says "Such was the funeral which took place during that winter, and with it the first year of the war came to an end" (ii. 47. 1). The advantages in dividing up the year into two unequal parts, the campaigning season (for "summer" here includes our spring and fall as well) and the off season are considerable in writing the history of a war, although Thucydides does not explain his reasons to us.[31] Considering the complications of the Athenian calendar, with intercalary months at irregular intervals and with the civil year divided into ten parts for administrative purposes, we should be grateful that he wrote as he did. As a method of writing a general history however most of these advantages would be lost, and it is interesting to see how difficult it is for us to work out an exact chronology for the Pentecontaëtia which he summarizes in Book I.

Book II begins with a surprise attack on Plataea by Sparta's ally Thebes before the Plataeans are aware that war has been declared. But the Plataeans extricate themselves by a little treachery of their own, and then prepare to stand siege by sending all non-combatants to safety in Athens. Then we are told of last-minute preparations by the Spartans and the Athenians, each seeking to win new allies wherever they might be found, among Greeks or barbarians. Both sent envoys to the Great King. Yet, strangely as it strikes us now, Thucydides writes that there was far more good-will among the Greeks towards Sparta than towards Athens, "for other reasons but particularly because the Spartans had proclaimed their intentions of freeing Greece" (ii. 8. 4). Thucydides has already described Sparta's early role in overthrowing tyranny in Greece (i. 18. 1), and she continues to pose as the friend of Greek liberty as the war proceeds. For example, when Brasidas urges the citizens of Acanthus on the Macedonian coast to open their gates to the Spartans he tells them that Sparta's only aim in the war is to free the Greeks (iv. 85. 1). Somehow this sentiment never lost its political appeal, whether proclaimed by Spartans, Athenians, Macedonians, or last of all, by Romans. It has an odd ring here following so closely on the information that Sparta, like Athens, has just sought help from the Persians!

Following a listing of the allies of Sparta and the allies of Athens we have a formal address by King Archidamus to the Peloponnesian forces before the invasion of Attica. We learn that the Spartan herald, refused a hearing in Athens, recrosses the border and remarks in truly epic style: "This day marks the beginning of great ills for the Greeks" (ii. 12. 3).[32] Meanwhile the Athenians have adopted Pericles' plan of evacuating the countryside to move inside the long walls, bag and baggage, but they did so with a heavy heart. Pericles prevented the assembly from meeting while the Spartans were still in Attica because he knew the Athenians were angry and might prove unmanageable. To us it is strange that a historian with such a strong interest in medicine, and one who had himself suffered from the plague, should not have commented on the relationship between this policy of Pericles and the spread of the plague. He does recognize that the plague never reached the Peloponnese, but only Athens, and next to Athens, "other most densely populated places" (ii. 54. 5).

The account of the plague is admirably precise and free of any tendency to theorize beyond the evidence. Perhaps the historian had read the Hippocratic treatise on *Ancient Medicine,* which we still have.[33] Thucydides traces the spread of the disease from Ethiopia to Egypt and Libya, from which it went on to penetrate most of the Persian Empire. He says it struck suddenly in Attica, first of all in the Piraeus, and recalls that at the time people said the Spartans must have put poison in the wells. When it reached Athens far more people died.[34] Remedies applied by physicians all proved completely ineffective, but Thucydides gives us the details in the hope that if the disease should return doctors might avoid making the same mistakes all over again (ii. 48). Thucydides' account is not confined to the medical aspects, but gives us a grim picture of the social effects as well. He concludes with a characteristic antithesis:

*The sufferings of the Athenians were enhanced by the fact that at the very time men were dying inside the city their land outside was being ravaged.*

Book II also contains Pericles' Funeral Address (ii. 35–46). This was delivered after the first year of the war just before the plague caused the death of so many Athenians including, on its second visitation, Pericles himself. The speech has long been accepted as the best pleading of Athens' case before the bar of history, and should be read all in one piece to be appreciated. The speech itself, superior to all the other examples of the genre that have come down to us,[35] is as controversial as some of Plato's Dialogues: where does Pericles end and Thucydides begin? Was it perhaps composed by Thucydides after the war was over as a lasting memorial to the Athens he had known? George Grote is right on one point. The historian was well aware when he wrote of the poignant contrast between the buoyant confidence of Pericles and the pestilence which came so soon afterwards.[36] To that extent at least this is a different oration than the one Pericles gave, and the very fact that Thucydides decided to include it in this context gives it an importance it cannot have had at the time. But we may reject the unworthy suggestion that there were not yet enough casualties to justify such a fine speech![37] Now Plutarch tells us that Pericles also gave the funeral oration after the Samian War in 439 B.C.,[38] and he adds, on the authority of Ion of Chios (a fifth century historian), that Pericles boasted he had outdone Agamemnon, for Agamemnon needed ten years to take one barbarian city while he, Pericles, had taken the most important city in Ionia in a mere nine months! Even though, as has been suggested, Ion is twisting this a little, and that in fact Pericles attributed this feat to the Athenians rather than to himself personally,[39] the statement remains bombastic, typical Fourth of July oratory. One more quotation from a funeral speech by Pericles is cited in Aristotle's *Rhetoric*, to the effect that the loss of the young men in the war was as though "the Spring had been taken out of the year."[40] Curiously enough Herodotus has Gelon of Syracuse tell the Greek envoys who were returning home without the hoped-for help against Persia, that "the Spring has been taken out of the year."[41] Stein, in my opinion quite correctly, rejects the idea that Herodotus has borrowed the phrase from Pericles' speech. Rather, it seems likely some earlier poet had coined the expression, which eventually became a cliché.[42] My own feeling, based on the small amount of evidence available to us, is that the funeral speech in Thucydides is a better speech than Pericles ever made. Too bad we do not have the text of the funeral oration delivered by Demosthenes for those who died at Chaeronea!

And now we must proceed more rapidly. The rest of Book II needs no special comment here, except perhaps to call attention to Thucydides' masterly account of the naval battles won by Phormio, the Athenian admiral stationed at Naupactus to keep an eye on Peloponnesian fleet movements in the Gulf of Corinth. There is no clearer description of naval warfare in any ancient writer, a description which preserves for us a vivid impression of the verve and expert seamanship that gave Athens her maritime empire.[43] The passage has a bearing also on our judgment of Thucydides as a naval officer. Could a man who so clearly understood naval matters have deserved to be exiled for incompetence? But this is a rhetorical question, and one which the Athenians were in a much better position to answer than we are. On the one hand, the very best technical training can be nullified by indecision; while on the other hand Athens needed a scapegoat, a role for which Thucydides, with his Thracian gold mines, was admirably suited.

The first ten years of the Peloponnesian War, the Archidamian War as it is usually called, ends with the Peace of Nicias in 421 B.C., a point reached by our historian in the early chapters of Book V. The dominant force in the government of Athens from Pericles' death until his own was undoubtedly Cleon the son of Cleaenetus, Thucydides' bête noire. We do not meet him, however, until the debate over Mytilene. Mytilene had led a revolt of the entire island of Lesbos, with the exception of Methymna, and that revolt was finally put down by Athenian forces under the command of Paches. The question under debate was whether to kill or enslave the entire citizenry, or merely to punish those who had been found guilty of fomenting the rebellion. As happened earlier with regard to the Corcyraean alliance, the Athenians met on a later day to reconsider a decision they had made earlier. Before, Thucydides gives us the proceedings anonymously as a debate between the Corcyraeans and the Corinthians, but this time we are told the names of the two Athenian speakers, each of whom had spoken on opposite sides of the question at the previous meeting. On that occasion the Athenians had followed Cleon in decreeing death or slavery for all the Mytilenians, and now, when they met to reexamine the question, Cleon speaks first. Diodotus, however, this time persuades them to change their minds, with the result that a galley has to be sent off in a hurry to prevent the execution from being carried out.[44] Diodotus is otherwise unknown to us, while for the historian, Cleon represents all that was wrong with Athenian policies after the death of Pericles. Is Thucydides writing maliciously out of hatred for the man who sent him into exile? Some have thought so, but anyone who reads the two speeches carefully one right after the other, is apt to find his sympathies—reluctantly but quite frequently—with Cleon, who argues that empire depends on force on the one side and fear on the other. If Athens intends to keep her empire she must make an example of all rebels. Otherwise she will have to spend so much time putting down rebellion among her allies that she will have no time left to deal with the enemy. Diodotus' speech, much longer and greatly admired, lacks the fiery quality of Cleon's, though it is a very skillful piece of rhetoric. It can be (and has been) used to support the thesis of Darrow and others that the death penalty is not a deterrent to crime. In neither speech, and this should be emphasized, is there any attempt to justify whatever action Athens might take on moral grounds. In fact, the milder terms demanded by Diodotus are really not mild at all. Over one thousand were to be executed, probably the entire membership of the oligarchical party except for those who had already been killed or made good their escape.[45] Two years earlier Potidaea had capitulated. The mild treatment of the Potidaeans was not, however, any indication of humanity on Athens' part, as is shown by the fact that criminal charges were instituted against the generals who arranged the terms.[46]

The surrender of Plataea gives us a chance to compare Athens with her enemy Sparta. On this occasion, the Plataeans were persuaded to throw themselves on the mercy of the Spartans. From the Spartan point of view this made their action voluntary, and if peace were finally made on the basis of each side returning conquered towns, Plataea would not have to be returned. Here, too, we have a pair of speeches, one by the Plataeans and the other by their enemies the Thebans.[47] Five men were sent out from Sparta to act as judges, before whom the Plataeans were required to confine their defense to one question only, whether or not they had helped the Spartans during the war. The Plataeans do not observe these limitations. Instead they appeal to history: their patriotism in the Persian War; the impossibility of obtaining protection from Sparta against Thebes; and their unwillingness to desert Athens when the war came. The Thebans then refute this historical argument on two grounds: that during the Persian War the Thebans were under a despotic government which acted against the wishes of the people, while the Plataeans had remained loyal to the Greek cause only because of their hatred for Thebes. Later when Athens, not Persia, threatened Greek liberty the Plataeans fought on the Athenian side, while Thebes, now under a free government, fought against tyranny. Therefore the alleged earlier patriotism of Plataea was proved to have been a sham. None of this has much to do with the legal responsibility of either Plataea or Thebes, as of course Thucydides was very well aware, but he may have intended here to show the grim contrast between the Spartan promises of freeing the Greeks with their conduct in destroying the heroic little city that had stood against the Persians at Marathon. There is no favoritism here. Both Athens and Sparta, despite brave words such as Pericles' funeral speech, have no scruples, recognize no higher law than expediency. Thucydides spells out his views on the deteriorating effects of war on all standards of decency, in his celebrated remarks about the Corcyraean revolution of 427 B.C.[48] In Corcyra the troubles are compounded by the fact that the oligarchs and democrats hate one another so bitterly that either would gladly admit the enemy in order to destroy the other faction.[49] The state of war between Athens and Sparta encouraged the leaders of any city opposition to call in the Athenians, if they were democrats, or Sparta if they were not. And Thucydides indicates that both Sparta and Athens did nothing to discourage the practice. For instance, it is probable that the Thebans who made a surprise attack on Plataea at the beginning of the war had been in touch with oligarchs inside the city, then these oligarchs were finally gratified by the slaughter of the surviving democrats by Sparta.[50] And on the other side, Diodotus had argued that the Mytilenian democrats ought to be spared if only to preserve Athens' image as the friend of the popular party.[51]

But let us return to Cleon, who was in no way discouraged by his rebuff over Mytilene. We meet him once again, emerging as the man who took credit for Athens' most spectacular military victory in the entire war, the capture of the Spartans on the island of Sphacteria. Thucydides' account of the affair of Pylos and Sphacteria will not be summarized here, merely the part played by Cleon. A series of circumstances that had not been foreseen by either side found the Athenians established on the mainland of Messenia at Pylos; while a Spartan force, cut off from the Peloponnese by an Athenian fleet, held the island of Sphacteria in the bay south of Pylos. Despite redoubled efforts by the fleet to maintain a close blockade some supplies reached the Spartans, and no one dared land on the island to drive them out. Winter was approaching, and if the Spartans could hold out a little longer they would be safe, because no Greek fleet could keep the sea during the winter. For this reason the Athenians were more and more worried lest the prize escape them, and Cleon was subject to recriminations. Earlier he had persuaded them to turn down quite generous Spartan peace proposals on the assumption that the island would be taken, and in case it was not, he would suffer politically. Cleon accordingly told the Athenians that capturing Sphacteria would be easy enough under good leadership. He added that if he were given the command he would either kill the Spartans or bring them back alive within twenty days. At this he was interrupted by loud laughter, and the Athenians insisted he take over the command of the reinforcements instead of Nicias—who expressed his willingness to resign in Cleon's favor. Thucydides says the Athenians insisted because they thought in this way they would either capture the Spartans or, better yet, get rid of Cleon! Malicious, yes, but so far as we can judge the *facts* are not distorted. Cleon sailed to Pylos, a fire broke out by chance on Sphacteria leaving the Spartans with no cover. They decided to lay down their arms, so that Cleon made good on his boast. Naturally the Athenians were elated, and peace seemed more remote than ever.[52]

In the meantime we begin to hear more about a very able Spartan soldier named Brasidas, who put new heart into the Spartans despite their loss of prestige at Sphacteria. Both Cleon and he found out the weak points in the armor of their respective enemies. Cleon (or perhaps better Demosthenes) exploited the advantages of holding a permanent Athenian base in enemy territory. It meant deserters from Sparta (helots or others) had an escape route open to them, and it raised the specter of a helot uprising backed by Athenian naval support. Brasidas, on the other hand, by his daring march north all the way to the Chalcidice, was able to offer an alternative to Athens' allies: they might now revolt and let the Spartans in. In the *Peace* Aristophanes aptly speaks of "War" as mangling the Greeks up in his huge mortar by the use of two pestles, "Brasidas and Cleon," whose loss made it possible for "Peace" to be brought back to the Greek world.[53] In fact, the capture of Amphipolis by Brasidas and the deaths of both Brasidas and Cleon in the battle in which Athens vainly tried to retake that city, led to the Peace of Nicias. Athens was now ready to talk terms, as the Spartans had been ever since Sphacteria. Thucydides had already gone into exile some three years before the peace was signed, and we have already seen that he wrote the "second preface" after the war was over.[54]

Thucydides' account of what happened after the Peace of Nicias suffers from a double disadvantage: first, the fact that he was an exile made it difficult for him to keep abreast of internal developments in Athens. Second, and even more important, he probably made no effort to gather information for a number of years. Later, when it was clear to him that the war had not in fact ended, he resumed his task, but must have found it hard to fill in the gaps. Still another problem arises from the format he had adopted for writing his history. A narrative based on campaigning seasons is more difficult to handle with the Athenians fighting in Sicily on a round-the-year basis, and with the Spartans permanently occupying Decelea in Attica. The war was no longer being fought as either Pericles or Archidamus had intended, but was greatly expanded, not only to Sicily in the west but even to Persia in the east. Also, while Carthage had declined Athens' offer of friendship at the time of the Syracusan expedition,[55] she took advantage of the chaotic conditions in Sicily after the Athenian disaster to return to the island in force. Thereupon, finding it in her interests to keep the Greeks busy fighting elsewhere, Carthage now sent an embassy to Athens suggesting an alliance![56] The struggle between two Greek cities and their allies was beginning to assume the aspects of a Mediterranean war. All of this complicated the historian's task of composing an intelligible narrative, while at the same time it made it harder for him to obtain the reliable data from so many different theaters of war. As Herodotus moves into the later books his theme narrows and becomes more manageable, while with Thucydides the reverse is true. Then, too, Herodotus lived long enough to finish the job, but Thucydides left behind an unfinished work. Nevertheless the last part of his *Peloponnesian War* is admired as much as the first. No greater compliment could be paid him in this regard than the charge later made against Philistus, a distinguished Syracusan historian, of borrowing his own account of the Athenian war in Sicily from Thucydides.[57]

Returning to the breakdown of the Peace of Nicias, we are given a number of different explanations. There was an unwillingness on the part of Sparta's allies to carry out the terms of the peace, which caused the Athenians to delay the return of Pylos to Sparta. Then, too, because the Spartans in Sphacteria had surrendered, which was not at all in accordance with the tradition of Thermopylae, it began to be whispered that after so many years the Spartan military abilities had finally declined. Cities like Corinth and Thebes that had done their best to force the war on Sparta were dissatisfied with the results, and their discontent suggested the formation of a third force that might be strong enough to challenge Sparta within the Peloponnese and Athens outside of it. Meanwhile in Athens Nicias tried to maintain the peace, only to find himself outreached by Alcibiades, who managed to put the Spartan envoys in an impossible position before the Athenian assembly, which resulted in their being sent home abruptly, while Athens made a dangerous alliance with Argos.[58] The crushing defeat of Argos and Alcibiades' Athenian contingent at Mantinea made it clear that Sparta was still master in her own house, while it encouraged Hyperbolus in Athens to revive the use of ostracism in an effort to get rid of Alcibiades. This test of strength in 417 B.C. turned out quite differently than expected, as Hyperbolus was the one who was ostracized as the result of a temporary alliance between Nicias and Alcibiades.[59] Strangely enough Thucydides tells us nothing about the matter when it occurred, although later on he says the oligarchical faction at Samos assassinated Hyperbolus, whom he refers to as a "wretched sort of person" who had been ostracized earlier but who was unworthy of such consideration![60] This may merely show the historian's contempt for an unimportant figure as Adcock suggests,[61] but I think there is more to it than that. Hyperbolus and Thucydides were probably on the Board of Generals together, aristocrat and parvenu, with very different political views. Hyperbolus came into greater prominence after Cleon's death and was dead set against making peace. As a leader of the war party, however, he could not hold his own against Alcibiades, and while Thucydides can hardly have approved of Alcibiades' policies he does respect his family background. One other possibility why the ostracism is not described by the historian is that he lacked the necessary information. The ostracism occurred at a time when he had ceased to gather information, believing that the war was over.

If the ostracism helped reestablish Alcibiades' position at home, the destruction of Melos was one way of reaffirming Athens' position abroad. Sparta might rule the Peloponnese, but she was helpless to assist her own colonists when such help had to go by sea. The "Melian Dialogue" in Thucydides,[62] where the speakers on each side remain unidentified is almost as difficult to explain as it is to forget. It can be argued that Euripides, democrat and patriot though he was, wrote the *Trojan Women* to express his horror over the slaughter of the Melian men and the enslavement of their dependents.[63] It was not an act of which the Athenians could feel proud, but does that mean Thucydides includes this heart-rending dialogue in order to appeal to the conscience of the Athenians? Obviously not. Long before this appeal to conscience could have any effect the war would be over, the appeal useless. Therefore he must have some more general purpose in mind. What if Mme. de Romilly is right in her main thesis, that Thucydides is really writing about imperialism?[64] Then, even after the war, the Melian Dialogue might serve as an illustration of the effects of imperialism on those who practice it, a warning to future statesmen anywhere who might be considering a policy of imperial expansion. Perhaps. I am more inclined to view it as a reaffirmation of his remarks on the eve of the first invasion of Attica, when he says: "most men were hostile to the Athenians, some because they wanted to free themselves from Athenian rule, others because they were afraid of being made subject to it."[65] Thucydides seems to be saying in the Melian Dialogue that nothing has changed. The rule of Athens had been feared by Greeks generally in 431 b.c., and the treatment of the Melians indicates that those fears had not been groundless. Presumably, then Thucydides still believes that, despite Plataea, public opinion in Greece continued to favor Sparta rather than Athens. Although the historian refrains from telling us what he himself thinks about this, the account shows his disapproval by its very tone. But is he writing primarily out of sympathy for the

Melians? Is he not rather thinking of Athens and the effect that such unnecessary cruelty will have on her popularity and thus, ultimately, on her position in the Greek world? The Athenians were a tough people. Soon "Melian hunger" becomes a catchword on the comic stage.[66] Athens had no lingering sense of guilt then, after the condemnation of Socrates, or at any other time.

The decisive turn in the war came with the Athenian expedition against Syracuse. This is not the place to discuss whether such an expedition per se was a blunder, but only to indicate how Thucydides regarded it. Athens' interest in the West was not new. Two years before the Archidamian War began the Corcyraeans pointed out to the Athenians how important an alliance with Corcyra would be in controlling shipping between Sicily and Magna Graecia and Greece, and also in preventing naval assistance from reaching Sparta from that quarter. Cleon's great moment at Sphacteria was a by-product of Athens' Sicilian policy. The Athenian forces that fortified Pylos had been detached from a fleet on its way to help Athens' allies in Sicily. The fleet turned around reluctantly when they heard that the Greek states in Sicily had made peace.[67] And now once more opportunity presented itself when the western Sicilian city of Egesta asked Athens to help her against neighboring Selinus. Thucydides says (vi. 6) unambiguously that this was merely a pretext, that Athens' *real reason* ($\dot{\eta}$ $\dot{\alpha}\lambda\eta\theta\epsilon\sigma\tau\acute{\alpha}\tau\eta$ $\pi\rho\acute{o}\phi\alpha\sigma\iota\varsigma$) was the desire to rule the whole island. But he does not go so far as Plutarch, who says the young bloods in Athens thought of Sicily as merely the beginning—they were drawing maps of Libya and Carthage in the sand![68] The prime mover in this enterprise was Alcibiades, the leading objector Nicias. Both were effective speakers, but the Athenians had so much respect for Nicias that to win his support they voted a much larger force than had originally been proposed, entrusting the command jointly to Alcibiades, Nicias, and a professional military man named Lamachus.[69]

And now we must pause for a moment over the strange episode of the mutilation of the Hermae, which occurred not long before the fleet left for Sicily. The images known as Hermae (not necessarily images of Hermes) that Athenians liked to set up before their houses were defaced one night while honest men were asleep. A wave of terror swept the city, chiefly because this act of vandalism was felt to be a bad omen for the expedition. The problem was to determine whether this was only the work of irresponsible pranksters or perhaps connected with a sinister plot against the state. Alcibiades' name was often mentioned because of acts of sacrilege committed in his youth, but he was refused a trial, his enemies preferring to charge him later when his many friends on the fleet would not be there to support him. Thucydides then continues with the narrative of the expedition to Sicily, which is again interrupted by the arrival of a ship sent from Athens to bring Alcibiades home for trial.[70] Then we are told that in Athens the investigation of the Hermae affair has been going on uninterruptedly, and that arrests have been made without any clear reasons, and that many leading citizens have been thrown into prison. At this point, Thucydides makes a long digression on early Athenian history, apparently supporting Herodotus' version of the assassination of Hipparchus, and refuting the views of Hellanicus.[71]

Returning now to Thucydides' account of the Hermae affair we find it somewhat disappointing, but this time we have another contemporary source as a basis for comparison, the speeches of Andocides. What is noticeable is not that Andocides has more details, for he was there while Thucydides was not, but that the historian refuses to be specific even about such facts as he has. Like Andocides, he says that one of the men arrested and held in prison was persuaded by another to turn state's evidence; but Andocides gives his own name as that of the informer and says it was his cousin Charmides who talked him around.[72] Both writers refer to an anxious night which the Athenians spent under arms, fearing treachery—presumably a plot to let enemy troops inside the walls.[73] Thucydides does say that it was not clear whether those denounced by the suspect, and punished, were guilty or not. But he adds (vi. 60. 5) that the city benefited greatly by having the matter settled. His reticence in naming names may be caused by an unwillingness to throw mud at the really old Athenian families. We have already seen how differently he treats the lamp-maker Hyperbolus.[74] Curiously, we have a bit from a lost speech by Andocides in which he says:

Shame prevents me from speaking about Hyperbolus, a man whose father was branded with an iron and who still works as a slave in the public mint, while he himself is a foreigner and a barbarian who makes lamps![75]

This is obviously not a statement to be relied on, but it does reflect the social background common to the orator and the historian. Thucydides could have told us a great deal about the oligarchical clubs that continued to work for the overthrow of the Athenian democracy, but he does not do so.[76] When Alcibiades reaches Sparta in his wanderings he refers to the democracy in no uncertain terms as something that all intelligent people understand for what it is, and he more than others as having the greatest reason to complain about it.[77] Granted that Alcibiades was a treacherous man, there is still something convincing in his allusion to democracy as a generally recognized evil. Here he speaks the language that must have been common in some circles even in Athens. While on the subject of the historian's aristocratic leanings, reference must be made to Antiphon, who was tried on a charge of treason, convicted, and executed. Thucydides, who was in exile when this happened, speaks of Antiphon's abilities in the highest terms, informing us that he made the best speech in his own defense of anyone he knew about. The contrast between this and his references to Hyperbolus, no traitor but the victim of traitors, can hardly be missed.[78] What surprises us today is the strength of the democracy in this atmosphere of oligarchical intrigue inside, and a formidable enemy without. The Old Oligarch, whoever he may have been, seems to have gauged the capability of the democracy more accurately than did Thucydides.[79]

In Sicily the recall of Alcibiades, who took refuge in Sparta urging the Spartans to renew the war openly, was shortly followed by the death of Lamachus, which left Nicias as supreme commander.[80] The siege of Syracuse is described as first a race in wall building—the Athenians trying to cut Syracuse off from the interior; the Syracusans building a counter wall to turn the Athenian wall. The arrival of the Spartan Gylippus put new heart into the defenders, and the situation began to deteriorate rapidly from the Athenian point of view. Nicias, who had been so much opposed to the expedition from the very beginning was in poor health, and asked to be relieved of his command. Instead the Athenians sent out another fleet almost as large as the first, under the leadership of Eurymedon and Demosthenes. This fleet went out in the spring of 413 B.C. despite the fact that a Spartan army under King Agis was now permanently stationed in Attica. But the situation in Sicily was beyond redemption. Demosthenes saw this clearly, after the failure of a night attack against the enemy lines, but neither he nor Eurymedon could persuade Nicias to sanction an immediate withdrawal. Thinking perhaps Nicias knew something they did not (perhaps an understanding with traitors inside Syracuse) the Athenians stayed.[81] There is no reason to dwell on the harrowing battle in the harbor or the terrible retreat overland—again delayed by Nicias—which resulted in virtually wiping out the entire force.[82] But it is worth noting that when Nicias meets his death at the hands of the enemy after surrendering himself, Thucydides speaks of him as "the man who least deserved such a misfortune of all the Greeks in my time, because he always tried to do what was right." Yet Nicias, more than anyone else, was responsible for the disaster in Syracuse. He was also, as Thucydides notes, a superstitious man.[83] Why then pay him such a tribute? I cannot accept the suggestion that it was because of his, "moderation and stability. . . . The mind is thus carried back to Pericles, whose stability Nicias alone possessed. . . ."[84] Was this not the stability Terentius Varro possessed, when after Cannae he did not despair of the Roman republic?[85]

Demosthenes, who has the best record of any Athenian general in the war and who had advised leaving Syracuse while it was still possible to do so, also died in the retreat, but without any suitable tribute from the historian. But he probably did belong to Cleon's war party and he must not have come from an aristocratic family. This is not intended as a reflection on Thucydides' impartiality as a historian, because he does full justice to Demosthenes as a commander at Pylos and elsewhere. It merely shows, I believe, that Thucydides had no personal regard for him, whether on political or social grounds it would be difficult to say. It is also interesting that Gylippus is mentioned with approval as having tried to save the lives of the Athenian generals.[86] Later, at the very end of the war, Gylippus was caught stealing public property. He either committed suicide or went into exile.[87] Probably Thucydides knew nothing of Gylippus' peculation when he wrote these lines, which suggests they were composed before the end of the war. Timaeus, writing much later, can afford to treat Gylippus with some contempt,[88] but he also has him intercede for the generals. I am not so sure as I once was that Timaeus was correct in saying so.[89] He must have read of Gylippus' intercession in Thucydides, but Thucydides may well have got his information from Gylippus or some other Spartan who put the blame for this violation of the rules of war on the Syracusans alone. Somehow it is a little reminiscent of Ctesias, whom we meet in the next chapter, explaining how he had done everything in his power to make life easier for the prisoner Clearchus. Who was there to contradict him?

Only three more topics, all of them from Book VIII, need be discussed: the Athenian response to the Syracusan disaster; the entrance of Persia into the conflict; and the oligarchical revolution of 411 B.C.

The first reaction in Athens was one of disbelief, which soon turned to anger directed at the politicians who had misled the people into such a suicidal expedition, and at the soothsayers who had prophesied the conquest of Sicily. But anger was soon followed by a sober appraisal of what lay ahead. There were nowhere near enough ships in the docks and not enough trained crews to row them if there were. Meanwhile they fully expected the Syracusan fleet to arrive any day before the Piraeus, and that their enemies would then attack them both by land and by sea while the allies would rise up in revolt.[90]

*Nevertheless they decided to do whatever present circumstances permitted, and not to give in, but instead to build another fleet with whatever resources they could bring together in the way of timber and money. Then, to make sure that the allied territory was fortified, Euboea above all, and to cut down expenses in the city by appointing a board of older citizens who were to take the proper measures to deal with the present situation.*[91]

The "board of older citizens," probably the ten probouloi of Aristotle,[92] no doubt represented men opposed to the expansionist policies of the extreme democrats, but there is no reason to question their loyalty to the government. However, although Athens was able to build a new fleet during the winter of 413/412 B.C., prevent widespread rebellion, and prepare to continue the war, a new and unexpected blow was added by the appearance of Persia with her moneybags on the scene. The Syracusan threat never materialized. True, a few ships were sent under Hermocrates which gave a good account of themselves, but Syracuse soon became occupied with her own internal problems and with the Carthaginian invaders. But the Persian threat was dangerous. With unlimited resources they could build fleets for Sparta and hire oarsmen to row them indefinitely, while if Athens lost her fleet she had no means to build another. This was a desperate situation, and there should be no doubt that under these circumstances, "the existence of the committee [i.e., the ten probouloi] facilitated the revolution of 411."[93] But it was not because they were oligarchs, but because they wished (unlike the oligarchs!) to save Athens at all costs.

Thucydides shows the rivalry between the two famous satraps Pharnabazus and Tissaphernes, each hoping by means of subsidizing the Spartans to recover lost territory and thus win favor with the king (Darius II) by restoring the tribute. We are told that Sparta preferred Tissaphernes' offer because it was backed by Alcibiades, who was the hereditary guest friend of the influential Spartan ephor Endius. When we remember that this is the same Endius whom Thucydides says Alcibiades had diddled (along with two fellow ambassadors to Athens) in 420 B.C.,[94] we can only conclude either that Thucydides was misinformed about the embassy of 420 or that Endius was an unusually gullible man. It appears probable that the historian did not have access to the facts. One can imagine stories about Alcibiades' cleverness making the rounds and losing nothing in the telling. The Treaty of Miletus, as it is called, was only the first of three treaties signed between Sparta and the Persians within a single year, and all are given by Thucydides.[95] The reason for cancellation then renewal of these treaties was Sparta's reluctance to pay the price, that is the recognition of the Persian rule over the Asiatic Greeks. Ultimately she did so, and that, in the last analysis, settled the war.

Closely connected with the entrance of Persia into the conflict was the oligarchical movement that led to the overthrow of the Athenian democracy in 411. Hignett makes the following statement: "Before the demagogues lost power they had embroiled

Athens with Persia as well as with Sparta by giving support to the rebellion of Amorges in Karia against the Great King."[96] He cites Andocides' speech *On the Peace*[97] as evidence, although Thucydides says nothing about it. Andocides cannot be trusted, particularly in this speech, because he is an interested party. He had been sent to Sparta to negotiate peace, and on his return in 391 he makes a speech urging that the terms be accepted. In the course of his remarks he looks back in time, and refers to a treaty of friendship the Athenians had once had with the Great King, which he says they had broken in order to help Amorges, "the King's slave and a banished man." However a passage from Ctesias' *Persica* puts matters in a different light.[98] A certain Athenian named Lycon supported Pissuthnes, the father of Amorges, in his rebellion against the king in 420 B.C. Later he was persuaded to go over to the Persian side; and when Tissaphernes obtained Pissuthnes' satrapy, Lycon was rewarded with land and cities as the price of his treachery. Lycon, therefore, was a free-lance mercenary captain, whose activities cannot be blamed on the Athenian government. Ctesias' knowledge of Persian history, plus the reticence of Thucydides entitle us to disregard Andocides despite Dalmeyda's ingenious attempt to save his credibility.[99] Therefore we need not believe with Hignett that the extreme democrats had "embroiled Athens with Persia." On the other hand, Persian support for Sparta after the debacle in Sicily was a deadly threat to Athens, and no Athenian—democrat, oligarch, or middle-of-the-roader—could fail to be aware of it.

Athenian naval operations were largely in Asiatic waters, where Samos was her chief stronghold and naval base. It is not my intention to try to unravel the tangled skein of intrigue that took place among the conspirators both in Samos and in Athens. There is a controversy over the details which took a new turn when Miss Mabel Lang published her important article in 1948.[100] She tried to show that our two chief authorities on the Revolution of 411, Aristotle and Thucydides, instead of contradicting one another could be combined in such a way as to give us a more accurate picture than either gives separately. She argued that Aristotle was interested in constitutional details for their own sake, Thucydides only when such details have an influence on the events. Reconciling them depends on working out a satisfactory chronology to accommodate the statements made by both writers. This Miss Lang attempted to do, but her solution was soon disputed by C. Hignett in 1952 and by others. Some new evidence then led Miss Lang to restate her case in another article in 1967, where the necessary references will be found as well as a revised timetable of events.[101] For our purposes it will be sufficient to note the high points in Thucydides' account.

The key figure is Alcibiades. He is no longer in the Spartan camp, because of the hostility of King Agis, and now hopes to turn his friendship with Tissaphernes to his political advantage in Athens. He soon learned of a plan by certain Athenian oligarchs to overthrow the government in Athens while at the same time gaining control over the Athenian fleet in Samos. In a series of conversations with some of the leaders of the movement from the fleet, Alcibiades intimated that Tissaphernes could be induced to change over to the Athenian side if the Athenians changed their form of government. Incidentally this was not an unreasonable hope, when we consider how fragile the ties were between Sparta and Persia, two treaties already having been abrogated. However, these hopes were destroyed when it was evident that Tissaphernes would not accept the terms for an agreement offered by the Athenians, which they transmitted for referral to Alcibiades. But the oligarchs had gone too far to back down. A reign of terror was instituted in Athens in which a number of leading democrats were assassinated. The revolution was finally accomplished by holding a meeting of the assembly a mile outside the walls at Colonus, thereby insuring a favorable majority. By a combination of plausibility and force the conspirators succeeded in having *de facto* powers of government transferred to a handpicked group of four hundred men, though it was expected that power would soon be vested in an assembly of the so-called Five Thousand. The Council of 500 was persuaded to abdicate on receipt of their salaries for the balance of the year. All now depended on Samos, where, however, the revolution failed and the Athenians at Samos promptly denounced the revolutionary government in Athens. This impasse was broken by Alcibiades, who had been invited back to Samos. He proposed a compromise to the government in Athens: the Five Thousand to be given power, and the Four Hundred to be dissolved. This, as Hignett says, was calculated to split the oligarchs down the middle.[102] It may be all that prevented Athens from being betrayed to the Spartans. The Four Hundred did fall, and the franchise was offered to anyone with a hoplite status (the so-called Five Thousand). Alcibiades succeeded in preventing the fleet from sailing at once to Athens to restore the unrestricted democracy, then led them to a great naval victory over the Spartans near Cyzicus. Thucydides' narrative breaks off shortly thereafter, with the arrival of a much perturbed Tissaphernes in Ephesus, where he offers sacrifice to Artemis.

Perhaps the most interesting statement is the one the historian makes about the Five Thousand, which he speaks of as easily the best government Athens had had in his day![103] This separates him from the extreme oligarchs like Antiphon, who preferred admitting the Spartans to the return of the old radical democracy. And since this was a government set up as a result of Alcibiades' mediation our curiosity is aroused as to what Thucydides' final judgment on Alcibiades would have been. Presumably he had already made up his mind when he wrote Book VIII. It remains probable that he regarded the second exile of Alcibiades as one more example of the deterioration of Athenian leadership after the death of Pericles.

Thucydides' influence on later historians remains second to none, for he was the founder of contemporary history, though Herodotus was the first historian (and long the only one) to concern himself with the total history of man. Of the later writers whose works have survived sufficiently for us to make a judgment, the greater number wrote contemporary history, although Ephorus and Timaeus are notable exceptions. In the next chapter we meet two historians who were born in the fifth century B.C. but wrote in the fourth, Ctesias and Xenophon. Of these Ctesias, like Herodotus, was an observer rather than a participant, while Xenophon, even more than Thucydides, was a man of action.

## Notes for Chapter Three

1. See the *Suda* s.v. Θουκυδίδης, 413.
2. For (1) see *Thuc.* i. 1; (2) ii. 48; (3) iv. 104–105; (4) v. 26.
3. Cf. Thuc. v. 26. 5; iv. 104, 107. See also A. W. Gomme, *A Historical Commentary on Thucydides* (Oxford, 1956), III, 579 (commenting on Thuc. iv. 106. 4); and H. D. Westlake, "Thucydides and the Fall of Amphipolis," *Hermes*, 1962, vol. 90, now in his *Essays on the Greek Historians and Greek History* (New York, 1969), 123 ff.
4. This is not certain, but it is assumed that a *strategus*, like the member of a jury or the Council must have been at least thirty years of age. See C. Hignett, *A History of the Athenian Constitution to the End of the Fifth Century B.C.* (Oxford, 1958), 224.
5. See Marcellinus, *Vita Thuc.* 31; and the comments of Sir Frank Adcock, *Thucydides and His History* (Cambridge University, 1963), 139.
6. Adcock, op. cit., 104 f.
7. See Marcellinus, *Vita Thuc.* 32–33. A similar example of a manufactured story of the murder of a famous writer is that in Hesiod, *Contest of Homer and Hesiod*, 323.
8. See Pausanias i. 23. 9; also Adcock, *Thucydides* 139.
9. Thuc. v. 26.
10. Sometimes called a "second introduction"; see Westlake, *Essays*, 3, n. 9. See also Jacqueline de Romilly, *Thucydide et l'Impérialisme Athénien* (Paris, 1947), 47 f., 161–164. Believing that the historian is writing about imperialism from the beginning, she denies that he can ever have regarded the Peace of Nicias as the end of the war.
11. See W. Schmid and O. Stählin, *Geschichte der griechischen Literatur* (Munich, 1948), I. 5⁷, 16 f. Schmid argues that while Thucydides speaks of writing an account of the entire war (Thuc. v. 26. 1), this is contradicted by his having three continuators (Cratippus, Theopompus, and Xenophon) who begin where our text of Thucydides leaves off. This view has been reexamined recently by W. P. Henry, *Greek Historical Writing* (Chicago, 1967), particularly with reference to Xenophon. See also Adcock, *Thucydides*, 96–106.

12. See *FGrH* (Cratippus) 64. F 1 = Dion. Hal. *Thuc.* 16.
13. See, e.g., Westlake, *Essays,* 35, where he says: "The eighth book is palpably an unrevised draft." On the eighth book, see also Eduard Schwartz, *Das Geschichtswerk des Thukydides,* (Hildesheim reprint, 1960), 72–91. Schwartz is primarily concerned with the documents now found in Book VIII.
14. Thuc. i. 22.
15. The most famous account in antiquity is the *De Thucydide* of Dionysius of Halicarnassus. John H. Finley, Jr., in *Thucydides,* 250–288, has a useful discussion of Thucydides' style.
16. Westlake, *Essays,* 1–38.
17. Thuc. vi. 54–59.
18. J. D. Denniston, after arguing against the general approach of Schwartz and Meyer (who agreed in trying to show development in Thucydides, but reached very different conclusions), handsomely acknowledges that, "the present writer's disbelief is as subjective as their belief" (*OCD*[1]. 904).
19. Dionysius of Halicarnassus (*Thuc.* 16) says Cratippus was contemporary with Thucydides. F. Jacoby denies it (*FGrH* ii c. 2. 6 ff.). See also Henry, *Greek Hist. Writ.,* 83, and n. 214.
20. For Dionysius, see previous note; for Plutarch, *FGrH* 64. T 2 = Plut. *De glor. Ath.* 1. 345 C–E. Plutarch does *not* call Cratippus a contemporary, neither does he regard him as a fraudulent writer.
21. See n. 12 above; also Henry, *Greek Hist. Writ.,* 65, n. 143.
22. Marcellinus (*Vita Thuc.* 43) has run into the report (which really shocks him) that Thucydides' daughter wrote Book VIII, also that it was written by Xenophon; see also Schmid-Stählin, V, 2[7], 136.
23. See *FGrH* 64. T 2 and Jacoby's comments (ii C. 2).
24. Gomme's comments on these chapters are indispensable (*Historical Commentary,* I, 89–157). Particularly helpful is the "Analysis" at the end (154–157).
25. See Finley, *Thucydides,* 95.
26. See Gomme, however, who finds the anonymity of the Corcyraeans (*Historical Commentary,* I, 166 on i. 30. 4), "the regular formula when the personality of the actual speaker was of no importance."
27. See Thuc. i. 68–71, 73–78, 80–85, and 86 respectively.
28. Again, for a different view, see Gomme, ibid., esp. 233, and on the passage as a whole, 233–246.
29. Thucydides says expressly the Spartan demand about the "curse" was aimed at Pericles (i. 128). The Athenians replied in kind with a request reminding Sparta of the scandalous death of Pausanias (i. 128). Athens rejected Sparta's demand that the boycott of Megara be rescinded (i. 139), yielding to Pericles' argument against making any concessions to the Peloponnesians (i. 140).
30. He does use these other systems when it serves his purpose, as when he wishes to place the beginning of the war in its chronological setting he includes Chrysis the Priestess of Hera, the Archon Pythodorus, and the Ephor Aenesias (ii. 2). For discussion, see Gomme, *Historical Commentary,* I, 8.
31. For a thorough discussion of Thucydides' use of "summers and winters," see Gomme, op. cit., III, Appen.
32. Cf. *Iliad* v. 62–63; xi. 604. Stein, in his edition of *Herodotus,* 1894, 6th ed. (Berlin, 1963), reprint, vol. III, p. 106, 1. 19, n., cites Hdt. v. 97 (. . . ἀρχὴ κακῶν ἐγένοντο Ἕλλησί τε καὶ βαρβάροισι). For other parallels, see Gomme, *Historical Commentary,* II, 15.
33. See W. H. S. Jones, *Hippocrates* (Loeb ed., 1923), I, 1–63; for influence on Thucydides, see esp. Charles N. Cochrane, *Thucydides and the Science of History,* 1929 (New York reprint, 1965), 14–34 (more emphasis on *Airs, Waters Places* which is also in Loeb ed. I, 71–137); and see Finley, *Thucydides,* 66–72.
34. Thucydides deserves our admiration for not attempting an estimate of the number of the victims. W. G. Lunt in his *History of England,* 3rd. ed. (New York and London, 1950), 240 f., discusses the mortality caused by the black death, and notes that contemporary chroniclers made estimates of from one-third to nine-tenths of the population. He adds that people living in Philadelphia during the influenza epidemic in 1918 had a similar impression of a high death rate. But for Philadelphia the statistics show that the number of

deaths per thousand rose only from 17.10 in 1917 to 24.37 in 1918. Thucydides, in the absence of such data, refuses to guess.

35. We still have part of Gorgias' oration (Diels, *Vorsokr.*[8] ii. 284–286), but this was a showpiece not a speech actually given on such an occasion; also there is an Epitaphios perhaps wrongly attributed to Lysias (Budé ed. of L. Gernet and M. Bizos, vol. 1, Oration II); another artificial funeral speech is Plato's *Menexenus*; still another, referred to as Demosthenes LX, is not accepted as genuine by anyone; and finally there is the Epitaphios of Hypereides which is genuine, and was given during the Lamian War (Budé ed. by G. Colin, discussion 273–290; text, 291 ff.).

36. See George Grote, *History of Greece*, 12 vol. ed. (London, 1870), V, 416.

37. See von Fritz, *GG* I, 666, where he says: "die berühmte Leichenrede . . . stehe der Grösse ihres Inhalts nach in keinem Verhältnis zu den Verlusten, die Athen damals erst erlitten hatte. . . ."

38. Plut. *Per.* 28. 4.

39. Also found in *FGrH*, 392. F 16; for Jacoby's suggestion, see ibid., iii b. (Text) 199.

40. Arist. *Rhet.* i. 7. 34.

41. Hdt. vii. 162.

42. See Stein, *Herodotus*[7], vol. IV, where he comments on Hdt. vii. 162. 6. Stein notes that Pericles applies the figure more aptly than Herodotus.

43. Thuc. ii. 83–92; see also F. E. Adcock, *The Greek and Macedonian Art of War* (University of California, 1957), 34 f.

44. See Thuc. ii. 37–40 (Cleon); 42–48 (Diodotus); and for the Hollywood finish, 49.

45. See Gomme, *Historical Commentary*, II, 325 f., who accepts the figure; Finley (*Thucydides*, 178, n. 40) on the other hand does not: "The figure 1000 given in the MSS seems almost certainly a copyist's error." It is not pleasant, but only too credible.

46. See Thuc. ii. 70. Gomme, op. cit. 204, argues convincingly that the charges failed.

47. See Thuc. iii. 53–59 (the Plataeans), 61–67 (the Thebans). Incidentally, the Plataeans are named (iii. 52. 5).

48. Thuc. iii. 69–85.

49. On the incomparably greater evils of civil war (*stasis*) compared with foreign war, see Plato, *Laws* i. 628–629.

50. See K. J. Beloch, *Griechische Geschichte*[2] (Berlin, 1927), II, 304. As is his wont, Beloch says the oligarchs in Plataea invited the Thebans, but gives no evidence. He is probably right.

51. See Thuc. iii. 47.

52. See Thuc. iv. 28; 30–39.

53. See Aristoph. *Peace* 261 (a clear allusion to Cleon) and 282 f. (obviously referring to Brasidas).

54. See nn. 9 and 10 above.

55. Thuc. vi. 88.

56. See B. H. Warmington, *Carthage* (Harmondsworth, England, 1964), 95; K. F. Stroheker, *Historia* (1954), III, 163–171.

57. See *FGrH* (Philistus) 556. F 51; this despite the fact that Philistus was an eyewitness of the siege of Syracuse (which Thucydides was not), see Plut. *Nic.* 19. 6.

58. See Thuc. v. 44–45, on Alcibiades' tricking the Spartan envoys; and v. 46. 5, on the alliance with Argos.

59. See Hignett, *Hist. Ath. Const.*, 266 f.; also Plut. *Alcib.* 13. 4–6.

60. Thuc. viii. 73.

61. See Adcock, *Thucydides*, 62.

62. Thuc. v. 84–114.

63. Aelian (*VH* ii. 8) tells us Euripides presented three tragedies and a satyr play in the year of the 91st Olympiad (416/415 B.C.), and that he received second prize, first prize going to Xenocles. Euripides' tragedies were *Alexander, Palamedes,* and the *Trojan Women*; the satyr play was called *Sisyphus*. Without the missing plays we cannot be sure of the allusions to Melos. But the time fits.

As Baldry says, it is hard to read the play, "without connecting it with the brutal Athenian conquest of the island of Melos in the previous year" (H. C. Baldry, *Ancient Greek Literature in its Living Context* (New York, 1968). Or is that the twentieth century speaking?

64. See her discussion of the Melian Dialogue (Romilly, *Thucydide*, 230–259).
65. Thuc. ii. 8.
66. See Romilly, op. cit., 237; and Aristophanes' *Birds*, 186. One is reminded of the *fames Perusina* (Lucan, *Phars.* i. 41).
67. This took place at the Congress of Gela in 424 B.C., and the credit goes to Hermocrates (Thuc. v. 58–65).
68. Plut. *Alcib.* 17.
69. On Nicias' views, see Thuc. vi. 9–14, 20–25. Lamachus was one of the signatories of the Peace of Nicias (Thuc. v. 19. 2), and in Pericles' time he helped Sinope get rid of its tyrant (Plut. *Per.* 20); which means that Lamachus was already a man in his fifties, little if any younger than Nicias.
70. See Thuc. vi. 27–29; 53.
71. See Thuc. vi. 54–59. This digression is introduced with little more justification than that the assassination of Hipparchus, like the Hermae affair, was variously interpreted. For Herodotus' view, see his *Hist.* v. 55; vi. 123. Thucydides has already briefly stated his own opinion (see Thuc. i. 20. 2; also Gomme, *Historical Commentary*, I, 136 f.). Westlake (*Essays*, 5) sees in this an example of Thucydides', "practice of inserting discussions on controversial subjects more or less connected with the war where he felt himself able to make a valuable contribution by putting forward views of his own or refuting those of others." But there is more to it than that, and it probably sheds some light on Thucydides' political views. The "tyrannicide" story, honoring Harmodius and Aristogiton was essentially anti-Alcmaeonid, designed to cut the feet out from under Clisthenes, who did overthrow the tyranny, but only with Spartan help. As Thucydides tells us (vi. 53), the Athenians were in no mood to be reminded that they owed their freedom to Sparta. Pericles is still sensitive on the subject, which is his reason for promising that if the Spartan invaders spare his land for old times sake, he will turn it over to the public (Thuc. ii. 13. 1).
72. See Thuc. vi. 60; Andoc. i. 48–53.
73. Cf. Thuc. vi. 61; and Andoc. i. 45.
74. Thuc. viii. 73.
75. See the Budé ed. of Andocides (by G. Dalmeyda), 132 (fr. 5).
76. On these clubs, see George M. Calhoun, *Athenian Clubs in Politics and Litigation* (University of Texas, 1913), esp. the last chapter on "The Clubs in the Political Field."
77. Thuc. vi. 89. 6.
78. For Antiphon, see Thuc. viii. 68; for Hyperbolus, see viii. 73.
79. See [Xenophon], *Ath. Const.*, esp. chap. 2. He notes only one weakness (2. 14), that the Athenians do not live on an island. For a translation, see T. S. Brown, *Ancient Greece* (New York, 1965), 116–126.
80. Thuc. vi. 103.
81. Thuc. vii. 49.
82. There is a story in Plutarch (*Nic.* 30) of how the news reached Athens. A stranger arrived in the Piraeus and stopped in at a barber shop, where he referred casually to the disaster. As a result he was arrested, put to the torture, and would have been killed had not other witnesses arrived in the nick of time to confirm his report.
83. See Thuc. vii. 86. 5; and vii. 54.
84. Finley, *Thucydides*, 246. Incidentally, Xenophon (*Vect.* 4. 14) says Nicias owned 1000 slaves whom he hired out to work in the silver mines. The number is suspect (see W. Linn Westermann, *The Slave Systems of Greek and Roman Antiquity*, Philadelphia, 1955, 8), but there is no reason to doubt Nicias' wealth or its source.
85. See Livy, *Historiae*, xxii. 61.
86. Thuc. vii. 86. 2.
87. See G. Schrot, "Gylippos," *Kl. Pauly* ii. 886; also Diod. Sic. xiii. 106. 9; Plut. *Lys.* 16–17 and *Nic.* 28; *FGrH* (Posidonius) 87. F 48 = Ath. vi. 234a.

88. See *FGrH* 566. F 100 abc.
89. See T. S. Brown, *Timaeus of Tauromenium* (University of California, 1958), 130, n. 89.
90. To this picture of woe may be added the loss of 20,000 slaves, most of them handicraft workers, who escaped during the Spartan occupation of Decelea (Thuc. vii. 27. 5). See Westermann, *Slave Systems,* 7 f.
91. Thuc. vii. 1. 1–3.
92. See Arist. *Ath. pol.* 29. 2.
93. See Hignett, *Hist. Ath. Const.,* 269.
94. See Thuc. viii. 6. 3 and v. 44. 3.
95. Viz., viii. 18 (Treaty of Miletus); 37 (Second Treaty); 58 (Third Treaty). For discussion, see A. T. Olmstead, *History of the Persian Empire* (Phoenix Books, 1948), 359–362.
96. See Hignett, *Hist. Ath. Const.,* 269.
97. Andoc. iii. 29.
98. See *FGrH* 688. F 15. 53; also Olmstead, op. cit., 359; H. W. Parke, *Greek Mercenary Soldiers* (Oxford, 1933), 23, n. 2; and "Lykon" no. 1, *Kl. Pauly* iii. 813.
99. See Budé ed. of Andocides (Paris, 1930), 96, n. 1, where he tries to reconcile Andoc. iii. 29 with Thuc. viii. 5. 5, 28.
100. Mabel Lang, *AJPhil* 69 (1948), 272–289.
101. See Hignett, *Hist. Ath. Const.,* 268–280, 336–378 (App. 12); Mabel Lang, *AJPhil.* 88 (1967), 176–187.
102. See Hignett, *Hist. Ath. Const.,* 278.
103. Thuc. ii. 97. 2.

## I. Ctesias

In the fall of 401 B.C. the Battle of Cunaxa
was fought between the forces of King
Artaxerxes Mnemon and those of his younger
brother Cyrus, a battle in which Cyrus lost
his life while his brother, who was wounded
early in the fight and had seemed to be on
the brink of defeat, emerged as the victor.
Ctesias and Xenophon were both present,
though on opposite sides, Ctesias as
physician to the king and Xenophon as a
volunteer serving under Cyrus. We may be
thankful, on purely selfish grounds, that
Cyrus lost, for had he won Xenophon might
have returned to Athens a rich man instead
of going into exile, and then he might never
have had the incentive to become a historian.
Ctesias, on the other hand, would probably
have had to leave Persia without gathering
the necessary materials for the *Persica.* The
importance of the battle in the lives of both
writers is shown in Eusebius' *Chronicle,* where
Xenophon and Ctesias are assigned to the
first year of the ninety-fifth Olympiad
(400/399 B.C.), the very year in which Cunaxa
took place.[1] And now we will begin with
Ctesias, who was probably older than
Xenophon, and who certainly preceded him
as a historian, since Xenophon cites him in
the *Anabasis.*[2]

    Ctesias was and is a controversial figure.
Among the ancients, Plutarch speaks of his
filling his books, "with a great farrago of
nonsense"; Arrian qualifies a reference to
Ctesias with ". . . if indeed his authority can
be accepted"; but it is Antigonus of Carystus
who strikes the shrewdest blow, refusing to
cite him in his own far from irreproachable
book on marvels, "because he tells so many
lies."[3] Among the moderns, George Grote,
with his customary independence, is inclined
to prefer Ctesias on occasion to Herodotus,
because of the excellent opportunities he had
for getting information;[4] but Felix Jacoby,
who has examined Ctesias more thoroughly

# CTESIAS
# AND
# XENOPHON

than anyone else, gives almost as unfavorable a verdict as Antigonus. Nor is his a tentative conclusion, for he states that, "we know the general plan of Ctesias' work better than we do almost any of the lost histories." For good measure, he not only finds Ctesias damned by the unanimous verdict of antiquity as untrustworthy, but he insists that, "Herodotus, who only spent a couple of months in Babylon and who perhaps never even laid eyes on Persia itself . . . gives us a fuller and better account of the land and its history than the royal physician. . . ."[5] A. R. Burn, in his widely read account of the Persian War, speaks of the high regard earlier scholars [nameless] once had for Ctesias as having been proved unfounded by the inscription of Darius on the rock at Behistun;[6] but Olmstead, a recognized authority on Persian history as well as the Behistun inscription, strikes a balance: "Ctesias gives us much information which we should otherwise seriously miss, though we must regret that he did not make better use of his opportunities."[7] More recently, in the first volume of a projected work on Greek historiography, Kurt von Fritz mentions Ctesias only in passing, though he does indicate some disagreement with Jacoby in detail.[8] Presumably his views will be made clearer in the next volume. However, Ctesias deserves consideration if for no other reason than that he was so widely read and had such great influence in antiquity. Nearchus, who knew Alexander about as well as anyone, says the disastrous march back from India through the Gedrosian waste was undertaken by Alexander out of a desire to outdo Semiramis,[9] whose adventures must have been known to him through reading Ctesias. A modern editor of Ctesias in speaking of that historian's influence remarks that he may have made a more important contribution to the course of history than to its elucidation.[10] Aristotle holds mixed views, for while he refers scathingly to Ctesias as an authority on animals, he is obviously fascinated by his account of Sardanapalus.[11]

Leaving these various opinions for a moment let us look at the facts. There is complete agreement that Ctesias came from Cnidus, a Dorian city at the tip of a promontory in southern Caria said to have been colonized at an early date by the Spartans, or else by a mysterious hero named Triopas, for whom the promontory was named.[12] No more appropriate birthplace can be imagined for a physician-historian: across the Gulf of Cos to the north lies Herodotus' Halicarnassus; while even nearer, in more of a northwesterly direction, Cos itself is visible, the island home of Hippocrates the founder of scientific medicine. Galen, last of the great Greek physicians, tells us that, as one of the Asclepiadae, Ctesias must have been related to Hippocrates.[13] We are entitled to assume that he was destined from birth for a medical career. This is all we can learn about Ctesias until the Battle of Cunaxa. Now Diodorus Siculus, who made extensive use of Ctesias' historical works, says that:[14]

*Ctesias the Cnidian was living at the time of Cyrus' expedition against his brother Artaxerxes and he was taken prisoner. However, he was retained by the king because of his medical knowledge and remained with him in an honorable position for seventeen years.[15]*

This will not do. The doctor who attended Artaxerxes at Cunaxa cannot by any reasonable person be thought to have fallen into Artaxerxes' hands at Cunaxa. Had he been a member of Cyrus' Greek entourage Xenophon could not have avoided mentioning it when he tells us that it was Ctesias who healed the king's wounds.[16] The most likely explanation is that Diodorus, who can be quite arbitrary in compressing his sources, has combined three separate statements into one: that Ctesias was a prisoner of war; that he dressed Artaxerxes' wounds at Cunaxa; and that he spent seventeen years in Persia as a court physician. Now, had he actually begun his duties in 401, then he could not have left—as he did—in 398 B.C.,[17] but there is nothing to prevent his having been made a prisoner at an earlier date, eventually becoming the physician who looked after Artaxerxes. Jacoby attributes the seventeen years to Ctesias' own statement, which Jacoby says is a lie.[18] Granted that Ctesias occasionally rounded out the truth, that does not prove that he has done so with reference to the seventeen years. What purpose would it have served? Assuming that the figures are approximately correct, then if he left the Persians in 398 he must have been taken prisoner in 415 B.C. or thereabouts. Unfortunately, our informants all speak of him as physician to Artaxerxes Mnemon, who came to the throne in 404 B.C. However, it is possible that it was only under Artaxerxes that Ctesias rose to the rank of personal physician to the king, and later on he might not refer to his earlier humbler status. But Jacoby also points out that Ctesias' *Persica* shows greater detail on the reign of Artaxerxes than on that of his predecessor.[19] Even this is not conclusive. We do not know when Ctesias decided to write a Persian history: if, for example, it was Cunaxa and his part in it that prompted him to do so, we would not expect the reign of Darius II to be covered in the same detail as that of his successor. In the present state of our evidence we ought to keep what we have if it is at all possible to do so, rather than to remove what we do not like by crying, "Liar!"

Regardless of how long he had been there, Ctesias left Persia in 398 B.C., after playing a significant part in the delicate negotiations between Artaxerxes, Evagoras of Cyprus, and the exiled Athenian admiral, Conon. They were delicate because Evagoras had openly defied the Persian government from the very moment he returned to Cyprus in 411 B.C. to make himself ruler of Salamis.

The Persians had only been waiting for a favorable opportunity to deal with him, yet instead they were persuaded to make use of his services and those of Conon to put an end to Sparta's naval supremacy. Keeping in mind that originally Persia had subsidized the Spartans in order to destroy the naval power of Athens, we can appreciate the skillful diplomacy that must have been employed to bring about the creation of a new fleet by Persia with an Athenian as admiral-in-chief! Ctesias' part in all this is known to us through two sources, Photius and Plutarch.[20] Photius, who is summarizing what he read in Ctesias, describes the historian as playing a very active role, with both Evagoras and Conon appealing to him by letter. We are told of a conversation of his with Artaxerxes on the subject of Conon, and learn that the king finally sent Ctesias away with confidential letters for Conon and for the Spartans. In this account, Ctesias is obviously the key figure in the negotiations. Plutarch, on the other hand, has Conon send his letter to Artaxerxes by messenger, with oral instructions to have it presented to the king by Zeno the Cretan (a dancer), or by Polycritus of Mende (a physician) if either were available; only as a last resort was he to apply to Ctesias! Further, Ctesias is said to have intercepted the messenger and inserted a request in the letter asking, "that Ctesias be sent to him as a useful man in maritime matters." "But," writes Plutarch, "Ctesias says it was the king who entrusted him with this task."[21] The name of Polycritus of Mende is of some interest, because we hear of a historian of the same name and nationality who lived about the same time, and who is credited with at least one historical work, on Dionysius the Younger.[22] The suggestion has been made that historian and doctor are one. In a fragment the historian refers to something he saw in Acragas when he was campaigning there,[23] something that must have occurred before Acragas was destroyed and would fit in very well with service in a mercenary force hired in 406 B.C. to defend that city.[24] It would not seem surprising to find this same Polycritus at Artaxerxes' court eight years later, except for Jacoby's objections that Polycritus was already at court in 406 (no reason given), and that "a well-known" (bekannter) doctor does not belong in a nameless group of mercenaries.[25] But he does believe the doctor and the historian are related.[26] Yet every army needs doctors, and nothing compels us to assume the future historian of Dionysius II was already "well-known" in 406 B.C. Xenophon speaks of every commander as providing himself with doctors as a matter of course.[27] Further, both the famous physician Democedes and Ctesias himself reached the Persian court as prisoners of war,[28] and the same thing may have happened to Polycritus. His presence at the Persian court at this time may help explain why Artaxerxes was willing to dispense with the services of Ctesias. It is tempting to hold Polycritus responsible for the account of Ctesias' tampering with Conon's letter, but for that of course there is no evidence. There must have been other Greeks in the Persian service who disliked him, and later on when his Persian history appeared, resentment was sure to have been felt at his toothsome account of court scandals.

Once he had left court in 398 Ctesias almost surely never returned. We are told that certain charges were made against him by Spartans when he reached Rhodes, but that he was exonerated. Eventually he came home to Cnidus and that is the last we hear of him.[29] In the course of time, Jacoby suggests, he may have missed the excitement of life in high places and hoped by his writing to make himself the center of attention.[30] However, this was no period when a competent physician need feel neglected, and it is more likely that Ctesias' return to Greece in the first place was motivated by the wish to write. Even though he did write in Greek it would not be safe to do so in Persia with so many Greek courtiers looking over his shoulder, and where the king himself must have been bilingual.[31]

Although Ctesias is credited with a number of publications, only two of them are well enough preserved for discussion here, the *Persica* and the *Indica*.[32] The latter, which was written in the Ionian dialect, was short, consisting of a single book.[33] Ctesias' *Indica* is the earliest such work to survive, though it is not unlikely that Scylax, the man who sailed from India to the Red Sea for King Darius I, had something to say about India which influenced Ctesias, either directly by a reading of his *Periplus*, or indirectly through Hecataeus,[34] but it is certain that every word written on the subject by Herodotus was familiar to the physician from Cnidus. Ctesias' relationship to the Father of History as a writer on India resembles that of Herodotus to his great predecessor on the history of Egypt, in that each greatly expanded what he found in the earlier account. Hecataeus had covered the Mediterranean world in a two-book *Periegesis*, while Herodotus devoted an entire book to Egypt alone; but Herodotus has merely a short digression on India in Book III along with scattered references elsewhere, which Ctesias expands into a monograph. Like Herodotus, he was later accused of plagiarism,[35] but the charge will not hold up so far as their respective accounts of Egypt and India are concerned even if Scylax is brought back into the picture. Had Scylax covered the subject of India in any detail this would be reflected in Herodotus. We know that Herodotus supplemented what he read by a visit to Egypt and conversations with knowledgeable persons he met there, who knew the Greek tongue, but here the parallel with Ctesias does not hold. Though we cannot be absolutely certain that he did not do so, Ctesias is not thought to have visited India. Presumably, had he made such a journey, he would have found occasion to mention it; but Photius sometimes leaves out just what we would particularly like to know. It is worth noting that no one says expressly that Ctesias did *not* visit India. Lucian, to be sure, says that he wrote about things in India, "that he never saw himself nor heard about from anyone else who was telling the truth,"[36] but he implies that Ctesias knew better—that the lies were deliberate.

The advantages Herodotus had in writing about Egypt, over Ctesias in describing India, were offset by the fact that he had no official standing in Egypt, while as the king's physician Ctesias was in a favorable position to learn whatever was known about India in government circles; and that may have been considerable when we remember Darius had once ruled a part of India. There must have been a coming and going of officials, probably of merchants as well, between the two countries. This would not have been possible without a staff of interpreters, whose services might have been available to anyone with Ctesias' credentials. The possibilities were there. What use did our doctor historian make of them?[37]

The most important evidence we have comes from Photius' summary of the *Indica*, which Bowman calls, "a careless and unsatisfactory performance."[38] In fact, the abridgment must have been quite drastic,[39] although we do have a few fragments preserved by other writers in antiquity which can be used to check against Photius.

India, for Ctesias as well as for Herodotus, is the most populous area in the world,[40] as well as the eastern limit of human habitation.[41] This naturally suggests, to a Greek writer, that such a region must have many marvels as well as great wealth. The gold, obtained according to Herodotus from the gold-digging ants,[42] has interested readers ever since, not less so when it is considered that India produces little gold now and produced even less in ancient times. W. W. Tarn has argued persuasively that the "ant gold" referred to actually came to India from Siberia, but that this trade was interrupted at some time between Darius I and the third century B.C.[43]—that is including Ctesias' day. The accounts of the ants and the gold-guarding gryphons will have been stories designed to keep the gold route, which came through Bactria, a trade secret.[44] Ctesias adds a reference to a spring from which liquid gold is collected once a year in clay vessels. When the gold hardens the clay is broken, leaving the precious metal intact.[45] This same spring also produces iron with the special property of protecting its possessor against hail and whirlwinds. Ctesias, himself, owned two swords made with this iron, one given to him by the king, the other by Queen Parysatis.[46] Other springs and ponds with remarkable attributes may still be found in the fragments of Ctesias: water so tenuous that no object will float upon it; a spring so resistant to intrusion that it hurls back to the bank those who venture to plunge into it; and another that makes strange noises, "like water boiling in a kettle."[47]

These and many other passages of a similar kind can be adduced to show that from one point of view Majumdar is entirely justified in excluding the *Indica* from his useful source book.[48] Nevertheless, this work would deserve fuller treatment in any study on classical ethnology. The size and remarkable traits of certain animals, including the elephant, the rhinoceros, the tiger, and the Indian dogs may be mentioned in passing.[49] In general, Indian fauna are larger, more deadly, swifter, or more useful than those of any other region. The people, too, are described in superlatives. Some are noted for their upright behavior, while others are distinguished by unusual physical characteristics such as the pygmies, or the Dogheaded Men who understand human speech but communicate only by barking. And here we are back on familiar ground, the already ancient world of epic tradition known to us through the Homeric poems, and even better known in the days of Ctesias through many poems that have since been lost. This by no means proves that Ctesias is a professional liar. Even had he visited India the unusual things he saw might well have convinced him, as they convinced Megasthenes who spent some time in India (as will be discussed later) that even more unusual sights were to be seen in the outlying areas of that country. Nor would a Greek visitor be in any position to check on the accuracy of his Indian informants—whom could he ask? And in what language? When Alexander the Great ventured deep inside the Iranian plateau it was expected of him that he find the Amazons—and he did so![50]

Let us now turn to the *Persica*, which not only deals with Persian history, but also contains an account of the ancient east before the Persian empire was established. And this brings Ctesias into competition, not only with Herodotus, but also with a much admired historian named Berossus, a native priest of Bel Marduk in Babylon who wrote a *Babyloniaca* in Greek and dedicated it to Antiochus I.[51] Schnabel says of Berossus that one of his greatest services was in refuting the lying accounts of Babylonian history written by Ctesias and his followers by supplying the Greeks with the "genuine" native tradition instead.[52] He is speaking particularly about the account in Ctesias of how Semiramis the Queen of Assyria built the city of Babylon.[53] But it seems probable that Berossus' anger against Ctesias was aroused less on historical than on religious grounds. His own version of the founding of Babylon would also be based on legendary material unsubjected to source criticism. It is interesting to note that Berossus and Ctesias are cited jointly on the subject of an annual Babylonian religious festival in which the slaves change places with their masters, one of them, the *zoganes* donning the robes of the king.[54] If we had this on the authority of Ctesias alone, no doubt scholars would reject it as just one more example of falsification by the unreliable Cnidian physician. The Semiramis story, on the other hand, was not invented by Ctesias, and there are good reasons for regarding it as the literary product of some Assyrian writer who wished to remind everyone of Assyria's past glories, in a period when she no longer ruled the east.[55] Other proud people, fallen on evil days, have done likewise. The Greeks, for example, living under Roman rule like to remember how they had treated Rome's ancestors in Troy. The account of Semiramis' life given in the opening chapters of the Second Book of Diodorus Siculus' *Historical Library* comes essentially from Ctesias, and it is detailed enough for us to appreciate the charm this historical romance must have had for ancient readers—including Alexander.

By way of contrast with Semiramis, a woman with all the derring-do of an epic hero, we have Sardanapalus as her unworthy descendant, a man who painted his face and wore women's clothes, an example of effeminacy cherished and occasionally imitated throughout antiquity. Yet at the very end he redeems himself. When all is lost he sets fire to the palace and dies in the flames, along with his many concubines and other prized possessions.[56] While this is not a tale to inspire confidence, Sardanapalus—like Semiramis—is a composite figure adapted in part to actual events under real rulers. Shamash-shum-ukin, for example, is thought to have burned himself alive in Babylon rather than fall into the hands of his brother Ashurbanipal, the King of Assyria.[57]

Ctesias also wove into his history a romantic story about Zarinaea, a princess of the Sacae, and a Median warrior named Stryangaeus.[58] There is every reason to accept this as a genuine eastern tale he heard during his years at the Persian court.

As we move on into the Persian history itself we note how frequently he gives us a different version of events than the one we find in Herodotus. Cyrus is said not to have been related to Astyages, the Median king whom he overthrew; while Herodotus says that Cyrus' mother was Astyages' daughter.[59] The capture of Sardis by Cyrus also takes place under different circumstances, for Ctesias has the Persians set images of warriors atop long slender poles, which were then elevated above the town in such a way that the Lydians, seeing them, thought their citadel was already in enemy hands.[60] The death of Cyrus is also different. He is carried off mortally wounded from the field of battle, but lives long enough to arrange for the succession and to make other last-minute appointments. The enemy here are not the Massagetae as in Herodotus but the Derbices; their leader is a king, not a queen; and Cyrus' mishap came as the result of an elephant ambush set by the Indian allies of the Derbices. The battle in which he fell was evenly fought, not a Persian defeat; and the drawn battle was speedily followed up by a second battle in which the Persians were victorious.[61] The reign of Cambyses also shows significant differences, particularly in the account of the magus who impersonated Cambyses' brother. In Ctesias, as in Herodotus, the magus bears a striking resemblance to the king's brother, but otherwise the accounts are quite different. It is the magus who falsely accuses Cambyses' brother, Tanyoxarces (instead of the Smerdis of Herodotus), of treason and persuades Cambyses to do away with him, concealing the evil deed by allowing the magus to impersonate the dead prince. As in Herodotus, Cambyses dies of a wound he accidentally inflicted on himself, but Ctesias' Cambyses dies in Babylon, after hurting himself while trying to carve a piece of wood with his dagger. In Herodotus he dies in Syria on the way home from Egypt as the result of his sword slipping out of its sheath when he was mounting his horse.[62]

There is no place here to make a detailed comparison between the account these two historians give of Persia. Jacoby is very harsh in his judgment, accusing the court physician of basing his narrative chiefly on Herodotus, borrowing his materials from his predecessor, then twisting them out of shape and putting them into a different context. In this way Ctesias hopes both to discredit Herodotus and at the same time to convey an impression of his own superior qualities as a conscientious historian. His references to the official Persian records are dismissed as merely a device to win credence for his account.[63] One example of his extraordinary carelessness may be cited. Ctesias gives Amyrtaeus as the name of the pharaoh conquered by Cambyses, while Herodotus correctly calls him Psammetichus; however, there was an Egyptian prince named Amyrtaeus who later headed a rebellion against Persia.[64] Yet Jacoby is not entirely fair. We have Herodotus' account in toto, while there is little else with which we can compare the *Persica* for the period where Ctesias and Herodotus overlap. This was not always true. There once was material in abundance, and various points of view must have been represented: both pro and anti Median, pro and anti Babylonian, pro and anti Egyptian and of course pro and anti Hellenic. The disappearance of all this makes Ctesias' narrative look like a clumsy variant of Herodotus' account, expressly constructed in order to refute it. Yet since Ctesias had a wide choice, just as did Herodotus before him, we need not assume he was so unimaginative as to write an entirely negative history. True, it is not as consequential nor yet as clearly thought out as that of the Father of History because, unlike Herodotus, he fails to subordinate his narrative to a central theme. But he does write with verve. He continued to be read, and was probably the most widely known authority on the ancient east in Greek and Roman times. Herodotus had many sides, including an instinct for getting his chronology straight and for reducing a complicated series of events to an understandable pattern; but he also had the old epic and Ionic love for an entertaining narrative and the acquisition of bits and pieces of information for their own sake. Thucydides trod the narrower path (though even he was occasionally tempted outside the limits he imposed upon himself). Ctesias, much more interested in entertaining his readers, takes the broad road. This does not mean Ctesias was no historian at all. He had a genuine curiosity about many things. For example, he argues against the theory that the Indians were black as a result of exposure to the heat of the sun, "because there are people there who are very white indeed . . . he says he himself saw two Indian women and five men of that type."[65]

To be sure his curiosity is not always to our liking, though perhaps it is understandable in a physician and a toxicologist. For example, he gives us a detailed description of the Persian punishment for convicted enemies of the state, a punishment which may be called "troughing"—involving a slow agonizing death in which insects play a leading role.[66] He seems to delight in poisons and poisoning. There is an unforgettable account of how the dowager Queen Parysatis manages to get rid of her hated daughter-in-law. Neither queen trusted the other, but Parysatis caught her rival off guard by offering to share a delicious little roasted bird with her. She divided it with a knife, one side of which had been smeared with a deadly poison, keeping for herself the uncontaminated half of the bird.[67] More innocent is the doctor's evident pleasure in telling us how the royal cattle employed to draw water for the royal gardens in Susa knew how to count. Each cow would draw one hundred buckets on a given day, then absolutely refuse to draw another bucket whatever threats or cajoleries were employed.[68]

On the details of political history Ctesias is unreliable, particularly, as Jacoby points out, when it comes to synchronizing the events of Persian and Greek history.[69] His account of the Persian War is carelessly put together and demonstrably inaccurate. For the later period, when it is more difficult to check the validity of his statements, he has become an important authority by default, though we wish it were otherwise. Nevertheless, he does reflect the atmosphere of life at court in the days of Artaxerxes, and he has a great flair for scandal and intrigue. We are forced to agree substantially with Jacoby's evaluation of the *Persica* as: "something in between a historical work and a novel—yet not a historical novel."[70] And now it is time to turn to Xenophon who wrote histories and at least one historical novel as well.

## II. Xenophon

Xenophon was fortunate in many things, not least in having his writings survive virtually intact, an honor he shares with only two other major Greek historians, Herodotus and Thucydides. Although he does not rank intellectually with either of them, he has a charm of his own: he really believes, like a loyal Socratic, that good will win out in the end, and that all problems can be solved by the application of common sense. And while we are reading him he has the rare ability to make us accept the world as he presents it, a much simpler world than the one to which we return after regretfully closing the pages of the *Anabasis,* or the *Cyropaedia.*

No one knows for sure the exact year when Xenophon was born or the year in which he died, though we do have a number of statements about him which, if we could rely on them, would provide us with satisfactory answers. The *Suda,* in the first of two separate notices on Xenophon, says that he "flourished" during the time of the ninety-fifth Olympiad (400/396 B.C.),[71] while the *Life* in Diogenes Laertius tells us he died in the first year of the one hundred and fifth Olympiad when Callidemides was archon and Philip son of Amyntas ruled over the Macedonians—which works out to the year 360/359 B.C.[72] If true, then he was born between 440 and 436 B.C., dying at a ripe old age of between seventy-five and seventy-eight. However, he is listed in the pseudo-Lucianic *Macrobioi* among the eminent men who lived to be over ninety years of age![73] Our confusion grows with a passage in the *Hellenica,* the genuineness of which is not open to question, in which Xenophon describes the assassination of Alexander of Pherae, an event which probably occurred in 358 B.C.[74] Finally, there is a treatise *On the Revenues,* which he also wrote, and which addresses itself to the economic hardships faced by Athens subsequent to the war with her allies which came to an end in 355 B.C.[75] In the *Anabasis,* Xenophon says he will not use his age as an excuse for shirking the responsibilities of high command should the soldiers elect him, a passage which has been used by Taylor to show that Xenophon cannot have been born before 426 B.C.;[76] but in my opinion the passage is not reliable as evidence. What election speech is? Just one more reference may be mentioned. An Athenian named Theopompus makes a short speech which brings this laughing rejoinder: "You sound just like a philosopher. . . ." If Meyer is right the young philosopher is Xenophon himself.[77] But, as will be shown presently, we do not need this kind of evidence.

There is general agreement that Xenophon was an Athenian of the upper class. His father was named Gryllus and he came from the same inland deme of Erchia which also claimed Isocrates, the

(*The Granger Collection*)

SOCRATES: TEACHER OF XENOPHON
Represents the philosopher in his later years, as Xenophon knew him.

great master of Greek rhetoric. There is a story, too often told to be repeated here, of how Xenophon first came under Socrates' influence.[78] Unfortunately, no date is given for the beginning of this association, but it necessarily terminated when Xenophon accepted the invitation of a friend of his, Proxenus of Thebes, to join the younger Cyrus as a gentleman volunteer. Socrates tried to dissuade him, and did obtain his promise to consult the oracle of Delphi before leaving, but Xenophon showed that he had learned something from his master after all. Instead of asking Apollo whether or not he should join Cyrus, he limited his inquiry as to the divinity to whom he should sacrifice before he left! Socrates was not pleased, but he recognized the folly of trying to stop him.[79] Surely this is all the evidence we need that the future historian was still very young at the time. The decision proved to be a critical one for Xenophon and perhaps for Socrates as well, though neither of them could have foreseen it at the time.[80] In 401 b.c., when Xenophon left Athens for so many long years, the city had not yet recovered from the disastrous Peloponnesian War or from the oligarchical reign of terror that followed it. Surprisingly enough, after the Athenian exiles returned in force demanding the over-throw of the oligarchs, the Spartans gave the Athenians as a whole the right to decide their own form of government which, as they must have known, meant the return of full democracy. We are not told in so many words how Xenophon felt about all this, but both as a member of the privileged class and as the friend of Socrates it would have been rather strange for him to have welcomed the return of the radical democrats. Nevertheless, he was capable of changing his mind. His writings show that he found much to ad-mire in Persia, in Sparta, and, at least late in life, in the Athenian democracy. These different stages of his thought may have had a practical motivation, for even though he appears to have a genu-inely high regard for Sparta and her institutions, the fact that they gave him an estate at Scillus puts his admiration in a somewhat different light.[81]

The death of Cyrus and the subsequent removal of the Greek mercenary leaders, including Proxenus of Thebes, provided Xeno-phon with an opportunity for leadership of which he took full advantage. Already an experienced soldier, perhaps beginning in the waning years of the Peloponnesian War, he soon showed him-self a consummate master of small-scale fighting, meeting each new crisis as it arose, whether from within or from without, with unfail-ing courage, ingenuity, and good humor. He also kept a weather eye out for new possibilities, and at one time toyed with the idea of establishing a colony on the Black Sea coast.[82] But this was not to be. Meanwhile, the reappearance of the Greeks after defying the armies of the Great King was a source of embarrassment to Sparta who owed her commanding position in the Aegean world to an alliance with Persia, in which she had agreed to give her ally a free hand in Asia—yet it was Clearchus a Spartan who had been Cyrus' chief supporter. Xenophon was resourceful enough to find temporary employment for the mercenaries which would keep them out of sight, in the service of Seuthes a Thracian kinglet; but the terms were unsatisfactory and the fighting conditions un-usually disagreeable. Fortunately for the mercenaries a sudden change in foreign policy led to the outbreak of open hostilities between Sparta and Artaxerxes, a circumstance which not only ended their pariah status but enabled them to enroll as a body under the Spartan banner. Xenophon intended to return home, for he tells us that, "the vote exiling him had not yet been taken in Athens."[83] The suggestion has been made in a recent article that this vote was taken in 399, not because of Xenophon's part in Cyrus' unsuccessful expedition, but because he had been closely associated with Socrates.[84] Lesky, on the other hand, insists that Xenophon was exiled because of his inexcusable act in fighting on the Spartan side against his own country in 394 B.C. at Coronea.[85] But in the passage just cited Xenophon implies that he intended to return to Athens when he took leave of the mercenaries. He may not yet have heard about Socrates' death and that news, perhaps even without the sentence of exile, may well have deprived him of any desire to return to his home or of any sense of loyalty to the government of Athens. Like Plato, he was deeply troubled by the death of his preceptor, a fact that is shown by his Socratic writings, notably the *Memorabilia*.

In 394 B.C. the Spartan King Agesilaus brought his army back to Greece from the Asiatic war and fought his way through the allied Theban and Athenian forces that stood in his path at Coronea. Presumably Xenophon took part in that engagement. Then for about twenty years he lived the life of a landed proprietor on his estate at Scillus. Here he could hunt as much as he pleased, and here he erected the shrine he had promised Artemis long ago, if he should live to return from the war.[86] Presumably this is also where he did a great deal of writing. But after Leuctra in 371 B.C. the long hand of Sparta was unable to protect her friends, so that Xenophon and his family had to leave Scillus, eventually settling down in the neighborhood of Corinth. Later, worsening relations between Athens and Corinth[87] brought Xenophon home again. The decree of banishment must have been cancelled, for his son Gryllus died fighting as an officer in the Athenian cavalry in 362 B.C.[88] The father survived him by a number of years, leaving his other son Diodorus and a grandson Gryllus to carry on the family tradition.[89]

Xenophon is said to have written some forty books,[90] though the term "books" (*biblia*) is ambiguous, sometimes indicating separate treatises and at other times a division equivalent to one papyrus roll. But in discussing him as a historian we need emphasize only two of his publications, the *Hellenica* and the *Anabasis*, each of which has come down to us divided into seven "books," though this arrangement does not go back to Xenophon in its present form. The two works are quite different, in that the *Hellenica* is a general history dealing, like Thucydides, with events that occurred in many different places over a relatively long period of time, while the *Anabasis* follows the fortunes of a single body of men for less than two years. Those two years are a part of the period described in the *Hellenica*, but the focus has been changed to give us an enormously magnified close-up of a small part of what went on, illuminated by the presence of the historian himself, both as an eyewitness and a leading participant. Yet it is not an official document like Caesar's *Commentaries*, because Xenophon represents no government, he is seeking no office. He owes no accounting to anyone for the leadership he exercises over a maverick force of heterogeneous Greek mercenaries. Had Thucydides written a separate account of his ill-fated generalship it would have been an invaluable source for the historian today, but it would also have been an official document with all that that implies. In point of fact, when the ancients bracketed Xenophon with Thucydides they were thinking of the *Hellenica*, so we will begin our discussion with it.

The *Hellenica* starts out abruptly: "Not many days after these things Thymochares arrived from Athens with a few ships." Not a word here or later on as to who the author was, and in adopting the device of anonymity (which seems to have deceived no one) Xenophon departs from the tradition of three generations of historical writing: the very first word written by Hecataeus, Herodotus, and Thucydides was the name of the author,[91] while Ctesias (whose opening remarks are missing) is always telling us about himself. Xenophon even goes one step further: he uses the *Hellenica* to provide himself with a pen name for the *Anabasis*, for he alludes to what most scholars regard as his own account of the retreat of the Greek mercenaries after the death of Cyrus as having been written by one Themistogenes of Syracuse.[92] There are obvious literary advantages in this procedure because it enables the writer to discuss events in which he took part with a detachment that would otherwise have been difficult to obtain. Writing as an officer serving in the war against Persia with the Spartan army, Xenophon would have found it difficult to make a critical appraisal of his commanding officers, including King Agesilaus, yet in the *Hellenica* he occasionally does so.[93]

The use of a pseudonym, or even anonymity, has its dangers, since the time may come when what was meant to be an open secret is no longer a matter of general knowledge. The survival of an important literary work might depend on a single manuscript. Some such circumstance may lie behind the statement in Diogenes Laertius to the effect that it was Xenophon who rescued Thucydides' history from oblivion;[94] that is he was credited with publishing the manuscript of the *Peloponnesian War*. In a recent study, W. P. Henry has been at some pains to examine the evidence for any relationship between Thucydides' work and the *Hellenica*, refusing to accept the usual view that the *Hellenica* was written as a continuation of Thucydides' unfinished work, but coming to no firm conclusion of his own.[95] Even Henry recognizes that the one work ends at about the point where the other begins,[96] and even granting that the join between the two is not satisfactory it still seems reasonable to regard the *Hellenica* as a continuation of Thucydides, at least until someone comes forward with a better reason for his beginning when he does. But there is a great deal more to Henry's argument than this one point. He gets in some shrewd blows against the critics of Xenophon who portray him as a man of limited intelligence with a naive view of the world. Henry shows that the simplicity of Xenophon is only apparent, that in fact it is calculated, an effect of which only a man with an unusually subtle mind would have been capable.

In one sense the *Hellenica* cannot be regarded as a continuation of Thucydides, because the latter tells us in the very beginning that he is going to describe a particular war. Logically then, his continuator ought to have stopped when the war came to an end. There might be some justification for carrying the narrative on down to the restoration of the democracy in Athens and the departure of Pausanias and his Spartans, but not any further than that; yet Xenophon continues his account for another forty years down to the Battle of Mantinea in 362 B.C. Xenophon concludes as follows:

*What has been written to this point is mine. Someone else will be apt to concern himself with what happened after these things.*

The ending is virtually an echo of the beginning,[97] and I find it hard to believe that the resemblance is accidental. Xenophon may be expressing the hope that some other writer will be found willing to continue his work, just as he has continued the work of his predecessor. If anyone did write such a continuation, his work has dropped out of sight.[98]

The conclusion of the Peloponnesian War with the establishment of a Spartan hegemony in Greece must have impressed many thinking persons as the end of an epoch, the beginning of a new and perhaps a happier period in Greek history. Xenophon's statement that the Athenians (perhaps the exiles are meant) pulled down their own walls to the sound of the flute, "thinking that day was the beginning of freedom for Greece," reflects the mood.[99] Yet events were soon to show that the rejoicing was premature, just as Thucydides had found earlier that the Peace of Nicias really ended nothing. Xenophon must have formed conclusions of his own about the continuity of history. He might have started a separate work, but he chose instead to expand what had been the history of a war into a general history of Greece. And this is not to be wondered at. When we consider that Herodotus began as a logographer and ended up writing an account of the Persian War, is it not equally appropriate that Xenophon should find the limits Thucydides had established for himself as no longer applicable? As though to emphasize his convictions (or disillusionment?) about the historical process, Xenophon goes out of his way—just before putting down his pen—to remark that in fact Mantinea decided nothing:

*After the battle confusion and indecision prevailed in Greece even more than they had previously.*

Much has been written in an attempt to unsnarl the knotty question as to when the various works of Xenophon were composed: whether the *Hellenica* precedes or follows the *Agesilaus;* how the *Anabasis* was written with relation to the others; and as to what parts, both of the *Anabasis* and of the *Hellenica,* were the earliest to be written. There is no space for discussing this question here, even if I felt competent to do so. It seems dangerous to rely on stylistic differences for judging the relative dating of works that belong to different literary genres. The *Agesilaus* is a biography, or rather an encomium. Naturally enough many passages in it, dealing with the same events, appear verbatim in the *Hellenica* as well. Essentially they differ by what the *Agesilaus* leaves out as inappropriate to its purpose.[100] The *Anabasis,* on the other hand, is *sui generis,* certainly at the time it was written.

For the first two books, Xenophon would have had his own memories of what went on as seen from inside the walls of Athens. As the war moved on to its desperate conclusion it would have been more and more difficult for those in the city to get reliable reports from outside. Xenophon's position is the reverse of that of Thucydides, who was on the outside looking in. Even later, when he began to write and would have been able to get information denied to him before, the perspective in which he viewed the war probably remained unaffected. There are a number of touches that still suggest personal experience. When Alcibiades finally returns from his long exile Xenophon gives us a picture of the feelings in Athens, both friendly and unfriendly. He adds as a picturesque detail that when Alcibiades' ship reached the Piraeus he hesitated before going ashore:

*But when he looked down and saw his cousin Euryptolemus the son of Peisianax together with others who were his friends and relatives then he went ashore and proceeded on up to the city, accompanied by an escort prepared to prevent anyone from laying hands on him.*[101]

He never gives us a judgment on Alcibiades himself. His last appearance takes place when, an exile again, he tries to warn the Athenian fleet in the Hellespont of the dangers of their position.[102]

His advice was not heeded and Athens lost her fleet and with it the war. Later we learn that Theramenes had opposed exiling Alcibiades.[103] And that is all.

The closest Xenophon comes to divulging his own political feelings is in his account of the Arginusae trials. Henry rightly argues that this episode has been arranged in such a way as to emphasize Socrates' singular courage in standing up for the rule of law, while the assembly is shown as more and more determined to take the law into its own hands. To achieve dramatic effect the facts have been slightly altered.[104] Therefore it is all the more significant when Xenophon has the mob cry out (in unison?), "that it was a shameful thing for anyone to stop the 'demus' from doing whatever it wanted to do![105] So Xenophon does have his prejudices. Yet he also says at the very end of Book II, that the democracy was restored and the "demus" took an oath to forget the past and not to hold the oligarchs responsible for their acts under the terror, and he adds that the people kept its word, "even up to the present time." That is a generous (or insincere?) statement for an Athenian with Xenophon's background to have made.

If one did not know who the author was there are many passages in the first two books of the *Hellenica* that might make us doubt where his sympathies lie. He is usually regarded as pro-Spartan, yet it is Critias, the most notorious of the notorious Thirty, who calls the Spartan form of government the finest in the world,[106] surely no recommendation to Xenophon's readers whether Spartan or Athenian. And then there is that high-minded Spartan Callicratidas who advocates peace with Athens, and an end to all this kowtowing to the barbarians in order to get money,[107] but who then leads the Spartan navy into the most humiliating defeat they suffered in the entire war!

Xenophon's description of the terror under the Thirty is justly celebrated as an excellent piece of historical writing which, coupled with Lysias' Twelfth Oration (*Against Eratosthenes*), gives us a three-dimensional view of what was happening, such as we also get for an earlier time when we read Thucydides' account of the mutilation of the Hermae along with Andocides' speech, *On the Mysteries*[108]— yet we must not forget that Xenophon was an eye-witness while Thucydides was not. Among the interesting survivals of the political language of those days is Xenophon's use of the term *kaloi kagathoi* (meaning literally "gentlemen," "men of the better sort"). Herodotus uses it without any political overtones: for example, he tells us Tellus of Athens died happy, and one reason for this was that his two sons had proved themselves to be *kaloi kagathoi*.[109] Thucydides follows the example of Herodotus, but on one occasion he uses the phrase *kaloi kagathoi* in the sense of members of the oligarchical faction, and he writes as though this were a new usage.[110] Xenophon is more specific. In speaking of the earliest period under the Thirty he says that they executed those known to have been hard on the *kaloi kagathoi* during the democracy. Then later Theramenes opposes killing men who had enjoyed favor in the democracy unless they had done harm to the *kaloi kagathoi*.[111] As a party term it seems not to have had a long history; perhaps coming into active use only late in the war it was evidently intended to put an attractive label on views that many Athenians had long found objectionable. This is made very clear in Theramenes' speech in his own defense, in which he accuses Critias and his supporters of arresting *kaloi kagathoi*.[112] That is, Theramenes, an oligarch himself, attempts to distinguish his own stripe of oligarchs as *kaloi kagathoi*, while those who went further than he did must be regarded as tyrannical. An interesting illustration of the way in which words tend to change their meaning in revolutionary times, as Thucydides had already indicated in general terms.[113]

With Book III the perspective changes: the war is over and Xenophon no longer views events from inside Athens. The last five books cover the following periods: Book III, 401–395 B.C.; Book IV, 395–389; Book V, 389–375; Book VI, 374–370; and Book VII, 369–362. Mosley believes that Book III was based largely on Xenophon's personal experiences under three Spartan commanders, and that Book IV was pretty much limited to what he could learn from Peloponnesian sources (presumably written at Scillus), while Book V was written in Corinth and the last two books in Athens.[114] But this is being much too precise, based as it must be purely on internal evidence. Xenophon says nothing about his own movements, which can only be inferred from what he says or does not say in his narrative. And in any given instance it is not easy to see whether an omission has been deliberate in order to please his Spartan friends or inadvertent because of ignorance. Then again he may not have regarded a certain development as significant or he may have omitted it simply out of carelessness. Under such circumstances anyone can read into the *Hellenica* a Xenophon of his own choosing. There are also annoying problems about the text as we have it, for it certainly contains interpolations by someone other than Xenophon as well as possible later additions made by the historian himself. For example, did he add the last chapter to Book II at a later date? And if so, when? The matter of interpolations will not be dealt with here except to say that in general they are explanatory rather than interpretive, but certain omissions do demand our attention. The most famous omission in the entire work is Xenophon's failure to mention the Second Athenian Confederacy, and this is simply inexcusable. News of its formation must even have penetrated the seclusion of Scillus. The "Charter" of the confederacy survives in an inscription dated quite exactly as of February or March in 377 B.C.,[115] and it must have been a common subject for conversation during the Olympic Games in 376 B.C., within easy walking distance for a sporting enthusiast like Xenophon. Leaving out any reference to it can hardly be attributed to malice. What purpose would it serve? It must, regretfully, be attributed to negligence, a negligence that finds no parallel in Herodotus or Thucydides. Hatzfeld maintains that Xenophon lacked the qualities of a true historian. He saw details but not the total picture; he was more interested in the how than the why.[116] However that may be, we must acknowledge that Xenophon lacks the architectonic qualities of a great historian, though Hatzfeld does him something less than justice in comparing him with Froissart,[117] for Xenophon was not unaware of the serious problems of his day. His other writings suffice to prove that.[118]

In antiquity Xenophon is often thought of as a philosopher rather than a historian, which may give us a clue to his deficiencies in both areas. As a historian he tends to oversimplify the problem, just as in some of his nonhistorical works he oversimplifies the solution. The idea of monarchy was being bruited about; and in the *Cyropaedia* Xenophon lays down the rules a successful monarch ought to follow, by exemplifying them in an imaginary biography of the founder of the Persian empire. The *Cyropaedia* was a best seller in classical times, as it deserved to be, and it has often been imitated since, for example in the *Télémaque* of Fénelon. Cyrus applies the rules of sweet reasonableness to the governing of mankind with the result that men not only obey, but obey him for their own good. This is the same quality Xenophon saw, or thought he saw, in Socrates, and served as the standard by which he measured the shortcomings of his own friend, the unforgettably human Agesilaus. In writing the *Cyropaedia* Xenophon had a theme which unifies that work in a way that is lacking in the *Hellenica*. The deficiency is less noticeable in the first two books of the *Hellenica* where Xenophon contemplates events from inside the city, a limited perspective that had the one advantage of presenting a unified picture. But in the later books the author faces a more difficult task which exceeded his abilities as a historian. He failed to group the complicated data available to him into a single pattern. Instead, he clutches at certain episodes which he does understand and presents them with great literary skill, while he ignores whatever he could not conveniently handle in that way. Probably that is why he ignores the Second Athenian Confederacy: there was no context in which he was forced to describe it. Nor does he tell us how the Boeotian Confederacy operated, either before or after the King's Peace, though here we are fortunate enough to have recovered a small part of a previously unknown *Hellenica* among the Oxyrhynchus papyri. The fragments give us an excellent account of the earlier constitution of the Boeotian Confederacy. Whoever the author may have been the loss of the rest of his history is most regrettable, as it would be helpful to be able to compare it with Xenophon in detail. Where we can compare the two works, the unknown writer is not always to be preferred; but the two tend to supplement one another in such a way that we learn much more than either can tell us alone. The period of overlap is very short, chiefly for the years 396 and 395 B.C.[119]

Another charge made against Xenophon concerns the Theban Epaminondas, who is not mentioned until quite late,[120] allegedly on grounds of prejudice. Xenophon had no love for Thebes (despite his friend Proxenus) but he did have admiration for Sparta, whose rule over the Greek cities was effectively destroyed by this same Epaminondas. Not only that, but Epaminondas was indirectly responsible for setting Xenophon on his travels again when the Elians felt strong enough after Sparta's defeat to move in on Scillus. And for good measure, Xenophon's son was killed fighting these same Thebans in 362 B.C. Yet Henry argues that because Xenophon pays a handsome tribute to Epaminondas, a tribute which, "so far from being that due the devil, is much more worthy of a saint,"[121] he admires him greatly. He has purposely held off giving his judgment to the very end and in order to make it more dramatic just as he had rearranged matters in connection with the Arginusae trials in order to pay tribute to Socrates. Here I cannot agree. Xenophon must have hated Epaminondas much as Clarendon hated Cromwell. Both however could appreciate the professional qualities of an enemy. Leaving Epaminondas' name out of the Battle of Leuctra was not done out of admiration for Epaminondas but out of sympathy for the Spartans. He makes amends later but he cannot bring himself to do so at the moment of Epaminondas' greatest triumph.

There is another side of Xenophon not touched on by Henry but of considerable importance for judging him as a historian, and that is his attitude towards the gods. Xenophon is a fundamentalist. There should be no mistaking the fact that he is a believer, not merely in the existence of the gods, but in their direct intervention in the affairs of men. His was no lip service only; religion is not regarded (as in Polybius) as merely a useful way to keep the masses in check. The gods are ready to help those who deserve their friendship. The *Cyropaedia*, perhaps our best guide to Xenophon's cast of mind, also gives the clearest statement on the place of religion in warfare, and it is put in the mouth of Cyrus' father, who gives his son a great deal of wholesome advice. A general ought to be expert in divination so he need not depend entirely on professional interpreters. But anyone who expects help from the gods must cultivate them in advance, for they take a dim view of those who approach them only in time of need. And the man who relies on the gods must also do his own part (Heracles and the Wagoner?). No one should ask the gods for victory in a cavalry engagement unless he has made himself an expert horseman—and so on.[122] A good example of the importance of all this is given in his account of the conspiracy of Cinadon. Agesilaus is still in his first year as king of Sparta when the official sacrifices reveal the existence of a conspiracy. Agesilaus has the diviner sacrifice again, and the signs become clearer and more specific. The warning was heeded and Cinadon arrested.[123] There is also no doubt that Xenophon thought of Socrates as having similar views, hence his oversimplification of Socrates' character and ideas. His religious predilections separate him by a wide margin from Thucydides and also from his contemporary, Ctesias. This characteristic is also exhibited in the *Anabasis*.

Like the *Hellenica*, the *Anabasis* lacks a preface, nor does the author reveal his identity. Plutarch, as we have seen, says that Xenophon attributed the work to Themistogenes of Syracuse, presumably on the basis of his reference to the Syracusan in the *Hellenica*.[124] Jacoby is sure, both that Xenophon attributes the work to Themistogenes and that this was merely a temporary attribution. According to him no exemplar ever bore Themistogenes' name, because there was no preface.[125] He is probably right on both counts though a nagging doubt remains. Why does the *Suda* tell us that Themistogenes of Syracuse is a historian cited by Xenophon for an *Anabasis of Cyrus* and also for *"some other writings about his own country"*?[126]

The *Anabasis* is an ideal subject for Xenophon. The movement of the army from one picturesque area to another provides the author with the opportunity to display his talent for describing new places, peoples, animal life, and native customs in a way emulated by a Francis Parkman. At the same time the dangers of writing an episodic history, so often succumbed to in the *Hellenica*, are avoided because all these details are relevant to the central theme, an army on the march. In the first book, the center of the stage belongs to Cyrus, a prince whose attractive personality as seen by Xenophon undoubtedly suggested many a detail for the historical romance he was to write about Cyrus the Elder. The shift in focus from Cyrus to Xenophon is managed with considerable dexterity, by means of a chance meeting between the two men just as the battle in which Cyrus loses his life is about to begin. The encounter concerns the taking of auspices. Cyrus tells the young Athenian to report that they are favorable. While they are talking, a confused noise reaches their ears from the Greek ranks, which Xenophon explains to Cyrus as the sound of the password for the day being passed from man to man: "Zeus and Victory!"[127]

The characterization of Cyrus which is given immediately

after the account of his death tells us more about the man who wrote it than about the Persian prince.[128] Here, in miniature, is the portrait of an ideal ruler which we find writ large in the *Cyropaedia.* Like his famous namesake, the younger Cyrus received an education that taught him modesty and respect for his elders. As he grew he excelled all his fellows in courage, in hunting skills, and in his ability to manage a horse. As a young governor of a province he demonstrated a sweet reasonableness which won him the trust of everyone with whom he had to deal. His highest hope was that he might live long enough to reward his friends and punish his enemies, like Sulla after him,[129] and, if Xenophon is to be believed, like the great Cyrus before him.[130] Socrates, at least Plato's Socrates, would have turned over in his grave. One touch of realism remains. We are told that the younger Cyrus was merciless in his punishments, cutting off the hands and feet of some wrongdoers and putting out the eyes of others as a warning that crime does not pay. Such men were often seen on the roads of Cyrus' satrapy.[131] Xenophon appears not to have been repelled by this barbarism. The elegance of his Greek prose cannot altogether hide a certain callousness in the writer that reminds us of the very rough life he had led. He was not a man to be squeamish about unpleasant necessities. The slaughter of children at school by marauding Thracians would probably not have upset him to the extent that it did Thucydides, just as it is certain Thucydides never felt the strange fascination in viewing dead bodies on a battlefield that is shown by Cyrus the Great (i.e., Xenophon) as a teen-ager.[132] In the eulogy of the younger Cyrus we are told that no one ever deserted him for Artaxerxes (with the exception of Orontas who failed to get away), though many abandoned Artaxerxes to join up with his brother. This is corroborated by Ctesias, one of the few occasions for comparing the two accounts.[133]

Book II, which need not detain us here, relates what happened between Cunaxa and the slaying of the Greek generals. It ends with a series of brief biographies of these men in which Clearchus, a competent soldier but a brutal person, is portrayed with obvious sympathy; while Menon, like Xenophon himself a friend of Socrates, is vilified. Ctesias offers independent testimony to the rivalry between Menon and Clearchus and to the low regard in which Menon was held by Cyrus, but he does not show partiality as Xenophon does.[134]

Book III begins with the crisis facing the Ten Thousand. Everyone is at a loss, not least a young Athenian named Xenophon who, however, receives guidance from above. He goes to bed filled with anxiety and in his sleep he dreams. He sees a bolt of lightning strike his family's house so that everything was illuminated by it. Waking up, Xenophon considers what the meaning of this dream might be. He soon discovers that it is capable of two divergent interpretations and comes to the conclusion that he will be able to learn which is the correct one by subsequent developments.[135] And this tells us something more about Xenophon's religious views. The dream is from a god, and therefore it does have significance. On the other hand (like Delphi itself!) it is ambiguous—whatever happens the prophetic accuracy of the dream will have been demonstrated. This point of view is less sophisticated than Artabanus' interpretation of dreams, in Herodotus, as apt to be brought about by what one has been thinking of during the day.[136] The next morning Xenophon makes an eloquent speech, during the course of which he alludes in specific terms to how Cyrus' body had been treated by his brother. The details are identical with those given in the *Persica*.[137] Did Xenophon borrow them from his medical counterpart? That is not unlikely. He can hardly be thought to have carried a copy of his speech with him during the rest of the march, so he must have composed a suitable speech years later, perhaps at Scillus with a copy of the *Persica* within easy reach.

The various scenes, many of them descriptive gems, that succeed one another in Xenophon's narrative of the expedition are too well known to be alluded to here, too well told to spoil by paraphrasing. One generalization may be made. These descriptions are less contrived and have much more of an authentic ring about them than those in the *Hellenica,* though even there we find occasional touches of realism. The account of Agesilaus' sufferings with his injured leg may serve as one example,[138] but usually the ugly side of life is kept in the background as in a Greek play.

In closing, two passages from the *Anabasis* may be singled out to illustrate what a mine of information the author has preserved for the modern reader in his *obiter dicta.*

The first of these is one of those casual references that tell us more than the author intended. The Ten Thousand have fought their way through the rough country and deep snows of Armenia. They are advancing rapidly through the hills of the land of the Macrones not far from Trapezus and the coast, and they have already been encouraged by their first glimpse of the ocean. They arrive at the bank of a river only to find a strange wild people carrying wicker shields and wearing hairy garments posted on the opposite bank to block their advance. At this point one of the light-armed soldiers in the Greek army came up to Xenophon and informed him he understood the language of these savages, "for I think this is my native land."[139] It seems the man had been a slave in Athens. How he obtained his freedom we are not told. Yet here he is, home again in this extraordinary fashion in the role of a Greek mercenary soldier, offering his services as an interpreter. Here is how slavery worked for one man, and here also is an example of how Hellenism spread. It is also interesting that Xenophon does not mention his name, evidently the man's story did not strike him as particularly unusual.

The other passage I have chosen concerns a Thracian people called the Melinophagi ("Millet-eaters") who live on the west coast of the Black Sea in the area around Salmydessus. This is a treacherous coast for shipping and many vessels are wrecked on the shoals when driven there by adverse winds. The natives profit by these misfortunes and regularly loot stranded craft. They used to fight over the spoils, but now have set up stones to establish recognized plundering districts for the different claimants. This says a good deal for the perils of Pontic trading ships in classical times, but what follows is even more suggestive.[140] Xenophon tells us that he and his men occupied Salmydessus, a harbor town, where they found all sorts of gear such as might have come from merchant ships, and this included many rolls of papyrus with writing on them, that is *books*. And this is one of the very few references we have about the book trade in the early fourth century B.C.[141]

This same fourth century B.C. was a good period for historians. We have met two of them, but as we move on into the century we will find others, the first of whom will be Ephorus of Cyme and the islander, Theopompus of Chios.

## Notes for Chapter Four

1. See *FGrH*, 688. T 5a.
2. See Xen. *Anab.* i. 8. 26.
3. See Plut. *Artox.* 1. 4; Arr. *Anab.* v. 4. 2; and Antig. *Hist. mir.* 15. For a discussion of this last work, see U. von Wilamowitz-Moellendorff, *Antigonos von Karystos* (Berlin, 1881), chap. 2 ("Antigonos der Paradoxograph").
4. See George Grote, *History of Greece,* 12 volume edition (London, 1869), IV, 112.
5. See F. Jacoby, "Ktesias" (1), *PW* xi. 2041 and 2046. The last remark is quoted approvingly by H. Bengtson, *Griechische Geschichte,* 2nd ed. (Munich, 1960), 148.
6. See A. R. Burn, *Persia and the Greeks* (New York, 1962), 11.
7. See A. T. Olmstead, *History of the Persian Empire* (Phoenix Books, 1948), 350.
8. See Kurt von Fritz, *Die Griechische Geschichtsschreibung,* Part I (in two volumes, *Text* and *Anmerkungen* respectively) (Berlin, 1967). For references to Ctesias see I (*Text*) 464; I (*Anmerk.*) 280; 339 and especially 354 f.
9. See *FGrH* 133. F 23a–b; also Jacoby, "Ktes.," *PW* xi. 2054.
10. See R. Henry, *Ctésias: La Perse, L'Inde: Les Sommaires de Photius* (Brussells, 1947), 8.
11. See, e.g., Arist., *HA* viii. 28, 606a. 8; iii. 22, 523a. 26; and Arist. *Pol.* 1311b. 40 ff.; *Eth. Nic.* 1095b. 19 ff. In neither passage is Ctesias cited by name, but see Jacoby, "Ktes.," *PW* xi. 2067.
12. For Ctesias' birthplace see *Suda,* s.v. Κτησίας; Diod. Sic. ii. 32. 4; Strabo xiv. 2. 15; for the Spartans as founders of Cnidus, see Hdt. i. 174; for Triopas, see Paus. x. 11. 1.
13. For Galen's statement see *FGrH* 688. T 4. The relationship may be taken with a grain of salt. All physicians are Asclepiadae and as such reputed to derive

from Asclepius the son of Apollo, just as all the Homeridae were proud of their descent from the great poet.

14. For a demonstration that Diodorus did use Ctesias and used him directly, see especially four illuminating articles by Paul Krumbholz which appeared as follows in *Rheinisches Museum:* 41 (1886), 321–341; 44 (1889), 286–298; 50 (1895), 205–240; and 52 (1897), 237–285.
15. Diod. Sic. ii. 32. 4.
16. See Xen. *Anab.* i. 8. 26; Plut. *Artox.* 11.
17. See W. Judeich, *Kleinasiatische Studien* (Marburg, 1896), 49 f.
18. See Jacoby, "Ktes." *PW* xi. 2033; but Müller prefers to assume a scribal error, where 17 years should be reduced to 7 years—see *Ctesiae Cnidii* etc. by Carolus Müllerus, pub. along with the Didot Herodotus, Paris 1862, p. 2, col. b.
19. See *PW* xi. 2033.
20. See Phot. *Bibl.* 72. 44b. 20 and Plut. *Artox.* 21. 2–4. Both appear in *FGrH* 688, as T 7c and T 7d respectively.
21. Plut. *Artox.* 21. 4.
22. See *FGrH* (Polycritus) 559.
23. Ibid., F 3.
24. See C. Müller, *Scriptores Rerum Alexandri Magni* (Paris, 1846), 130 (though Müller wrongly gives Dinocrates of Sparta instead of Dexippus as their leader).
25. See *FGrH* iii B. Commentary (notes) 305. n. 5.
26. See Ibid. Commentary (text) 516. 19–22.
27. See, e.g., Xen. *Cyr.* i. 6. 15—οἱ στρατηγοὶ τῶν στρατιωτῶν ἕνεκεν ἰατροὺς ἐξάγουσιν κ.τ.λ.
28. For Democedes see Hdt. iii. 125; for Ctesias, Diod. Sic. ii. 32. 4.
29. It was natural for the Spartans to take a lively interest in a man who stood as close to their enemy Artaxerxes as Ctesias did. There were also sure to be questions about Clearchus, the Spartan who commanded the Greek mercenaries at Cunaxa and who fell into Persian hands at a later date, and was put to death by them. Our information on Ctesias' return comes from Photius (i.e., Ctesias) *Bibl.* 72. 44b. 20–42 = *FGrH* 688. F 30.
30. See *PW* xi. 2046.
31. Olmstead, who misses very little, remarks with specific reference to Ctesias, "note how many Greeks held positions at court." (*History of Persia,* 379). Presumably Artaxerxes received the same education as his brother Cyrus, and Cyrus must have known Greek, for we find him exchanging words with Xenophon before the battle (Xen. *Anab.* i. 8. 15).
32. Jacoby arranges the fragments under ten headings, included here for the convenience of the reader (*FGrH* iii c. 688. 420–517).

| | | |
|---|---|---|
| 1. *Persica* (book given) | FF | 1–33 |
| 2. *Persica* (book not given) | | 34–44 |
| 3. *Indica* (specific reference) | | 45–45t |
| 4. *Indica* (reference inferred) | | 46–52 |
| 5. *Revenues in Asia* | | 53–54 |
| 6. περίοδος | | 55–60 |
| 7. Reference without title | | 61–66 |
| 8. Medical works | | 67–68 |
| 9. Of doubtful authenticity | | 69–72 |
| 10. Spurious | | 73–74 |

The "spurious" fragments come from the *De fluviis,* itself a spurious work attributed to Plutarch. In his edition Müller anticipates category no. 10 and rejects no. 5; so does J. A. Bowman in his dissertation, *Studies in Ctesias,* see *Summaries of Doctoral Dissertations,* Northwestern University, VI, 7. This is not the place to discuss the matter as we are not concerned with no. 5.
33. See *FGrH* 688. T 10 = Phot. *Bibl.* 72. 45a. 20.
34. See Chapter 1 above.
35. See Euseb. *Praep. Evang.* x. 3. 23.
36. See Lucian, *Ver. Hist.* i. 3.
37. R. C. Majumdar, *Classical Accounts of India* (Calcutta, 1960), xi–xii, excludes

Ctesias on principle, citing Rawlinson as saying that he, "adds practically nothing to our knowledge of India," and those are harsh words.

38. See *FGrH* 688. F 45; and Bowman, op. cit., 7.
39. There are only 14 pages of Greek text in the Budé edition of Photius, while the fragments of Book XII of Polybius (also in the Budé format) amount to 54 pages. The extent of our loss may be approximated by comparing these figures with the 129 pages in the Budé edition of Herodotus' Second Book.
40. Cf. *FGrH* (Ctesias) 688. F 45. 2 with Hdt. iii. 94 and v. 3.
41. Cf. *FGrH* (Ctesias) 688. F 45. 4 with Hdt. iv. 40.
42. Hdt. iii. 104–105.
43. See W. W. Tarn, *Greeks in Bactria,* 2nd ed. (London, 1951), 106.
44. Ibid. See also *FGrH* (Ctesias) 688. F 45. 26 for the gryphons.
45. *FGrH* (Ctesias) 688. F 45. 9.
46. Ibid.
47. See *FGrH* 688. F 45. 49 for the last two and F 47b for water where nothing will float. This last spring is evidently the Silas river of Megasthenes (*FGrH* 715. F 10a–b), though it is spelled differently (*Side,* with variants) in Ctesias. There is another fabulous river known to us through an Indian text, called the Çila river, which means "stone." The Indians believed there was such a river on the northern edge of India which turned everything to stone—and naturally the stones would not float. For references and discussion, see E. A. Schwanbeck, *Megasthenes Indica* (Bonn, 1846—reprinted in Chicago, 1967), 37, n. 32. The repelling waters also turn up in Sicily, oddly enough in the work of Polycritus of Mende (*FGrH* 559), who may or may not be Artaxerxes' physician of the same name. In the Polycritus fragment (*FGrH* 559. F 2) the pond is even more remarkable. Normally no larger than a shield it obligingly keeps on enlarging itself to permit one bather after another to enter its waters, but when the fiftieth bather jumps in then the pond hurls all fifty bathers back to the shore and reverts to its original dimensions.
48. See n. 37 above.
49. For the elephant see *FGrH* 688. F 45b; for the rhinoceros ("wild ass") F 45. 45; for the tiger (?) ("Martichora" = "Man-eater") FF 45. 14 and 45d (vouched for by Aristotle, Aelian, Pausanias, and Pliny the Elder); and for the dogs F 46a–b.
50. Plutarch, living in a less imaginative age, uses the references to the Amazons as a test to separate the unreliable Alexander historians from the rest (Plut. *Alex* 46). For a more sympathetic judgment see Erwin Rohde, *Der Griechische Roman,* 1914, 4th ed. (Hildesheim, 1960 reprint) 176, n. 3.
51. Perhaps he wrote during the joint reigns of Seleucus Nicator and Antiochus, certainly after 293/292 B.C. The fragments are in *FGrH* no. 680; also in Paul Schnabel's *Berossos und die babylonisch-hellenistische Literatur,* 1923 (Hildesheim, 1968 reprint).
52. Ibid., 184.
53. See *FGrH* 680. F 8. 142.
54. See *FGrH* 680. F 2 and 688. F 4 = Ath. xiv. 44. 639c.
55. See M. Braun, *History and Romance in Greco-Oriental Literature* (Oxford, 1938); also my discussion in *AJPhil.* 76 (1955), 25.
56. See *FGrH* 688. FF 1n–q.
57. See Sidney Smith, *CAH* III, 124; A. T. Olmstead, *History of Assyria,* (Chicago, 1923), 475.
58. See Rohde, *Griech. Roman,* 39; also *FGrH* 688. FF 5. 34, 7, 8a–b.
59. Cf. *FGrH* 688. F 9 with Hdt. i. 75. Ctesias insists on calling him Astyigas rather than Astyages. He may be right.
60. See *FGrH* 688. F 9c; cf. Hdt. i. 84.
61. See *FGrH* 688. F 9. 7–8; cf. Hdt. i. 214, where Herodotus remarks he has chosen one version from many available to him.
62. See *FGrH* 688. F 13. 9–14; Hdt. iii. 30, 61, 64.
63. See Jacoby, "Ktes.," *PW* xi. 2048. Diodorus refers to Ctesias' use of these records twice, first as βασιλικαὶ ἀναγραφαί, and again more precisely as βασιλικαὶ διφθέραι (Diod. Sic. ii. 22. 5 and 32. 4). This is curious, though not noted by Jacoby, because Herodotus tells us the Ionians used to call books

διφθέραι because in ancient times when papyrus was hard to come by they used hides as a writing material (Hdt. v. 58). In calling the Persian records διφθέραι, is Ctesias borrowing out of context from Herodotus with a view to making these Persian documents seem very old and therefore authentic? Or *did* the Persians use hides for writing purposes at one time? Recovery of the Dead Sea Scrolls suggests the need for caution in our judgment.

64. Cf. Hdt. ii. 140; iii. 15 with *FGrH* 688. F 13.
65. See *FGrH* 688. F 45. 19.
66. See ibid., FF 14. 34; 26. 16.
67. See ibid., F 27. 70. Ctesias himself must have been an expert in mixing drugs, and he lived in a period of rapid medical advance in preparing medicines. In fact, he tells us how he has no hesitation now in mixing *hellebore* for use in prescriptions, though in his grandfather's time it could not be done safely (F 68).
68. See ibid., F 34. The cows were as good at counting as the pond in Sicily, see n. 47 above.
69. See *PW* xi. 2059.
70. See *PW* xi. 2063.
71. See the *Suda*, s.v. Ξενοφῶν, Γρύλου, ᾿Αθηναῖος (47).
72. See D.L. ii. 56—the archon is really Callimedes.
73. See [Lucian] *Macrob.* 21.
74. See Xen. *Hell.* vi. 4. 36.
75. See A. Lesky, *Geschichte der griechischen Literatur,* 2nd ed. (Munich, 1963), 667; and E. Zeller, *Socrates and the Socratic Schools,* 3rd ed. transl. by O. J. Reichel (New York, 1962), 239, n. 2.
76. See Xen. *Anab.* iii. 1. 25; A. E. Taylor, *Socrates the Man and his Thought* (Garden City, 1956), 13, n. 1.
77. See Xen. *Anab.* ii. 1. 12–13; Eduard Meyer, *Geschichte des Altertums,* 3rd ed. (Berlin, 1921), V, #833.
78. See D.L. ii. 48.
79. See Xen. *Anab.* iii. 1. 4–7.
80. Xenophon's presence in Athens just might have prevented the tragedy. If anyone could have persuaded Socrates to a more sensible course he was the man to do it!
81. See D.L. ii. 52.
82. See Xen. *Anab.* v. 6. 15.
83. See Xen. *Anab.* vii. 7. 57.
84. See D. J. Mosley, "Xenophon" No. 1 in the *OCD²*, 1141.
85. See Lesky, *Gesch. griech. Lit.,* 664.
86. See Xen. *Anab.* v. 3. 5–13, for the whole account of this Scillan idyll. Perhaps she was the divinity to whom he sacrificed on the advice of Delphi before setting out.
87. See Xen. *Hell.* vii. 4. 4 on the expulsion of Athenian garrison troops from Corinth in 365 B.C.
88. See Paus. i. 3. 4; his reputation, or rather that of his father, is shown by the *encomia* by Isocrates and others (see D.L. ii. 55). Jacoby is skeptical both about the decree exiling Xenophon and the one which rescinded it. Ister says both were introduced by the same man, Eubulus. See *FGrH* 334. F 32, and Jacoby's comments (ibid., iii b, supp., 646); also W. P. Henry, *Greek Historical Writing* (Chicago, 1967), 90 f.
89. See D.L. ii. 54, where we are told Diodorus fought at Mantinea himself, but without distinction (i.e., he survived), and that Diodorus had a son named Gryllus.
90. See D.L. ii. 56; and *Suda, s.v.* Ξενοφῶν (47).
91. Hecataeus' preface is discussed in Chapter 1 above, see esp. n. 50.
92. Xen. *Hell.* iii. 1. 2. Another account was written by Sophaenetus of Stymphalus. See the *Testimonia* on Themistogenes (no. 108) and Sophaenetus (no. 109) in the *FGrH* as well as Jacoby's comments; also Lesky, *Gesch. griech. Lit.,* 665 for other references. It is worth noting that while Sophaenetus is mentioned in the *Anabasis,* Themistogenes of Syracuse is not.
93. This has been pointed out recently by W. P. Henry in *Gk. Hist. Writ.,* 154.

94. See D.L. ii. 57.
95. See W. P. Henry, *Gk. Hist. Writ.*, 210, where he says: "Before determining how, why, when, and where the ancients wrote, we must first discover what they wrote."
96. Ibid., 21, n. 41.
97. He begins with, μετὰ δὲ ταῦτα κτλ, and ends with, τὰ δὲ μετὰ ταῦτα ἴσως ἄλλῳ μελήσει.
98. Theopompus and Cratippus are also credited with having written a continuation of Thucydides (see *FGrH*, nos. 115 and 64 respectively), while Callisthenes' *Hellenica* starts later than theirs but overlaps that of Xenophon, covering the period from the King's Peace to the outbreak of the Phocian War (see *FGrH*, no. 124; also W. Spoerri, "Kallisthenes," no. 1, *Kl. Pauly* 3, 85.
99. See Xen. *Hell.* ii. 2. 23.
100. Here I agree heartily with Henry (*Gk. Hist. Writ.*, 133); see my *Onesicritus: A Study in Hellenistic Historiography* (University of California, 1949), 16 f. for a comparison between the treatment of Agesilaus in the two works.
101. See Xen. *Hell.* i. 4. 19.
102. Ibid., ii. 1. 25.
103. Ibid., ii. 3. 42.
104. See Henry, *Gk. Hist. Writ.*, 196–200. But his conclusion that here Xenophon has come to realize the true greatness of Socrates whereas in the *Memorabilia* he has not is a *non sequitur*, both because Xenophon has a different notion of greatness than we have, and because the two literary forms require different treatment.
105. See Xen. *Hell.* 1. 7. 12.
106. Ibid. ii. 3. 34.
107. Ibid., i. 6. 7.
108. Cf. Thuc. vi. 26–29; Andoc. i. 34–55.
109. Hdt. i. 30.
110. See Thuc. viii. 48. 6; for nonpolitical usage, Thuc. iv. 40. 2. The "Old Oligarch," who wrote a little earlier and whose *Athenian Constitution* was falsely attributed to Xenophon, uses the term χρηστοί ("worthy men") in the same partisan way to designate the oligarchs. See also Aristophanes' *Knights* line 185, where *kaloi kagathoi* implies good birth.
111. See Xen. *Hell.* ii. 3. 12, 15.
112. Ibid., ii. 3. 38.
113. See Thuc. iii. 82. 4.
114. See "Xenophon," no. 1, *OCD²*, 1142.
115. See M. N. Tod, *Greek Historical Inscriptions* (Oxford, 1948), vol. 2, no. 123.
116. See Hatzfeld's introduction to the Budé edition of the *Hellenica*, vol. 1, 15 f.
117. See ibid., 18.
118. See, e.g., Jean Luccioni, *Les Idées politiques et sociales de Xénophon*, pub. by Ophrys, no date (1947?), for discussion.
119. The literature is enormous. The reader is referred to I. A. F. Bruce, *An Historical Commentary on the Hellenica Oxyrhynchia* (London, 1967), for references and discussion. The most complete text is now the Teubner text of V. Bartoletti, *Hellenica Oxyrhynchia* (Leipzig, 1959); see also *FGrH* 66 along with Jacoby's commentary. A number of guesses have been made as to the author. Jacoby thinks it was written after 387 but before 356 B.C. and he says his identification of the author with Daimachus of Plataea (*FGrH* 65) is "as good as certain" (*FGrH* ii C. 7. 4–5). Bruce reviews the long arguments as to the authorship and concludes by saying that the author is probably someone we already know about, "and if we do it is more probably Cratippus than Daimachus" (Bruce, op. cit., 22–27). It is also interesting to compare G. L. Barber's article on "Oxyrhynchus, the historian from" in the 2nd edition of the *OCD* in 1970 with the one he wrote for the first edition in 1949. Perhaps the most important point is that scholars find evidence for the use of this work in Diodorus Siculus. That means Ephorus must have read it. Knowing, as we now do, that the Oxyrhynchus *Hellenica* is a reliable work we can have more confidence in Diodorus when he gives us information not to be found in Xenophon, than we did before.

120. See Xen. *Hell.* vii. 1. 41, in connection with the Theban invasion of the Peloponnese in 366 B.C.
121. See Henry, *Gk. Hist. Writ.,* 201.
122. See Xen. *Cyr.* i. 6. 3–6.
123. See Xen. *Hell.* iii. 3. 4.
124. See Plut. *Moralia* 345 E; also Xen. *Hell.* iii. 1. 2.
125. See *FGrH* ii D. 349.
126. See *Suda,* s.v. Θεμιστογένης; Müller (who is not quite satisfied), *FHG* ii. 74.
127. Xen. *Anab.* i. 8. 15–16.
128. Ibid., i. 9.
129. See Plut. *Sulla* 38 *ad fin.* Frank remarks that Sulla's epitaph, "breathes the true spirit of the petty politician"—Tenney Frank, *A History of Rome* (New York, 1923), 245.
130. See Xen. *Cyr.* i. 4. 25.
131. Ibid. i. 9. 13. The same Persian practice was observed later by Alexander's army, see Curtius Rufus v. 5. 5.
132. Thuc. vii. 29. 5; and Xen. *Cyr.* i. 4. 24.
133. Cf. Xen. *Anab.* i. 9. 29 with *FGrH* 688. F 16. 63; for Orontas see *Anab.* i. 6. 1–11.
134. For Ctesias see *FGrH* 688. F 16. 63; for the biography of Clearchus, see Xen. *Anab.* ii. 6. 1–15; for Menon, ibid. 21–29; also ibid. i. 5. 11–17. For more on Menon see A. E. Taylor, *Plato the Man and his Work* (New York, 1936), 129 f.
135. See Xen. *Anab.* iii. 1. 11–13.
136. See Hdt. vii. 16 β. 4; for another example of a prophetic dream in Xenophon, see *Anab.* iv. 3. 8; for sneezing as a good omen, ibid., ii. 2. 8–9.
137. Cf. Xen. *Anab.* iii. 1. 17 and *FGrH* 688. F 16. 64.
138. Xen. *Hell.* v. 4. 58.
139. See Xen. *Anab.* iv. 8. 4.
140. See ibid. vii. 5. 12–14.
141. See Sir John E. Sandys, *A History of Classical Scholarship,* 3rd ed., (London, 1921), 86; and Frederick G. Kenyon, *Books and Readers in Ancient Greece and Rome,* 2nd ed. (Oxford, 1951), 24. We would like to know where these books were being sent and, above all, we wish Xenophon had told us something about them. Treatises on farming? or perhaps the poetry of Homer? Socrates' student should at least have looked at them.

## I. Ephorus of Cyme

Not one of the historians considered in this chapter survives at all except in fragments, nor do we have even a condensed version of any of their works to be compared with Photius' summaries of Ctesias. Yet at one time these historians did not lack for readers. In fact Ephorus, Theopompus, and the Alexander historian Callisthenes appear on a late canon of the ten leading Greek historians.[1] Some important writers were necessarily left out of such a list, but for a man to have been included means that that man's reputation must have been high. The period we have now reached is a transitional one between the old Greece in which the city-state, though subject to serious challenges, remained the cultural, economic, and political center of the Greek world, and a new period of wider geographic horizons with large territorial states that resulted from Alexander's conquest of the Persian empire. Ephorus and Theopompus represent the older tradition while the Alexander historians already reflect the new Hellenistic age. Probably no historian in the fourth century B.C. was more popular than Ephorus of Cyme.

Ephorus' reputation made it necessary for the Alexandrians to provide him with a *vita*, but we can see from what remains of their efforts that they found little information to work with. One fact is beyond dispute: he was born in Cyme, an Aeolian Greek city in Asia Minor, the citizens of which were so dull, according to Strabo, that whenever it rained a town crier had to order them to take shelter.[2] Ephorus was proud of his city, however, mentioning it whenever possible in his writings. He also supported the local tradition that Hesiod was born there, while some Cymeans claimed Homer as well.[3] As to when he lived, the data given in the *Suda* are untrustworthy, for if he did in fact flourish during the ninety-third Olympiad (or 408/405 B.C.), then it is absurd to add that this

# EPHORUS; THEOPOMPUS; THE ALEXANDER HISTORIANS

5

was before the reign of Philip of Macedon (360–336).[4] Schwartz has the most likely explanation. As the continuator of Thucydides, Theopompus was appropriately given a floruit at the end of the Peloponnesian War, with the result that Ephorus, always bracketed with Theopompus, was given the same date.[5]

Another statement almost always made about Ephorus is that he studied under Isocrates. Isocrates lived so long (436–338 B.C.) and he had such a commanding reputation as a teacher of rhetoric that he attracted an unusual number of students. Hellenistic scholars were as well aware of this as we are today. They must sometimes have been tempted, if a writer of that day showed any similarity in style with Isocrates to attribute this similarity to a student-teacher relationship. There is no reason, therefore, to think that Ephorus did not study under Isocrates, but the unreliability of our information about his life in general prevents us from being sure. The famous story that Isocrates compared his two favorite pupils, Ephorus and Theopompus, saying that the one (Theopompus) needed a bridle and the other a spur is not of a kind to inspire confidence. The same judgment is also said to have been made of his students Aristotle and Xenocrates by Plato, and by Aristotle in turn of Callisthenes and Theophrastus.[6] However that may be, we ought to reject out of hand any idea that it was Isocrates who persuaded Ephorus and Theopompus to become historians, selecting for each a type of historical writing suited to his talents.[7] As Schwartz says, this is merely converting a stylistic judgment into a biographical fact.[8] And all these comparisons with Theopompus are at Ephorus' expense. He is regarded as a dull, plodding, unimaginative writer, compared with the dash and excitement to be found in Theopompus' work.[9]

Although Ephorus wrote other books, his reputation depends entirely on his History, which has a special importance for modern investigators because it was a leading source for Diodorus Siculus' *Historical Library*—which means that Ephorus is responsible for a great deal of what we know about the political history of Greece.[10] And it also is through Diodorus that we learn most of what we know about the organization of Ephorus' History and the period which it covers. Diodorus tells us that when Ephorus wrote his general history he decided to leave out the remote mythological period and begin with the Return of the Heraclidae.[11] The work was completed by Ephorus' son Demophilus who added an account of the Sacred War (356–346 B.C.), which his father had left out.[12] But we also hear the History contained thirty books and that it ended with the siege of Perinthus (340 B.C.).[13] Some embarrassment is caused when we find Demophilus cited for Book XXX.[14] For if the Sacred War was treated in Book XXX then we would naturally assume that the siege of Perinthus was also treated in Book XXX since it takes place after the Sacred War. There is one more small piece in the puzzle: Diyllus of Athens wrote his own history as a continuation of Ephorus, but he begins it with the Sacred War![15] Why did he not begin it with 340 B.C.? Jacoby evades the issue by finding this "very understandable."[16] However, R. Drews makes an attractive suggestion, starting from a key statement in Diodorus about the organization of Ephorus' History.[17] Everything hinges on just what Diodorus means by a history describing events "according to their *genos*," which C. H. Oldfather (the Loeb editor and translator) interprets as a *topical* history. Drews argues that *genos* refers not to a topic but rather to a geographical area. In other words, Ephorus proposes to write a general history subdivided geographically. When he wrote, Macedonian history might well have been considered separately from the history of Greece to the south. Under such circumstances he might narrate the history of Macedonia as far as 340 B.C.—then turn to Greece, whose history he had brought down only to 356 B.C. before his death. In other words, he did not deliberately omit the Sacred War. There are still difficulties, as it is hard to keep Macedonia and Greece as separate areas during the Sacred War which began as a Greek war but ended up with the victory of Philip. However, there is no time to discuss this further here; the reader will find the necessary references in Drews' article.[18]

Moreover, Ephorus is not a theoretical historian. He follows a different method for early historical times because of the nature of the sources at his disposal: when they present the past as a series of episodes, he writes episodic history. Later, when precise details multiply he makes use of regional history. On the Peloponnesian War he divides his subject much as Thucydides does, because that is the easiest way to handle the material.[19]

Ephorus is also credited with dividing his History into books and providing each book with a separate introduction,[20] and he may have been the first historian to do this. Diodorus Siculus emulates him in both practices, but his books are not usually geographically distinct. Instead, Diodorus is interested in having each book a unit which will make it more useful to overworked students. The sixteenth and seventeenth books of Diodorus are centered around the reigns of two great men, Philip and his son Alexander. Book V, however, does retain a geographic orientation, concerning itself with "islands," but it gives up any idea of a synchronized history such as Ephorus attempted. Instead each island is treated separately.[21]

So far we have not tried to establish an approximate date for the death of Ephorus, except to point out his mentioning the siege of Perinthus in 340 B.C. There is one other statement about him which, if true, would extend his life a few more years. Plutarch says some writers blamed Callisthenes for accompanying Alexander, while they praised Ephorus, Xenocrates, and Menedemus for declining to do so.[22] I am inclined to accept this as evidence that Ephorus was still alive when Alexander crossed over into Asia in 334 B.C., partly because the other two writers are prominent members of Plato's Academy,[23] and the Academy would know about them. There were three great epochs for the Greeks looking back: the Trojan War, the Persian War, and Alexander's expedition. It was embarrassing for any Greek state to have to explain her absence from the Catalogue of Ships (and no doubt this has had its effects on our text of the *Iliad*). It was equally important to be able to show that one's own city took part in repelling Xerxes and his millions (the Cretans, all appearances to the contrary not-with-standing, said they *were* there at Salamis). States like Argos and Thebes that were known to have sided with Persia always found this a talking point for their enemies. Alexander's expedition was different, in that some thought of the Macedonians as tyrants who destroyed Greek freedom (and here certainly Demosthenes' orations helped), while others were proud of the triumph of Greek over barbarian arms. But without exception they recognized the supreme importance of Alexander's conquests. Also, in the late fourth century there had been an increasing interest in the individual and less preoccupation with the city-state. This is reflected in the development of biography. In writing up the life of a prominent man-of-letters, be he philosopher or historian, it became necessary to ascertain how he stood with Alexander; and Ephorus' reputation must have been high for him to be associated with two names as well known as those of Xenocrates and Menedemus. Had he died before 334 B.C. the story would not have been fabricated.

There is a considerable literature on Ephorus, including attempts to work out the plan of his History, and up to a certain point progress has been made. No one who looks at the arrangement of the fragments made by the brothers Müller in 1841 and compares it with that of Jacoby in 1926[24] can fail to be gratified by the improvement. Discarding the minor works, spurious fragments, and references to Demophilus' continuation we have some 184 fragments from the History, but they are very uneven in value. In order to restore the plan of the work we need references citing the number of the book to which they allude. As assembled by Jacoby there are only eighty-three fragments which meet this requirement, and forty-four of those come from the first five books, books which Jacoby himself regards as preliminary to the main scheme of the History.[25] After that the pickings are very slim indeed, sometimes only one reference for each book through Book XII, then no references at all to XIII, XIV, or XXIII. Yet, on this basis, Jacoby has attempted to restore the economy of the work, including a final section on Contemporary History (XXVI–XXX). This is very interesting and suggestive but far from conclusive, when we remember that we have only one specific reference to Book XXVI, two for XXVII, and one each for XXVIII and XXIX! The four references to XXX help only for Demophilus. Into this very leaky receptacle Jacoby pours some 110 unmarked fragments,[26] hoping they will remain in place. Only for the first five books does his plan have sufficient support. Here it is particularly fortunate that in references to Book IV, it is sometimes cited as the book about *Europe,* while even when the double title does not appear all references to Book IV fit such a context. Jacoby therefore calls IV and V primarily books on the geography of Europe and Asia respectively.[27] The first three books he assigns to the *Time of Migrations (Zeit der Wanderungen),* and that too fits the references we have. But the rest of his reconstruction is pretty much speculation, though by an expert.

There are also six fragments that relate to Ephorus' prefaces, that tell us something about that historian's views. The first is from Photius, who says only that Ephorus' prefaces resemble those of Theopompus, which he explains by their having had the same starting point in history, no doubt an allusion to their both having studied under Isocrates. Had Photius only given us some excerpts from these prefaces we would be more beholden to him![28] In another passage, Polybius upbraids Ephorus for speaking of music as having been invented for the purpose of bewitching and deluding mankind.[29] This shows us Ephorus at his philosophizing worst, perhaps emulating Plato's criticism of the arts in Book III of the *Republic.* The next passage, from Harpocration, is more substantial. Here Ephorus seems to be imitating another great writer, this time a historian, when he says that those who provide the most precise details about contemporary events are very reliable, while anyone who describes ancient times in that way is completely untrustworthy. Jacoby sees in this an echo of Thucydides' complaints about the difficulty in getting accurate information about what happened a long time ago because the evidence has disappeared.[30] Another excerpt from a Preface informs us that Ephorus thought the barbarians had a longer history than the Greeks, a view which Diodorus is not willing to accept—though it does fit in very well with Herodotus.[31] The next reference comes from Polybius, who cites Ephorus approvingly as having emphasized the value of a historical account based on first-hand experience.[32] Because we know that Diodorus Siculus drew heavily on Ephorus for long sections of his *Historical Library* there has been a temptation to attribute much of the prefatory remarks in the *Historical Library* to the same source, a temptation which even Jacoby does not entirely avoid.[33] But all we know is that Ephorus made one or two obvious generalizations which would not have been any revelation to Hecataeus, let alone Herodotus or Thucydides. What Diodorus says later on may owe something to Ephorus—it would be strange if it did not—but Diodorus also knew and made use of the writings of Polybius and Posidonius, whose authority continued to carry great weight with Strabo.[34] Strabo is better evidence for this than Diodorus, because of his admirable habit of citing his authorities. Polybius undoubtedly was adapted by Diodorus to his own purposes and Polybius expresses the very views Jacoby attributes to Ephorus.[35] Ephorus was not the founder of "pragmatic" history—his claims are much humbler than that—but he was the first Greek historian we know of to attempt a World History, and one which purports to omit the very early days because the evidence is unsatisfactory. Diodorus, on the other hand, is frankly summarizing earlier histories for the convenience of students—so they will not have to thumb their way through long detailed accounts. Polybius, as we shall see later, is also writing a World History but one limited to a particular time in which, as he sees it, the separate histories of earlier days all flow into one common stream, the Roman Tiber. Ephorus' place in historiography lies somewhere in between Diodorus' Outline Series and Polybius' critical appraisal of the history of his own times.

The quality of Ephorus' mind may best be shown by discussing some of the individual fragments. There is one which Macrobius has transcribed for us verbatim; it concerns the Achelous river. He says that while only people in the neighborhood offer sacrifice to other rivers all men pay honor to the Achelous; that while other rivers have no common name applied to them instead of their local names the name of this river has become a common term for water. While we often use general names instead of particular names in other instances—Hellenes for example for Athenians or Peloponnesians for Spartans—in this case the oracle of Dodona is responsible, for it usually requires a sacrifice to the Achelous. As most interpret this as meaning not the Acarnanian river of that name but water in general, they imitate the oracle. And that is how the water of the Achelous comes to be invoked in oaths, prayers, sacrifices, and all matters concerning the gods.[36] This may be accepted as fairly typical of Ephorus' tendency to rationalize old customs, supplying us with an explanation for anything which in the modern world seems to require one. Although this particular example has little intrinsic interest for us it is curious to find a writer like Macrobius, in the fifth century A.D., so fascinated by it that he inserts it in Greek in the midst of a Latin text! It is also rewarding to compare Ephorus' digression on the Achelous with that of Thucydides. The latter is concerned with the effects of the sediment brought down by the river, which he predicts will eventually connect the Echinades islands with the mainland.[37] This kind of scientific curiosity, already rare in Thucydides, seems to be lacking entirely in Ephorus. Another instance of rationalizing is in Ephorus' explanation of the *Apaturia*, an Athenian festival. He connects it with an early victory of the Athenian champion over the Boeotian champion in a duel to settle a boundary dispute. The Athenian won by employing "deceit" (*apate*).[38]

Ephorus must have written at some length on the Return of the Heraclidae (with which his historical period begins), and in doing so gave full rein to his interest in prosopography—the names and connections of famous persons. A part that survives deals with the exploits of Oxylus. Oxylus was descended from Aetolus who had gone to Aetolia (which of course he named for himself) only after being driven out of Elis. Wishing to regain his homeland, he first helps the Heraclidae—Temenus in particular—in forcing their way back into the Peloponnese. In return they provide him with an army to win Elis for himself. When the army of Oxylus faced his enemies it was agreed (as with the Athenians and Boeotians just considered) to settle the matter by single combat. The Aetolian champion had a sling and a wallet filled with stones, while his opponent, who was armed with a bow and arrow, was expected to win easily. But it turned out otherwise. The sling was a very recent Aetolian invention, and the missiles it discharged had a longer range than the bow and arrow of his foe.[39] This serves as a reminder that Ephorus also wrote a monograph on inventions (*heuremata*), and it also tells us something of his attitude to the subject. He is an armchair observer obtaining his data from books. He does not tell us how the weapons compared with one another in his own day as to speed and accuracy, though that would have been of great interest. He makes use of rhetorical ingenuity rather than historical imagination.[40]

An interesting passage from Book IV (on Europe) has come down to us through three different writers, two of whom, Strabo and Cosmas Indicopleustes, purport to give us his exact words. Where they overlap, it is gratifying to note that there is virtually no difference between them. Cosmas lived in the sixth century A.D. during the reign of Justinian. He traveled widely (as his name of "Indian Voyager" suggests), and we welcome this further testimony to his accuracy.[41] Ephorus has moved in the direction of an elongated world, not the flat one advocated by Cosmas, but presumably a sphere. Yet the old Babylonian idea of a circular shape for the land mass has yielded, first to a square and now, as exemplified by Ephorus, to a rectangle. The long sides are the north and south, with Scythians in the far north balancing Ethiopians in the deep south. The shorter east and west sides have Indians and Celts respectively, at their extremities. This is one stage in a long controversy which continued in the Hellenistic period, when attempts were made to determine the circumference of the earth. Ephorus gives no estimate of distances, and that is to his credit. His other best known geographic theory has to do with the old puzzle of the reasons for the Nile flood, but his solution is even more bizarre than those known to Herodotus.[42]

Fate has not been particularly kind to Ephorus in preserving the later part of his History. Many of the references come from lexicographers who merely cite him for a particular statement about a place or its inhabitants or the spelling of a name. Sometimes such a short passage has significance, as when we learn that Cimon paid the fifty-talent fine (levied against his father Miltiades) by marrying a rich woman.[43] Fifty talents is an enormous sum of money, so the historian feels obligated to give us a plausible (not necessarily accurate) explanation of how the money was paid. There must be no loose ends.

Of more importance is a longer passage in Diodorus Siculus, in which Ephorus is cited as saying that Pharnabazus had Alcibiades put to death (404 B.C.) because Alcibiades was about to warn Artaxerxes of Cyrus' revolt. But Pharnabazus preferred to get credit for this warning himself—so he killed Alcibiades. This is another example of Ephorus' lack of historical insight, as Eduard Meyer points out with his customary acuteness. Pharnabazus had Alcibiades put to death surreptitiously, not to get credit for warning the king, but to avoid compromising his own relations with Cyrus![44]

As might be expected Ephorus comes off badly when he writes on the same subject as Thucydides. We have a long passage from Diodorus dealing with the causes of the Peloponnesian War, in which he is following Ephorus. Here we find Pericles' position in Athens endangered by the attacks of his political enemies. Charges against friends of his like Phidias and the philosopher Anaxagoras are mentioned, and also Pericles is worried over being held to account for spending the public money entrusted to him. Alcibiades advises him to avoid having to render an accounting, so Pericles decides to go to war to take men's minds off internal matters. Ephorus cites and elaborates on passages from Aristophanes in support of this view.[45] While Thucydides has been criticized for leaving all this out, for it was part of the contemporary scene, this is nothing compared to the deficiencies of Ephorus. He has no counter interpretation carefully thought out as an explanation for the war. On the other hand he does preserve evidence we should otherwise lack and which Thucydides does not give. Today we need everything we can get.

We will leave Ephorus with one last citation from Plutarch:

*As when one of us happened to have read two or three books of Ephorus*

*and proceeded to wear everyone out, and ruined every festive occasion by*
*continuing to go on about the Battle of Leuctra and the events that*
*followed which made Epaminondas famous.*[46]

Evidently Epaminondas was not neglected in Ephorus' History as
he had been in Xenophon's *Hellenica*. Diodorus preserves much of
the detail and something of the tediousness of the original.

## II. Theopompus of Chios

Theopompus of Chios was a stormy petrel. Opinion about his
merits is sharply divided in antiquity, some having a very low
regard for him as a writer, others praising him with almost as much
enthusiasm as he praised himself; but hardly anyone attempts an
objective appraisal. The ancients could judge him when all—or
most—of his historical writings were still extant. Therefore it is
unlikely that today when we have only fragments, numerous
though they are—we can arrive at a satisfactory judgment. For a
short time, when the soil of Egypt yielded her rich harvest at
Oxyrhynchus and the *Hellenica Oxyrhynchia* was first published it
looked as though Theopompus' reputation would be enhanced,
because Eduard Meyer, the leading ancient historian of his day,
pronounced this fascinating survival to be the work of Theopompus.[47] Since that time others have suggested Ephorus, Cratippus, or Daimachus with the possibility growing that the author may
have been a historian previously unknown to us. So now Theopompus' reputation must stand or fall on the basis of the fragments
alone, because the Oxyrhynchus historian, whoever he may be, is
not Theopompus.[48] Before taking up the fragments, however, let
us see what is known about the man himself.

Our two most useful Byzantine sources, the *Suda* and Photius,
do not fail us. Reversing the chronological order we will begin
with the late tenth century *Suda*, then turn to the ninth century
Patriarch of Constantinople. The article on Theopompus may be
translated as follows:

*Theopompus of Chios, orator, the son of Damasistratus: lived [was born,*
*or rather flourished?] at the time there was no archon in Athens*
*(404/403 B.C.) during the ninety-third Olympiad (408/405). He studied*
*under Isocrates along with Ephorus. He wrote an* Abridgment of
Herodotus' History *in two books; a* Philippica *in seventy-two books;*
*a* Hellenic History—*which follows those of Thucydides and Xenophon*
*and contains eleven books describing events following the Peloponnesian*
*War—and other works.*[49]

This notice in the *Suda* well illustrates the weaknesses of that
indispensable work. The date is as valueless as the forms in which

it is given are inconsistent. Someone worked out a floruit for Theo-pompus on the basis of his being a continuator of Thucydides, obviously the only fact he had to go on. But this does not end the confusion. The *Hellenica* was actually in twelve books not eleven, the *Philippica* in fifty-eight, so that as Jacoby indicates, the seventy-two books here represent the sum of two books (*Abridg-ment*), twelve books (*Hellenica*) and fifty-eight books (*Philippica*).[50]

Now let us see whether Photius is more helpful:

*Theopompus is a Chian by birth. He is said to have been exiled from his native land along with his father, who was convicted of acting in the Spartan interest. He came back to his country after his father died, when Alexander, King of the Macedonians, brought about his return by writing a letter to the Chians. At that time Theopompus was forty-five years old. After Alexander's death when he was beset on every side he went to Egypt. Ptolemy, the king of that land, refused to admit him, and would have put him to death as a trouble maker had not friends interceded and begged him off.*[51]

So far as the date is concerned, we know that Alexander did order the Chians to take back their exiles in 332 B.C.,[52] and this would give us an approximate birth date for Theopompus of 377 B.C., not at all unlikely in itself and certainly better than the *Suda's* wild guess. But there are difficulties. Alexander was overthrowing the oligarchs and setting up a democracy in Chios, yet Theopompus' father (and he himself) were violently antidemocratic!

Leaving this question unresolved for the moment, what else can we find to help out in dating Theopompus? There is the state-ment that when Mausolus died (at the time of the 106th Olympiad) his widow Artemisia held a contest in his honor for the best speech commemorating the deceased. Among the competitors were the orators Theodectes of Lycian Phaselis, Naucrates of Erythrae, Isoc-rates of Apollonia, and Theopompus. Theodectes won first prize, but some ancient authorities say Theopompus won.[53] Now Mauso-lus died in 353/352 B.C. (which would be the last year of the 106th Olympiad),[54] when (following the earlier calculation as to his birth in 377) he would have been only twenty-four or twenty-five years old. And that is not too wide of the mark, even though difficulties remain. The same scholars in two editions of the *OCD* indicate doubts about the nature of Theodectes' contribution (". . . the treatment is unknown"), yet Theodectes presumably composed an oration. He was equally famed as an orator and as a writer of tragedy, just as his son made his reputation both in history and in rhetoric. The son also composed an encomium on Alexander of Epirus.[55]

Isocrates of Apollonia, who also entered the competition, studied under the famous Isocrates. And this led, later on, to some of his speeches being confused with those of his great namesake. Similarly, because Theopompus is reported by Photius as flourishing at the same time as Isocrates of Athens, Theodectes of Phaselis, and Naucrates of Erythrae, an earlier textual error probably substituted "of Athens" for "of Apollonia"—some scribe attempting to correct what he thought was a mistake.[56] If that is so then nothing prevents Theopompus from having studied under the Athenian Isocrates.[57] And returning to the earlier statement that he was forty-five years old when Alexander wrote the Chians on his behalf, we find the corresponding date for his birth in 377 B.C. as approximately right. We may assume that Alexander did write such a letter for him. Theopompus would not be covered by the general orders to the Chians to bring back their exiles and reestablish the democracy, for he loathed democracy. But neither would he have gotten along with the outgoing oligarchy because they were on the Persian side.

Only one other facet of Theopompus' many-sided life needs comment here, and that is his bad relationship with Plato's Academy. Theodectes, his rival in the Mausolus competition, was a student of Plato's; and Theopompus points out with some complacency that while he and Naucrates were men of means, Isocrates and Theodectes had to write for money.[58] The Academy was a formidable enemy. Surely one reason Philip chose Aristotle as Alexander's tutor was to influence Greek opinion through the powerful Academy. The backbiting among intellectuals for favor at court is illustrated at its worst in one of the *Socratic Letters*, a collection that cannot be relied on for historical accuracy but which does reflect contemporary attitudes. This particular letter is written to Philip by Plato's successor Speusippus, who says:

> I have heard that Theopompus is with you, an ineffectual person, who makes slanderous remarks about Plato, as though Plato had not prepared the way for your rule back in the time of Perdiccas, and as though he had not taken it very hard whenever he heard anything contrary to brotherly affection had happened to you. But in order to put a stop to Theopompus' truculence ask Antipater [a rival historian] to read aloud to him from his own Hellenica, for then Theopompus will learn how he is quite rightly forgotten by everyone and that he does not deserve the good things he receives from you.[59]

The tone of this letter (spurious or not)[60] is important, because it heralds the advent of the court historian. That title fits none of the other writers we have considered, for Ctesias, who lived at court, wrote for Greek readers after he left Susa. Another example might be Philistus, historian of the tyrant Dionysius of Syracuse, if enough remained of his work for judgment.[61] In the Hellenistic period court historians became common, and as historians they could not help writing differently than they would have as plain citizens of a Greek city, whether residents or, as seems to have been more usual, as exiles. Theopompus was no typical court historian. He was rather a transitional figure, a stormy petrel as was suggested, in this as in all things. He appears to have compensated by plain speaking about Philip's private life, for the admiration he felt obliged to express for his political achievements. But this may in itself have been a form of flattery. Philip was an unusual man without the kind of personal vanity one might have expected. He could afford to allow a historian great latitude.[62]

Among the known facts about Theopompus' life is that he remained in Chios while Alexander campaigned in Asia, but that after his return and death the historian was forced into exile once more, narrowly escaping death in Egypt. The general picture is that of a restless man with a sarcastic tongue who made strong friends and equally strong enemies. He traveled extensively, though not always of his own choice; and he must have enjoyed considerable vogue as an orator for special occasions.

In recent years a sadly mutilated book list has reached us in a Rhodian inscription dated about 100 B.C. This list is arranged alphabetically by authors and the restoration of some of Theopompus' titles is conjectural. A number of these are titles of speeches, such as: a "Laconicus," a "Corinthiacus," a "Maussolus," an "Olympicus," a "Panathenaicus," and others. There is also a work attacking Plato, an encomium (either of Philip or of Alexander), and an "Address to Alexander."[63]

Not all the questions posed by this list can be answered. If Theopompus wrote an encomium of Philip, it was presumably written just after Philip's death and would bear roughly the same resemblance to the *Philippica* as Xenophon's *Agesilaus* bears to his *Hellenica*. On the other hand, if this is to be restored as an encomium of Alexander, as Jacoby urges,[64] the existence of another work, a *Censure of Alexander*,[65] suggests an entirely different parallel. The historian Callisthenes, who accompanied Alexander as his official chronicler and who was later put to death by him, once aroused the antagonism of the Macedonians by this same sort of rhetorical ambivalence. He made two speeches, one praising and one censuring the Macedonians, the latter of which may have cost him his life.[66] Is it not conceivable that Theopompus may have shown off his rhetorical virtuosity by writing companion pieces, one praising and one damning Alexander? With an eccentric like Theopompus this is always possible. And after Alexander's death both views would have found ready acceptance, but it would be well to sound out the audience in advance. Perhaps he neglected to do this in Alexandria.

Of his major works, the *Hellenica* was written before the

*Philippica*, all of it, so far as we can determine, while Philip was still alive. Diodorus tells us he wrote it as a continuation of Thucydides, extending over a period of seventeen years down to the Battle of Cnidus (394 B.C.) in twelve books.[67] Noting that this was an excellent place for a pro-Spartan history to end, Jacoby implies that Theopompus completed the *Hellenica* as originally planned.[68] Not much remains, and its interpretation presents no particular problems. But the *Philippica*, which soon eclipsed the earlier work, poses many questions despite the fact that we still have an imposing number of fragments. First of all we would like to know when it was written.

An important inference about the time of composition has been drawn from two statements, one attributed to Theopompus, the other to Callisthenes. The lexicographer Harpocration reports that in the twenty-fifth book of the *Philippica* the historian claimed that the treaty with "the barbarian" was fraudulent, because it was inscribed in Ionian letters rather than in Attic letters.[69] It is common knowledge that the official change in the alphabet in Athens was made during the archonship of Euclid (403/402 B.C.). Presumably treaties inscribed before that year would be in the Attic alphabet, those thereafter in the Ionic script. Therefore, the treaty in question between Athens and Persia was examined by Theopompus and found to be an anachronism. In another fragment, Theopompus accuses the Athenians of falsifying a "Hellenic Oath" (which they claimed the Greeks swore to before Plataea) and a treaty they signed with the king, adding that in general the Athenians bragged about their achievements in the Persian War.[70] However, Callisthenes is reported by Plutarch as denying that there was any formal treaty between Athens and Persia in which Persia agreed not to send warships into Greek waters—and so on—as a result of Cimon's victory at the Eurymedon. But Callisthenes did say that, while there was no formal agreement, the Persians observed the terms of the alleged treaty out of fear.[71]

On this slender basis it has been maintained that Book XXV must have been known to Callisthenes when he made his statement, and that the proper place for him to have mentioned it was in describing Alexander's campaign in Lycia and Pamphylia![72] However, it is much more likely to have been mentioned in Callisthenes' earlier work on Greek history, and if this is so, then the *Philippica* must have been well under way long before Alexander came to the throne. But Wade-Gery thinks that the *Philippica* was not published until after Philip's death, because of Fragment 27[73] from the Preface, where Theopompus remarks that "Europe had never borne a man comparable with Philip the son of Amyntas."[74] Wade-Gery has no interest in Theopompus per se, but only in the existence or nonexistence of the Peace of Callias. For the purposes of his argument he needs to have Callisthenes aware of Theopompus' attack on the genuineness of the treaty. Therefore, in his efforts to find a way by which Callisthenes could have read Theopompus before any part of the *Philippica* was published, he constructs a theory of his own. He argues that what he calls "the two anti-Athenian 'pamphlets' which Theopompus *inserted* [my italics] into Philippica X and XXV had done service as propaganda . . . long before the publication of the complete history."[75] And I find this unacceptable. We may quite reasonably assume that Theopompus was speaking about the Peace of Callias and that Callisthenes disagreed with his interpretation. So far so good, but we must not use this conjecture as though it were a solid basis for further assumptions. If we believe Callisthenes read this in time to controvert it, we must accept the likelihood he controverted it in his Greek history, where it belongs, not in his Alexander history. Further, it is only fair to assume that Book XXV had appeared when he wrote, rather than to invent two *pamphlets* by Theopompus that preceded the *Philippica* but have only come to light in the twentieth century. Then we must assume Philip was alive when this work was written, and that as Theopompus well knew, he was a very remarkable man to allow his historian to write as he chose.

This preoccupation with the Peace of Callias has led us rather far afield, but this may be excused since digressions were also part of Theopompus' stock in trade,[76] less evident in the *Hellenica*, perhaps because the influence of Thucydides kept him within bounds. We have only a few references for evaluating the *Hellenica*. Beginning where Thucydides stops, Theopompus describes the remainder of the military events, and devotes considerable space to the misfortunes of Athens under the Thirty,[77] but the distribution according to books is not clear. A passage in Book VI dealing with troubles in Oropus has tentatively been put in 402/401 B.C.[78] Then there is an interesting fragment from Book VII on the origin of the Spartan helots which may have a connection with the Conspiracy of Cinadon in 399.[79] Book IX is cited only once, mentioning a man named Sisyphus of Pharsalus, who played a role in Thessalian politics.[80] Book X contains a typical encomium of Spartan virtues as embodied in Lysander, who was master of himself, never given to overindulgence in wine or women,[81] while in XI Agesilaus displays a similar contempt for high living.[82] There is no certain reference to XII, and few other fragments can be assigned specifically to the *Hellenica* except by indirect means. And now something must be said about the *Philippica.*

Despite its reputation the fifty-eight books of this major work did not all survive, even in antiquity. Diodorus Siculus, writing in the first century B.C. with access to Roman libraries, says five books have disappeared, and Photius some nine hundred years later confirms this, while denying that any further losses have occurred.[83] We still have some 219 fragments where the book number is given, and on this basis Jacoby provides a Table of Contents, beginning with Book I which he says contained the Preface as well as a general account of the conditions in Greece at the time Philip became king (360/359 B.C.); and ending with Books LV–LVII, dealing with events in 337 B.C. There is no apparent logic in Theopompus' division into books, though some indication of geographic organization—for example, Books XII–XVIII deal primarily with the east, and so on. Book LVIII, no fragment of which survives, must have dealt with the last plans and death of Philip. The highly personal, not to say arbitrary, arrangement of his material by Theopompus makes analysis difficult. However the summary of Book XII by Photius does show that Theopompus did have a plan of his own and that he adhered to it. A commentary on each of the longer fragments, though rewarding, would require too much space, so I will select a few passages to illustrate different aspects of the History.

The final section of Book X of the *Philippica* has been given a special subtitle (which by no means implies separate publication), "On the Athenian Demagogues," a digression that goes all the way back to Themistocles and comes on down to the fourth century financial wizard Eubulus. The great, perhaps even excessive interest of modern scholarship in fifth century Athens has magnified the importance of this group of fragments out of all proportion to their value. That value lies more in the historian's judgment on Athenian leaders in his own day, when he had good evidence. He seems to have read back this estimate of fourth century politicians into the earlier period. Given a choice between two possible interpretations of the conduct of an Athenian public figure Theopompus always takes the less creditable one. For example, he says Themistocles bribed the ephors to prevent interference with rebuilding the walls of Athens.[84] His views on Cimon have survived. We hear how Cimon curried favor with the common people by letting them pick his fruit and help themselves to his garden produce; he also invited all comers to dinner, helped the poor to pay for burying their dead, and sometimes exchanged clothes with a citizen who was shabbily dressed. All this might be favorably interpreted, but Cimon is also said to have been a great thief and to have set an example of bribery for others to emulate.[85] Other interesting details are given about Cleon and Hyperbolus.[86] Our real loss is what Theopompus had to say about fourth century leaders. We do have part of an eloquent speech by Aristophon, leader of the war party in Athens who, unlike Demosthenes, bitterly opposed making peace with Philip. Yet this is the only reference in literature to this Athenian politician.[87]

(*The British Museum*)

COIN OF PHILIP II OF MACEDON
The obverse represents the god Zeus, not Philip. Kings were not yet depicted on their coins, though their features may have been. Philip was the central subject of Theopompus' major work. The reverse, of a Macedonian boy rider, reminds us of Philip's interest in horse racing and also of his son Alexander, who tamed Bucephalus.

Another fragment deserves to be translated in full:

*During the siege of Methone his [Philip's] right eye was put out by an arrow while he was inspecting the machines and the sheds for the besiegers, as Theopompus relates in the fourth book of his History.*[88]

This is circumstantial enough to suggest that Theopompus may have been there when it happened. The siege took place in 354/353 B.C. If Jacoby is right, this means he accompanied Philip on one of his Thracian campaigns.[89] He must have been very conscious of what Xenophon had written about Thrace in the *Anabasis*, for like Xenophon, Theopompus was an amateur ethnologist, and probably wrote something about Thracian mores. His method is illustrated by a well-known description of the Etruscans which fortunately survives.[90] There is much exaggeration. He has a particular interest in their sexual promiscuity, which he found only slightly more repellent than their habit of shaving all the hair off their bodies instead of merely getting a haircut. He notes the spread of this practice even among Greeks living in Italy. Are his sources entirely literary? We cannot tell.

One of the best known parts of the *Philippica* is a long digression in Book VIII called *Thaumasia* (*Marvels*), which for some reason best known to the author is inserted in the narrative of events along the Hellespont. Among the topics treated was Persian religion. We are told that in time Ahriman (*Areimanus*) is doomed to be destroyed along with famine and pestilence, when the earth will become entirely smooth. Theopompus says that according to the Magi the gods rule and are ruled in turn for 3000 years, and that for another 3000 years they fight and make war and destroy one another. But in the end Hades will lose and mankind will be happy, needing no food and casting no shadow—and so on.[91] Here Theopompus reflects the interest in Zoroaster that is typical of his day.

According to Jaeger, Plato was concerned with such matters during his last decade and transmitted this interest to the Academy, including Aristotle. The Academy sought confirmation for Plato's views in the wisdom of the east.[92] That was certainly not Theopompus' object, but we do not know what that object was. Also in the *Thaumasia* section Theopompus relates a fable about the Land of the Meropes, interesting as showing the author's cynical view of the world. The very worst of his mythical people from another world, after observing the customs of the Hyperboreans—the very best people of our world—turn back in horror to the land from which they came.[93]

The historian took pride in the land of his birth. There are a number of allusions to Chios in the fragments. One of these informs us the Chians were the first to make dark wine, having been instructed in that art by Oenopion the son of Dionysus, who colonized the island. From them the knowledge was transmitted to other men.[94] He also tells us, with no evidence of disapproval, that next to the Thessalians and the Spartans the Chians were the first Greeks to own slaves, but that unlike the others they had barbarian slaves whom they bought for cash. This suggests he held strong views on the superiority of the Greek. But so too did Aristotle and Plato, and also Isocrates (for all his brave words on civilization depending on education rather than on race.)[95] So did not Diogenes the Cynic whom Theopompus may have met, nor yet Zeno who was soon to establish the most influential philosophic school in the ancient world.

Theopompus' curiosity was all-embracing, as has been suggested by passages already discussed. He was specially concerned with morals in the restricted sense, and bad behavior was a subject that attracted him more than virtuous conduct.

Although such examples show him to be a man of many interests they give no clear indication of his worth as a historian. The chief difficulty lies in separating style or manner from substance. Gilbert Murray's essay on Theopompus[96] has the great merit of concentrating on what went on in the mind of the historian rather than on the facts about Greek history that can be recovered from the fragments of his work. In doing so he may, and I think he does, give Theopompus more credit for sensitivity than he deserves. As we read along, the fourth century historian begins to take on more and more the character of modernity. The real Theopompus continues to elude us. He was unmistakably a moralist of sorts; but did his interest in the symptoms of moral deterioration cause him to reduce history to a formula? He has much to say about "flatterers" and the influence they have in corrupting the men of power. Philip is surrounded by men to whom debauchery was a way of life. For Murray this means Theopompus is a pessimist with a deep sense of the irony of history. And that is possible. But there is one fragment that suggests the historian went farther than that. We are told that Philip observed the weakness of the Thessalian leaders for partying and overindulgence. He took full advantage of this circumstance by entertaining them lavishly and playing the buffoon, and by this means he got a stronger hold over them than he could have obtained by giving them expensive presents.[97] This may mean that for Theopompus Philip rose above his environment, that instead of becoming the victim of flatterers he made use of them to serve his own ends. If that does represent Theopompus' interpretation of Philip's character then he may have been a better historian than the bulk of the fragments suggest.

## III. The Alexander Historians

Polybius criticized Theopompus for subordinating the history of Greece to the deeds of Philip,[98] but the Alexander historians carry this tendency a long step further. Alexander is not merely the leading protagonist on the stage of history, but a new kind of history is written in which everything that happens is seen from the perspective of the Macedonian army on the march. And this is reminiscent of the viewpoint of the *Anabasis,* but with this important difference. When the outside and inside worlds converge as they do more and more after the Ten Thousand reach the coast of the Black Sea, it is the inside world that begins to come apart. Not so with Alexander's army. When Antipater defeats the Spartans in a bloody battle near Megalopolis, Antipater's concern and that of the Hellenic League as well, is centered on Alexander. How will he take it? Will he feel annoyed that a subordinate has exceeded his instructions? A report is sent off promptly to him, and the Spartans are told to send envoys to the king to plead their case before him in person.[99] Alexander, unlike Cyrus the Younger or his historian, is the focal point for the history of his time. We are reminded of Diogenes who, taunted with having been condemned to exile by the Sinopeans replied, "But I have condemned them to stay at home!"[100]

That this change in the Greek world should also be reflected in the history of the period was only to be expected, but Alexander made sure of this by taking along with him a number of writers.[101] However, not everything went off according to plan. The best-known literary figure, perhaps the only man with any reputation as a historian, was Callisthenes of Olynthus, who soon fell out of favor.

There was nothing wrong with Callisthenes' credentials when he joined the expedition. He came doubly recommended, as a historian of some standing and as the kinsman of Aristotle,[102] who introduced him to Alexander.[103] It is possible that as the student of Aristotle he had already come to know Alexander, but the sequel was to show that he did not know him well enough. He must have been a good deal older than the king, probably old enough to have gone to Assos with Aristotle when the latter left Athens following Plato's death to accept Hermias' invitation.[104] The privilege to read and study Homer in the very land of Troy and with Aristotle as a teacher was not granted to everyone, and we may be sure the opportunity was not wasted on Callisthenes. Aristotle evidently regarded his kinsman with affection, but this did not blind him to Callisthenes' very definite limitations. He might do for a rhetorician, even for a historian, but he was not cut out to be a philosopher.[105] Callisthenes had served his apprenticeship by writing a number of monographs, including an account of the First Sacred War,[106] and a periplus which must have been at least two books long. He had also collaborated with Aristotle in drawing up the list of victors in the Pythian Games, a service for which both were officially honored in an inscription we still have.[107] The fact that Alexander carried with him a copy of the *Iliad* prepared by Aristotle is well attested, and Callisthenes is said to have had a hand in preparing it.[108] The *Hellenica* was Callisthenes' chief historical work, a general history in ten books, extending from the King's Peace down to the beginning of the Phocian War (387–357 B.C.).[109] The remaining fragments show a truly Peripatetic range of inquiry, from the exact month and day of the Fall of Troy to the old problem of the Nile flood.[110]

As an Alexander historian, Callisthenes proved more tractable than Theopompus in describing the deeds of his patron. Everything the king does appears to be presented in a heroic light. Callisthenes undoubtedly approved of the masquerade at the site of Troy where Alexander emulated his ancestor Achilles while Hephaestion played the part of Patroclus, though we do not have a named fragment on this. The gods show their favor to the Macedonian conqueror when he and his escort were in danger of losing their way in the desert while seeking the oracle of Zeus-Ammon at Siwah, when miraculously crows appeared to guide them. Alexander is said to have gone to Siwah because he learned that Perseus and Heracles had been there before him.[111] Earlier, in marching past Mt. Climax along the Pamphylian shore we are told that the waves withdrew, prostrating themselves before Alexander.[112] Before the decisive Battle of Gaugamela, the last appearance of Darius at the head of an opposing army, Alexander is said to have prayed to Zeus to aid him, "if he were in fact descended from Zeus."[113] Small wonder that later writers refer to Callisthenes as a "flatterer," though not many were as blunt as Timaeus, who said that Callisthenes got what he deserved for doing his best to corrupt Alexander.[114] It does seem ironical that the man who wrote about Alexander in such glowing terms should have incurred his hatred over what was chiefly a matter of court etiquette, yet so it was. Willing that Alexander should be accepted as a hero, and later presumably as a god, Callisthenes could not reconcile himself to the servility, as he regarded it, of the Persian custom of prostrating oneself before the king on state occasions, and he paid for his unwelcome frankness with his life.[115]

None of the other Alexander historians published their histories until after the king's death. There is of course a question about the *Ephemerides,* some sort of a daily record kept by the king's secretary, Eumenes, which was not intended for publication. Presumably it survived both the fire in Eumenes' tent[116] and the confusion following Alexander's death. It was published later in an altered form.[117]

Only four of these Alexander historians will be considered here, namely: Onesicritus, Aristobulus, Ptolemy, and Clitarchus. The text of these and of others will be found in Jacoby and are also available in translation.[118] Of the four I have selected, Onesicritus was the first to publish, and under a distinctive title (πῶς Ἀλέξανδρος ἤχθη), which may be paraphrased as *How Alexander Lived His Life,* and was meant to suggest Xenophon's idealized account of the great Cyrus. If Callisthenes represents Alexander as the embodiment of the heroic qualities of Achilles, it was Onesicritus' intention to represent Alexander as a king guided by Cynic principles, "a philosopher in arms."[119] Onesicritus came from Astypalaea (presumably the island) and he makes quite a point of his association with Diogenes of Sinope.[120] Whether it was this that recommended him to Alexander we do not know, but he was also destined to be closely associated with another personage of that day, Alexander's boyhood friend Nearchus "the Cretan," who was legally a Macedonian. Presumably his father came to Macedon to make his fortune, like many another restless Greek in the days of King Philip. Be that as it may, Nearchus was one of those five friends whose loyalty to Alexander had led to their being banished by Philip.[121] Later Alexander did all he could to further their careers. Nearchus was put in charge of the fleet that sailed back from India all the way to Babylonia, and Onesicritus was a prominent member of his staff. This suggests that Onesicritus was also a skilled seaman, as Alexander would not have sent him along to discuss philosophy with Nearchus! The two men disagreed about the proper course to steer when nearing the Persian Gulf and this may have led to a permanent rupture between them. Nearchus, so far as we know, never wrote an Alexander history but he did write an account of his voyage and included in that account some remarks about India.[122] Onesicritus, on the other hand, wrote an Alexander history in which he included an account of the same voyage, which survives only in one passage from Pliny's *Natural History*.[123] Whether he made use of Callisthenes' unfinished work is uncertain, but the chances are that he did. This much we do know. He shows considerable interest in the exotic plants and animals he saw in India and, like Ctesias before him, he denies that the black color of some peoples was caused by their exposure to the hot sun, not because some Indians were white (as Ctesias said) but because the children were born black, and this of course happened before they had been exposed to the sun! He explains this by the water they drank.[124] One characteristic of Onesicritus' account seems to have been a desire to show that India produced more marvels than any other land, and when there was duplication, for example in producing elephants, then the Indian species is larger, more formidable, and longer lived than its Libyan counterpart.[125] Despite some exaggerations, he was able to give us a recognizable description of what he saw, including cotton and the banyan tree.[126] Like others he was interested in how the heavens behaved in such a distant land. The effects of traveling farther and farther south on the way shadows fall, with the expectation that eventually the sun at noon will lie directly overhead and there will be no shadow at all on the sundial, came to his attention.[127]

He was also intrigued by the customs of the Indians. His best-known passage describes a meeting he had with a group of Indian sages, the famous Naked Philosophers (Gymnosophists), who conversed with him about their views and listened politely to his account of Greek philosophy, all this as relayed through a battery of interpreters.[128] One particular Indian kingdom on the lower Indus, the Land of Musicanus, made such an impression on him that he pictures it as a kind of Cynic paradise, where righteousness prevails, lawsuits are unknown, slavery does not exist, gold and silver are despised, and the only science studied is that of medicine.[129] Onesicritus' history must have made for interesting reading, and whoever read it ended by being better informed than he had been, although there was also a great deal of exaggeration and a certain amount of nonsense. Nearchus continues to play a role in the period after Alexander, not so Onesicritus. He is reported (on doubtful testimony) to have spent some time at the court of Lysimachus,[130] but the last occasion where we can be reasonably sure of his presence is when the Indian wise man who accompanied Alexander back from India became ill and had the king provide him with a funeral pyre on which he was consumed before a large audience, without showing any sign of pain. This was one of the sages Onesicritus had interviewed.[131]

Equally unknown after Alexander's death was the historian

Aristobulus of Cassandrea, whose fragments occupy twice as much space in Jacoby's text as those of Onesicritus and half again as much as those of Ptolemy. Considerable ingenuity has been called upon in an effort to bring Aristobulus back to life, but without conspicuous success. One reason for a special interest in Aristobulus is that of the five major accounts of Alexander that have reached us—namely: Arrian's *Anabasis*, Diodorus Siculus' *Historical Library* Book XVII, and Plutarch's *Alexander* in Greek; and Justin's *Epitome of Trogus Pompeius* and the History of Q. Curtius Rufus in Latin. Arrian's is by far the most reliable, and Arrian himself professes to follow two authorities above all others, Aristobulus and Ptolemy. Where they agree he has no doubts, where they differ he uses his own judgment.[132] Müller, noting that Aristobulus was given the task of restoring Cyrus' tomb after it had been looted by vandals during Alexander's absence in the Indian campaign, and also noting that the historian is called a Cassandrean, suggests that Cassander made use of Aristobulus' professional services in building the city of Cassandrea.[133] This evidence has been expanded by Pearson to justify a chapter entitled, "The Technical Expert, Aristobulus."[134] He suggests that Aristobulus is really a Phocian who came to live in Cassandrea, citing a Delphic inscription conferring guest friend-ship on a certain Sophocles, *whose father Aristobulus lived in Cassandrea,* and this is certainly possible, though his argument against Cos as an alternative is weak.[135] But Aristobulus' version of the Cutting of the Gordian Knot does seem worthy of a "technical expert,"[136] just as his observation of the effects of a change in course of a flooded Indian river, and his comments on cultivating rice point to a professional interest in irrigation.[137]

Other passages indicate that he was not given to flights of rhetoric, in fact he seemed quite literal minded. We see this clearly enough in the curious incident in Babylonia when the king is inspecting the canal system. His diadem blew off and came to rest on a giant reed growing in the water. The usual story, according to Arrian, is that the sailor who rescued the crown, by clapping it on his head and swimming back with it, was given the mag-nificent reward of a talent for his dexterity, only to have his head cut off for presuming to wear Alexander's crown! Aristobulus, however, says he received a talent and was then flogged for his presumption.[138] The "usual story" sounds as though it had been inspired by Herodotus, who has Xerxes reward the captain with a gold crown for saving his life, then cuts his head off for occa-sioning the death of so many fine Persians.[139] Another version given in Arrian is that the man who saved Alexander's crown was not a sailor at all, but Seleucus the future king, and naturally all the proper inferences are drawn from that. Aristobulus tones down the story to make it more plausible. But a man who did not begin to write his account until he was going on eighty-four, would not have trusted to memory for minor incidents, even assuming he had been an eye-witness. The chances are that he accepted this story because he found it in his written sources, all of which may have been fictitious, then tried to work out his own "reasonable" version.[140] One more fragment may be cited to show his dependence on other writers. In describing Alexander's trip through the desert he follows Callisthenes in having crows come to the rescue, but adds a characteristic touch: there were exactly *two crows* that flew on ahead of the army.[141] Such precision is admirable.

His portrait of Alexander seems to be uncritical, as is natural, but it also avoids the impossible. It need hardly be mentioned that he was not one of those writers who described Alexander's encounter with the Queen of the Amazons,[142] though it is less certain what Alexander himself might have wished. It is hard to disassociate this in one's mind with Cyrus' meeting with Epyaxa. Of course Callisthenes had not lived to describe (or ignore) this episode, imaginary though it was.[143]

Another peculiarity in Aristobulus' account of Alexander did not escape Tarn—nor had Müller missed the implications—he represents Alexander as a man who avoided excessive drinking.[144] Tarn, who had his own ideas about Alexander, seized on this interpretation with avidity because it agreed with his own. This is not the place to take a position in the controversy over Alexander, though I may say in passing that I do not regard it as settled. What matters here is that Tarn's interest was always in Alexander, not in his historian Aristobulus. And here he ran into the prevailing view expressed by Eduard Schwartz, to the effect that Aristobulus was to all intents and purposes a secondary historian who merely worked over materials provided for him by others. That would mean his remarks about Alexander's temperance carried no weight. Whoever may have been right about Alexander, I find Schwartz far more convincing about Aristobulus. Tarn has exaggerated his intimacy with Alexander and his knowledge of the king's character. Aristobulus is a thoroughly second-rate historian, though he may have been a competent engineer.[145]

Ptolemy the son of Lagus, like Nearchus, was one of the five friends of Alexander's once banished by Philip, and like Aristobulus he is a main source for Arrian's *Anabasis*.[146] If the *Macrobioi* attributed to Lucian is right, Ptolemy lived to be eighty-four years old,[147] and since we know he died in 283 B.C., two years after turning over the burdens of government to his son, he must have been born in 367 B.C., which makes him some eleven years older than his boyhood friend Alexander! When the army crossed over into Asia he was already thirty-three to Alexander's twenty-two—a mature man even by Spartan standards. Still assuming this is correct there is something rather strange about Ptolemy's slow progress towards the top. It was a time when military reputations could be made in a hurry, yet Ptolemy's career is unspectacular until Alexander's death. As his close friendship with the king cannot be doubted, we can only conclude him to have been a man of very modest military abilities, something of a loner in fact. But his diplomatic and financial astuteness served him so well that he is the only one of the Successors to die in his bed. He obtained Egypt for himself in the first distribution of satrapies at Babylon; and once he had obtained it nothing could force him to give it up, neither the regency when it was offered to him after Perdiccas' assassination nor a full-scale invasion led by Antigonus and Demetrius. Although Ptolemy won few battles he lost no wars, and despite his embarrassing absence at Issus in 301 B.C., he left behind him the strongest kingdom in the Mediterranean when he died. It must have been in his old age, perhaps after retirement, that Ptolemy sat down to write the history of Alexander. In doing so he had advantages denied any other historian, not only his unrivaled knowledge of the man whose history he was writing, but also his own life-long experience in the practical side of government. He had the wit to see at the outset of his own independent career that Alexander's importance did not end in Babylon. He saw to it that the king's body was transported to Egypt for burial (despite Perdiccas) in Alexandria, where it still remains. We may be sure Ptolemy's history of Alexander, like the tomb he built for him, would also serve the dynastic interests of the Ptolemics in Egypt.

Unfortunately the fragments are few and disappointing. Much that we read in Arrian belongs to Ptolemy, but too little can be specifically assigned to him to allow us to sense the writer's personality. Like Callisthenes and Aristobulus, Ptolemy describes Alexander's trip through the Libyan desert to Siwah, but there are two notable deviations from other accounts: the Macedonian king was saved not by crows, even *two* crows, but by *two snakes*, making hissing noises; and the return journey was made by a different route, straight across the long and dangerous stretch of desert to Memphis rather than by the shorter coastal route.[148] Both deviations are suggestive, the first for its possible religious connotation, the second because, if true, it represents a pointless recklessness we would not expect on Alexander's part, and also because then he must have chosen the site of Alexandria on the way out. If he did so, then his consultation of the oracle at Siwah had nothing to do with founding the city. It seems likely that Ptolemy did not accompany Alexander to Siwah. He has edited Callisthenes' account for purposes of his own.

There are a number of passages in Arrian in which Ptolemy is mentioned, though not all these need come from Ptolemy's history. He is clearly the source for Arrian's account of the betrayal of Bessus the regicide and for Ptolemy's exploit in bringing him in alive to Alexander,[149] and this was probably the high point of his military services to Alexander. However, in later years he acquired the epithet of "Soter" (Savior). One explanation was that he had saved Alexander's life in the desperate fighting inside the Malli town. It speaks well for Ptolemy the historian that he either denied expressly having done so, or that he describes his own activities somewhere else at the time when that episode occurred.[150] Another plus for Ptolemy is his failure to mention the Amazon queen.[151] Not surprisingly, like Aristobulus, he takes an official attitude on the guilt of Callisthenes as well as the treason of Philotas, Parmenion's son.[152] To judge by what remains, Ptolemy's history was a straightforward account with few digressions on ethnography or plant and animal life, or Indian wise men. But it is unsafe to generalize on the evidence we have. The Ptolemies, including Ptolemy Soter in all probability, did more as patrons of learning than any other Hellenistic rulers. It may be that Ptolemy preferred to keep history and these other matters in separate compartments. From reading Arrian's account of Alexander we would never suspect that Arrian was also a Stoic philosopher, the chief source for our knowledge of his teacher Epictetus. Such interests do not surface in his *Anabasis,* and the same may be true of Ptolemy.

Clitarchus, the last Alexander historian to be considered here, is quite different from any of the others. Although he did not accompany Alexander (or surely we would know it) he is thought by some to have written his history of twelve books or more before either Ptolemy or Aristobulus. What makes him particularly important is that he is the source underlying what has been called the "vulgate" account of Alexander, which is the chief ultimate authority behind Diodorus Siculus, Q. Curtius Rufus, and Justin; he was also used by Arrian and Plutarch. No one is sure when he was born or when he wrote, but there are strong opinions. He seems to have lived in Egypt and presumably would have written nothing to displease the court. He belongs to the category of historians who wrote to entertain rather than to inform their readers. He tells some good stories, notably the one about firing the Persian royal palace in which the chief actor is not Alexander, but Ptolemy's mistress the Athenian courtesan Thais.[153] Resemblances between statements attributed to him and to other Alexander historians have raised questions about priority. Did Aristobulus use him? Did he use Aristobulus? Tarn, anxious to discredit Clitarchus' testimony because he does not accept his picture of Alexander, argues that Clitarchus wrote later than the others, chiefly on the grounds that he made use of Patrocles' account of his explorations of the Caspian Sea.[154] Tarn adds that Clitarchus would never have contradicted

Ptolemy Soter during that king's lifetime, and Ptolemy says he was not one of those who saved Alexander's life in the Malli town while Clitarchus credits him with doing so. Although this would not have suited Ptolemy Soter, according to Tarn, his son Philadelphus would not have objected to a pious forgery.[155] The whole argument is an excellent example of special pleading, including an elaborate but unsubstantial "proof" that Clitarchus made use of Patrocles. As might be expected, Clitarchus joins Onesicritus in Plutarch's list of the liars who vouch for the story of Alexander's meeting with the Queen of the Amazons.[156] He also describes Alexander and his soldiers as reeling their way back to the rendezvous in Carmania in Bacchic revel, drowning their memories of the terrible sufferings endured in Gedrosia. This is sensational reading, like the later Alexander Romance, but cannot be taken seriously as history. We may appropriately close this brief consideration of Clitarchus by echoing Tarn's hope: "I trust that less may be heard of him in future."[157]

## Notes for Chapter Five

1. See *FGrH* (Ephorus) 70. T 34; on the Alexandrian Canon see Sir John Edwyn Sandys, *A History of Classical Scholarship*, 3rd ed. (London, 1921), I, 131.
2. Strabo xiii. 3. 6.
3. Ibid.
4. See the *Suda* s.v. Έφιππος (3930) (scribal error for Έφορος); Müller tries to reconcile the two statements, but his argument is tenuous (see *FHG* i. lviii).
5. E. Schwartz, "Ephoros," *PW* vi. 1.
6. See D.L. iv. 6; v. 39; also Schwartz, "Ephoros," *PW* vi. 1.
7. See *FGrH* 70. T 3a,b,c.
8. See Schwartz, op. cit.
9. See e.g., *FGrH* 70. T 28a = *Suda* s.v. Έφορος (3953); also *FGrH* ii c. 23.
10. Ephorus' writings include one dealing with prose style, another on inventions (Εὑρήματα) and a third collecting traditional material about Cyme (Ἐπιχώριος)— see *FGrH* 70. FF 1–6; Schwartz, op. cit., 2–3. The work on inventions was attacked in a separate treatise by Alexinus of Elis, a philosopher of the Megarian school noted for literary feuding—(see F. Susemihl, *Geschichte der griechischen Literatur in der Alexandrinerzeit* (Leipzig, 1891), I, 19). For Diodorus' use of Ephorus see Schwartz, "Diodoros," *PW* v. 679–682.
11. See Diod. Sic. iv. 3. This is often taken as the beginning of the historical period. Today we associate it with the Dorian invasion. See G. L. Huxley, *Early Sparta* (London, 1962), 102, n. 71; also "Herakleidai," by F. Kiechle in *Kl. Pauly* ii. 1037–39.
12. See Diod. Sic. xvi. 14. 3.
13. Diod. Sic. xvi. 76. 5, where we learn that the entire period covered in the History was about 750 years.
14. See Athenaeus, Deipnosophistae vi 22. 232D = *FGrH* 70. T 9b.
15. See Diod. Sic. xvi. 14. 5 = *FGrH* 73. T 1; Diod. Sic. xvi. 76. 6 = T 2.
16. *FGrH* ii c. 112.
17. See R. Drews, "Ephorus and History written κατὰ γένος," *AJPhil.* 84 (1963): 244–255; also Diod. Sic. v. 1. 4.

18. See also H. Gärtner, "Ephorus," *Kl. Pauly* ii. 299–301. In the second century B.C. two major historians, Polybius and Agatharchides recognize the usefulness of dividing history into areas. Agatharchides speaks of a division of the *oecumene* into four regions, North, South, East, and West. He names a leading historian for each and says his own specialty has been the South—see *De Mari Erythr.* 64, in Carolus Müllerus, *Geographici Graeci Minores*, 1855 (henceforth *GGM*) (Hildesheim, 1965 reprint) I, 156. See also Strabo viii. 1. 1, who compares Ephorus with Polybius.

19. See Drews, op. cit., 249 f., esp. n. 13.

20. See Diod. Sic. xvi. 76. 5 = *FGrH* 70. T 10.

21. Agatharchides had a special interest in islands, the people who inhabited them and their discovery—presumably islands in the south (land of the Troglodytes)—but reluctantly gave up the idea of writing about them because of his advanced age. See *GGM* i. 194. 110.

22. Plut. *De Stoic. repugn.* 20. 6 (1043 D).

23. Xenocrates became head of the Academy and Menedemus of Pyrrha was his nearest competitor. See H. Dörries, "Menedemos" (7) *Kl. Pauly* iii. 1205.

24. Cf. *FHG* i. 234–277 (Carolus apparently left Ephorus to his brother Theod.—see p. ii—but he himself made some corrections and additions in vol. iv—see pp. 626, 641 f); and *FGrH* ii a. 70. 43–109. According to Schwartz, Müller simply took over an earlier edition by Marx which was already obsolete (Schwartz, "Ephorus," *PW* vi. 4).

25. See *FGrH* ii c. 27. 34–38. Jacoby uses the term προκατασκευή—which Polybius was to use for the first two books of his own history. For the 44 fragments see *FGrH* ii a. 70. 45–57. FF 10–53.

26. Viz. *FGrH* 70. FF 112–221.

27. This is accepted by F. W. Walbank. See his *Commentary on Polybius*, (Oxford, 1957), I, 466 (on Polyb. iv. 20. 5).

28. *FGrH* 70. F 7.

29. Ibid., F 8.

30. See *FrGH* 70. F 9 = Harpocration s.v. 'αρχαίως; also see Thuc. i. 1. 2; 20. 1.

31. See *FrGH* 70. F 109 = Diod. Sic. i. 9. 5.

32. See *FrGH* 70. F 110 = Polyb. xii. 27. 7; Jacoby sees a reflection of Thuc. i. 22. 2, but Gomme, discussing this same passage in Thucydides, says this is precisely where Ephorus failed—see A. W. Gomme, *A Historical Commentary on Thucydides* (Oxford, 1945), I, 142.

33. See *FGrH* ii c. 43.

34. A comparison of the references cited by Strabo from Ephorus and Polybius respectively, as well as the nature of those references will make this clear. See the Index of the Didot Strabo (*Strabonis Geographica*), ed. by C. Müllerus and F. Dübnerus (Paris, 1853).

35. See *FGrH* ii c. 43.

36. See *FGrH*. 70. F 20.

37. Thuc. ii. 102.

38. *FGrH* 70. F 22—and this was not original with Ephorus. We have met the explanation much earlier in Hellanicus. See above, Chapter 1, n. 81.

39. *FGrH* 70. F 115.

40. Here the contrast with Thucydides' approach to early times is most revealing. See Thuc. i. 3–6, where technological change is treated much more broadly as a part of social history. Thucydides is often wrong, that was inevitable, but he thinks in historical terms.

41. He also copied an inscription of Ptolemy III at Adula which otherwise would be unknown. See W. Dittenberger, *Orientis Graeci Inscriptiones Selectae* (Leipzig, 1903), vol. 1, no. 54; see also W. W. Hyde, *Ancient Greek Mariners* (New York, 1947), 300.

42. See *FGrH* 70. F 65. Strange that it appears in Book XI instead of in Book V, as Jacoby points out in his commentary on this fragment.

43. See *FGrH* 70. F 64.

44. See *FGrH* 70. F 70 = Diod. Sic. xiv. 11; also Eduard Meyer, *Geschichte des Altertums*, 3rd. ed. (Berlin, 1921), vol. 5, #750, n.

45. See *FGrH* 70. F 196 = Diod. Sic. xii. 38–41. 1. Jacoby argues that xii. 38 comes

from a different source, but Schwartz argues even more persuasively for attributing the entire passage to Ephorus (Cf. *FGrH* ii c. 92 (on F 196), and Schwartz, "Diodoros," *PW* v. 680; see also A. W. Gomme in *Historia* 1953, II, 13 n. 1.

46. Plut. *De garr.* 22. 514 c = *FGrH* 70. F 213.
47. The text was first published by B. F. Grenfell and A. S. Hunt in *The Oxyrhynchus Papyri* (London, 1908), V, 110–142, and the editors attributed it to Theopompus; E. Meyer's *Theopomps Hellenica* was published in Halle in 1909, strongly supporting the same view. See now I. A. F. Bruce, "Theopompus and Classical Greek Scholarship," *History and Theory*, 1970, IX, 86–109.
48. For references see present work, chap. 4, n. 119 above.
49. Translated from the *Suda*; see *FGrH* 115. T 1, esp. *ap. crit.* for line 16.
50. For the fragments and testimonia on Theopompus see *FGrH*, No. 115. For the 12 book *Hellenica* see Diod. Sic. xiii. 42. 5; xiv. 84. 7.
51. See *FGrH* 115. T 2 = Phot. *Bibl.* 176. 120b. 19.
52. See M. N. Tod, *Greek Historical Inscriptions* (Oxford, 1948), II, no. 192. In his discussion Tod alludes to another letter from Alexander to the Chians in behalf of a "friend" (ibid., p. 267); V. Ehrenberg (*Alexander and the Greeks*, Oxford 1938, 30, n. 1) denies that this can refer to Theopompus.
53. See *FGrH* 115. T 6a–b.
54. For the date see K. J. Beloch, *Griechische Geschichte*[2] (Berlin and Leipzig, 1923), III, 2[2], 143–145.
55. See *OCD*[2] article on "Theodectes," by A. W. Pickard-Cambridge and D. W. Lucas; also see Albin Lesky, *Geschichte der griechischen Literatur*, 2nd ed. (Berlin and Munich, 1963), 619, 679; also the *Suda* s.v. Θεοδέκτης nos. 138 and 139.
56. See Phot. *Bibl.* 176. 120b. 30 = *FGrH* (Theopomp.) 115. F 25. On the mix-up between the orations of the two Isocrates see Susemihl, *Gesch. gr. Lit. Alex.*, 1892, II, 450 n. 3.
57. As the *Suda* article (translated above) says; see also Gellius, *NA* x. 18. 6 = *FGrH* 115. T 6b; Jacoby *contra*, *FGrH* ii d. 352.
58. See *FGrH* 115. F 25. 12 ff.
59. See *Epist. Soc.* 30. 12 (Epistolographi) = *FGrH* 115. T 7.
60. See Susemihl, *Gesch. gr. Lit. Alex.*, II 586 f. and nn. 27, 28.
61. See *FGrH* 556 for Philistus' fragments. Philistus is a special case since the tyrant was under obligations to him rather than the other way around. Philistus believed in dictatorship.
62. Philip could profit by free speech at his expense, if we can accept the Demades story (Diod. Sic. xvi. 87. 1–2).
63. See *FGrH* 115. T 48.
64. See *FGrH* 115. T 48, F 255, and *ap. crit.*
65. See *FGrH* 115. T 8 = *Suda* s.v. Ἔφορος.
66. The incident is described by Plutarch, *Alex.* 53. 3–6.
67. Diod. Sic. xiii. 42. 5.
68. See *FGrH* ii d. 355. Jacoby believes the *Hellenica* was not begun before, or not much before 350 B.C., and he thinks Theopompus was eager to enter the lists against Xenophon.
69. See *FGrH* 115. F 154.
70. See *FGrH* 115. F 153.
71. See Plut. *Cimon* 13. 4.
72. This wild conclusion is drawn by the usually reliable Eduard Schwartz in an article in *Hermes*, vol. 35, 109, as quoted by Wade-Gery, *Essays in Greek History* (Oxford, 1958), 204, n. 1; see also Jacoby, "Kallisthenes" (2), *PW* x. 1965.
73. *FGrH* 115 F 27 = Polyb. viii. 9. 1.
74. See Wade-Gery, *Essays*, 236 n. 1. Incidentally, the different ways this is interpreted are educational. Gilbert Murray takes it literally, as meaning there was no one like Philip—and he was "utterly dissolute"; he also finds the same cynical touch in the *Encomium of Philip* (". . . if Philip continued as he had begun he would end by being King of Europe")—see Gilbert Murray, (*Greek Studies* (Oxford, 1946), 164 f. and 162 alluding to F 256). But Walbank has another view—that Theopompus was advocating a policy restricted to Europe

as against the expansionism favored by Isocrates, so that he approves of Philip just so long as he followed that policy—see F. W. Walbank, (*A Historical Commentary on Polybius* (Oxford, 1967), II, 80).

75. See Wade-Gery, *Essays*, 204.
76. See *FGrH* 115. T 31 = Phot. *Bibl.* 176. 121a. 35. We are told that Philip V had an abstract made of the 58 book *Philippica* containing only the parts about Philip and that these (without abridgment) amounted to only 16 books!
77. See *FGrH* 115. F 5a. It would be interesting to know whether, like Xenophon, he wrote anonymously.
78. See F 12, and Jacoby's commentary (*FGrH* ii d. 356); cf. Diod. Sic. xiv. 17. 1–3.
79. See *FGrH* 115. F 13. There are some helots who come from Messene, others who live in a part of Laconia once called "Helos."
80. See *FGrH* 115. F 18. Westlake thinks he may have turned against Sparta in a movement of revolt which picked up momentum after the Theban victory at Haliartus (395 B.C.). See H. D. Westlake, *Thessaly in the Fourth Century B.C.* (London, 1935), 61—but Book IX should be earlier than 395 since Lysander still appears in Book X.
81. *FGrH* 115. F 20. This is a warm tribute to a statesman, rare in Theopompus. Xenophon is cool towards Lysander, no doubt out of loyalty towards Agesilaus, and Theopompus may be correcting him.
82. See *FGrH* 115. F 22. The other reference to Book XI (F 21) comes from Porphyry, who compares the way Xenophon and Theopompus described the meeting between Pharnabazus and Agesilaus (see Xen. *Hell.* iv. 1. 29–40) to the disadvantage of Theopompus. Though sharply divided on some matters Xenophon and Theopompus are alike in denouncing luxury in any form, especially gourmet eating. See Xen. *Cyr.* i. 3. 4, where the boy Cyrus reproves his self-indulgent Median grandfather for going to such a deal of trouble to fill his stomach, when the object could be accomplished so much more easily!
83. See *FGrH* 115. T 17 = Diod. Sic. xvi. 3. 8; T 18 = Phot. *Bibl.* 120a. 6. Photius refutes the charge that Book XII was missing by giving us a careful summary of the contents, a most useful passage for anyone studying Theopompus. We may be grateful to the unknown writer—a certain Menophanes—who aroused the prelate's ire.
84. See *FGrH* 115. F 85.
85. See *FGrH* 115. F 89 for the less damaging portrait, and F 90 for the scurrilous one, reported with relish by St. Cyril. The latter (a Patriarch of Alexandria) was a master of invective in his own right.
86. On these fragments see now W. Robert Connor, *Theopompus and Fifth-Century Athens* (Washington, D.C., 1968), who gives a text with translation and commentary (pp. 19–76); he also does this for the four fragments of Book XXV which deal with the fifth century (see pp. 77–98).
87. See *FGrH* 115. F 166. See also Beloch, *Gr. Gesch.*[2] III, 1[2], 504 f.
88. *FGrH* 115. F 52.
89. See *FGrH* ii d. 353. 11–14.
90. See *FGrH* 115. F 204 (from Book 43).
91. See *FGrH* 115. F 65 = Plut. *De Is. et Os.* 47.
92. See W. Jaeger, *Aristotle: Fundamentals in the History of his Development*, 2nd ed., Eng. tr. (Oxford, 1948), 131–134.
93. See *FGrH* 115. F 75c, esp. c. 6.
94. See *FGrH* 115. F 276.
95. See Isoc. *Paneg.* 50. See also F. M. Snowden, Jr., *Blacks in Antiquity* (Cambridge, Massachusetts, 1970) 170.
96. "Theopompus, or the Cynic as Historian," in Murray, *Greek Studies*, 149–170.
97. See *FGrH* 115. F 162.
98. Polyb. viii. 11. 3.
99. See Curtius Rufus vi. 1. 16–21; Diod. Sic. xvii. 73. 5–6.
100. See Diog. Laert. vi. 49.
101. None of the original Alexander historians survives except in fragments. These will be found in Jacoby's *FGrH* nos. 117–153; most of them are also available in English translation, see C. A. Robinson, *The History of Alexander the Great* I

(Providence, 1953); for a scholarly discussion see the excellent book of Lionel Pearson, *The Lost Histories of Alexander the Great*, "Philological Monographs" XX of the American Philological Association, (London and Beccles, 1960).

102. See *FGrH* (Callisthenes) 124. T 2 = Plut. *Alex.* 55. The *Suda*, s.v. Καλλισθένης, calls him his great-nephew.

103. Ibid., T 4 = Diog. Laert. v. 4–5. Here the general term of "kinsman" (συγγενής) is used. On Callisthenes in general see F. Jacoby, "Kallisthenes" (2) in *PW* x. 1674–1707; Pearson, *Lost Hist.*, 22–49; and E. Mensching, "Peripatetiker über Alexander," *Historia* 1963, XII; T. S. Brown, "Callisthenes and Alexander," *AJPhil.* 1949, LXX, 225–248 (reprinted in *Alexander the Great*, ed. by G. T. Griffith, Cambridge, 1966).

104. See note 103 for references.

105. See *FGrH* 124. T 5. But the real evidence is in Plut. *Alex.* 54. 2 = *FGrH* 124. T 7, where Aristotle says of Callisthenes, λόγω μὲν ἦν δυνατὸς καὶ μέγας, νοῦν δὲ οὐκ εἶχεν ("he was forceful and eloquent but lacked intelligence"). I agree with Pearson (*Lost Hist.*, 23). For a different view, see J. R. Hamilton, *Plutarch: Alexander, A Commentary* (Oxford, 1969), 149. Walbank may be said to have laid the ghost of the idea of "tragic history" as something specially associated with the Peripatetic school (to which Callisthenes belonged). See his article, "History and Tragedy," *Historia* 1960, IX, 216–234.

106. This was fought in the late sixth century to protect Delphi from interference by neighboring Crisa. There is a fragment preserved by Athenaeus (xiii 10. 560 BC = *FGrH* 124. F 1).

107. See Dittenberger, *Sylloge Inscriptiomum Graecarum*[3] (Leipzig, 1915–1924), 275 = Tod, *Gk. Hist. Inscrip.*, vol. 2, no. 187.

108. See Strabo xiii. 1. 27; also Plut. *De Alex. fort.* i. 10.

109. See *FGrH* 124. T 27.

110. *FGrH* 124. FF 10 and 12 respectively.

111. See *FGrH* 124. F 14. On the masquerade at Troy see Arr. *Anab.* i. 11. 6 to 12. 2.

112. See *FGrH* 124. F 31. Callisthenes may be borrowing from Xenophon here, who represents the Euphrates river as acknowledging Cyrus in the same way (Xen. *An.* i. 4. 18). If so it was not a very good omen, but the *Anabasis* was a classic; connecting Alexander with it was meant to be a tribute.

113. See *FGrH* 124. F 36.

114. See Polyb. xii. 12b. 2.

115. See the references in note 103 above.

116. See Plut. *Eum.* 2.

117. For references and an opinion see Hamilton, *Plut. Alex. Comm.*, 58–60.

118. See note 101 above.

119. See in general my *Onesicritus, A Study in Hellenistic Historiography* (Los Angeles, 1949) and *FGrH* no. 134. The phrase is put in the mouth of an Indian sage, who says Alexander was the only king of this kind he had ever known (μόνον γὰρ ἴδοι αὐτὸν ἐν ὅπλοις φιλοσοφοῦντα) from *FGrH* 134. F 17a = Strabo xv. 1. 64.

120. See *FGrH* 134. F 17b.

121. See Arr. *Anab.* iii. 6. 5.

122. Nearchus' account of his voyage is summarized in Arrian's *Indica*. Even in this abbreviated form it is one of the best accounts of exploration that has come down to us from the ancients. Onesicritus was also honored along with Nearchus and others at Susa (Arr. *Anab.* vii. 5. 6).

123. Pliny *HN* vi. 96–100.

124. On Ctesias, see Chapter 4, p. 86 above and n. 65; for Onesicritus see *FGrH* 134. F 22, esp. c. 24. Both writers offer proof: Ctesias had seen Indians who were white; Onesicritus says foreign cattle changed color after drinking the Indian water.

125. See *FGrH* 134. F 14.

126. See *FGrH* 134. F 22.

127. See *FGrH* 134. FF 9–11. Perhaps the Zoroastrian idea of men who cast no shadows in a future age of bliss helped confuse Greek speculation on the subject. See pp. 122–123 and n. 91 above, in connection with Theopompus.

128. See *FGrH* 134. F 17ab.
129. Ibid., F 24. Diogenes the Cynic also felt medicine and philosophy alone worth studying (see Diog. Laert. vi. 24; also his dislike of other studies, ibid., 73 *ad fin.*). Onesicritus, an avowed Cynic, reflects Diogenes' views on medicine, so he may also reflect his views about slavery. The Cynics are often treated in a patronizing fashion even by modern scholars. The ancients called Diogenes "a Socrates gone mad" (ibid., vi. 54); but that is a caricature, perhaps a refusal to take an uncomfortable doctrine seriously.
130. See Plut. *Alex.* 46.
131. See *FGrH* 134. F 17a *ad fin.* Even if he was not there, he must have talked to someone who was.
132. See Arr. *Anab.* Proem 1.
133. See Müller's *Scriptores Rerum Alexandri Magni,* bound up with Dübner's edition of Arrian (Didot, Paris 1846), 94.
134. See Pearson, *Lost. Hist.,* chap. 6.
135. Ibid., 151; and 106. Pearson's argument that Cos was not cited by Aristobulus at all, but by Onesicritus, because Onesicritus lived in Astypalaea and Astypalaeans looked to Cos as their nearest important city, is not valid. Onesicritus probably came from the *island of Astypalaea,* not the small town of the same name *on the mainland near Cos.*
136. See *FGrH* (Aristob.) 139. F 7ab.
137. See Pearson, *op. cit.* 174 for discussion and references.
138. See Arr. *Anab.* vii. 22. 4 = *FGrH* 139 F 55 *ad. fin.*
139. Hdt. viii. 118 *ad fin.*
140. See [Lucian] *Macrobioi* 22 for Aristobulus' advanced age; he is said to have lived to be over 90.
141. See *FGrH* 139. FF 13–15 = Arr. *Anab.* iii. 3. 6. Further discussion on the Siwah incident will be found in A. Gitti, *Alessandro Magno all'Oasi di Siwah: il problema delle fonti* (Bari, Italy, 1951); and C. Bradford Welles, "The Discovery of Sarapis and the Foundation of Alexandria," *Historia* 1962, XI, 271–298.
142. Plut. *Alex.* 46.
143. On Epyaxa, see Xen. *Anab.* i. 2. 12. Callisthenes appears to have had the *Anabasis* in front of him (or in his memory) when he wrote (see note 112 above), and this might also fit Onesicritus. See Hamilton, *Plut. Alex. Comm.* 123 f. for a different interpretation and references.
144. See Müller, *Scriptores,* 94, where he remarks: "nam primum absolvit regem a crimine vinolentiae . . . Aristobulum historicum per me licet adulatoribus regis aggregari" etc.
145. On Aristobulus see W. W. Tarn, *Alexander the Great* (London, 1948), II, esp. 29–43; and E. Schwartz, "Aristobulos," *PW* ii 911–918 [reprinted in his *Griechische Geschichtsschreiber* (Leipzig, 1959), 119–129]. For other references see G. Wirth, "Aristobulos" (7) *Kl. Pauly* 1964, i. 564 f.
146. See Arr. *Anab.* iii. 6. 5, and Proem 1.
147. See [Luc.] *Macrob.* 12.
148. See *FGrH* (Ptolemy) 138. FF 7 and 8. See note 141 above; also Hamilton, *Plut. Alex. Comm.,* 69–70.
149. See *FGrH* 138. F 14 = Arr. *Anab.* iii 29. 6 to 30. 5.
150. Cf. *FGrH* 138. F 26a and F 26b. The difference is important. If Ptolemy *denied* he was there he was contradicting Clitarchus, if he simply mentions what he was doing when Alexander was wounded by the Malli he was not.
151. See *FGrH* 138. F 28. This equates him with Aristobulus and separates him from Onesicritus.
152. See *FGrH* 138. FF 16 and 17.
153. For Clitarchus in general see: F. Jacoby, "Kleitarchos" (2), *PW* xi. 622–654; *FGrH* no. 137; Pearson, *Lost. Hist.,* 212–242. For Thais see *FGrH* 137. F 11.
154. See Tarn, *Alexander the Great,* II, esp. 16–29.
155. See ibid., 26–28.
156. See *FGrH* 138. F 15 = Plut. *Alex.* 46.
157. Tarn, *Alexander the Great,* II, 132.

The third century is a period of uneasy
equilibrium in the Greek world. The heroics
of Alexander's conquest of the Persian
empire have melted into the distance,
remembered dimly and idealized, much as
Alexander's generation looked back to the
men of Marathon, Thermopylae, and Salamis.
The dream of one empire had proved
illusory. Instead there were three major
monarchies ruling in Macedonia, Syria, and
Egypt, with Pergamum a poor fourth,
followed by a growing number of still smaller
dynasties such as Bithynia and Cappadocia all
the way down to microcosms like
Commagene. Nor had the city-state
abandoned the struggle entirely. Autonomy
prevailed in many of the older centers such
as Athens and Sparta, while Rhodes
continues to remind us of what a determined
citizen body could still accomplish in
competition with giant states. There were also
various kinds of leagues; some of them,
notably the Aetolian and the Achaean leagues
in mainland Greece, were making interesting
experiments with federal government,
attempting to solve the old Greek problem of
how to combine complete freedom at home
with political effectiveness abroad. This is the
very heart of the Hellenistic period. Scientific
achievements were greater than ever before,
stimulated by the competition of rival courts
which provided libraries and generous
support for research on a scale unheard of in
earlier times. There was a rising production
of literature on all levels, for scholars, for
dilettantes, and for those who asked only to
be entertained. But it was not a period that
produced great historians. Whether, as Bevan
thought, this was an age that lacked a sense
of purpose cannot easily be answered,[1] but
historians do not seem to have quite the
sweep that characterized their colleagues in
previous ages. On the other hand, we have
an abundance of learned men, polymaths, for
whom that third century giant Eratosthenes
of Cyrene may stand as a worthy representative.

# MEGASTHENES AND TIMAEUS

THE LIGHTHOUSE OF ALEXANDRIA AS IT ONCE WAS
Planned perhaps by Alexander, begun by his friend the historian Ptolemy I, it was
completed under Ptolemy II. The architect, Sostratus, came from Cnidus, home of
Ctesias as well as Agatharchides. The building symbolized the new Hellenistic age
and outlasted the Roman Empire.

An expert in so many fields: mathematics, chronology, astron-
omy—a great librarian and a poet of sorts—he was probably the
leading geographer in antiquity. But the historians seem not to have
been either first-rate scholars or public figures of the stature of
Xenophon or Ptolemy Soter who wrote about their own times from
personal experience. The chief exception might be Hieronymus of
Cardia, who lived even longer than Isocrates and must have out-
lived an entire generation. He wrote a general history of the period
from Alexander's death to the death of Pyrrhus, a history which
had great influence on Diodorus Siculus and on the "Lives" written
by Plutarch. But Hieronymus wrote in the shadow of a patron. Most
of his long life was spent in the service of the Antigonids, first
under the One-Eyed Antigonus who seemed well on the way to
reuniting Alexander's empire until Seleucus' elephants stopped him
at Ipsus in 301 B.C. But Hieronymus continued to serve Demetrius,
Antigonus' son and Antigonus Gonatas, the son of Demetrius,
under whom he finally settled down to write his history. But what
remains of Hieronymus suggests a chronicle of events rather than
a critical analysis, the materials from which a history might have
been written rather than a history in its own right. Nevertheless,
he has many admirers. The chief value in Books XVIII, XIX and
XX of the *Historical Library* of Diodorus Siculus lies in what Diodorus preserves from Hieronymus. After that Diodorus, himself,
is reduced to fragments. Our skimpy knowledge of the period after

Diodorus breaks off makes it clear that the loss of Hieronymus is a major one.[2]

Other historians also come to mind, whose works have disappeared, but not without leaving some indication of their importance: men such as Dicaearchus who wrote a *Life of Greece* and concerned himself, among other things, with finding out the altitude of mountains; Duris of Samos who, like Dicaearchus, was a Peripatetic but who was also the ruler of Samos; or Aristoxenus of Tarentum, sometimes called the first true biographer and certainly the chief authority we have on Greek music; and Phylarchus, an Athenian who became involved in a Spartan revolution; and many more.[3] But I have selected to represent the third century here, two historians: Megasthenes and Timaeus, writers we associate with opposite ends of the classical world, India and the East and Sicily and the West. We may begin with the historian of India.

## I. Megasthenes

Megasthenes wrote what has come to be accepted as the most reliable account of India produced in antiquity. Yet this is perhaps less a tribute to his accuracy than a recognition of the breakdown in communications between India and the Greek Mediterranean that took place not long after he wrote. Alexander's conquest of the Punjab gave promise of closer relations with the East, but that promise was only partly fulfilled because of adverse political developments. The Seleucids, who inherited claims to the Macedonian East, had to devote more and more time to their enemies in Egypt and the West. A strong Indian monarchy replaced the small states in northern India once conquered so rapidly by the Macedonian invaders; also the Parthians and other intruders made their presence felt in the very heart of Iran; and finally the Romans put the quietus on a revival of Macedonian imperialism in the East or anywhere else. For these and other reasons, few Greeks after Megasthenes wrote about India on the basis of first-hand experience and none of them, so far as we can tell, made as good use of his opportunities as Megasthenes had done. The Greeks in Bactria and their descendants did come to know India well, but their own dramatic history has to be worked out tentatively and precariously chiefly on the basis of the coin evidence. They left no histories behind them.[4] The *Suda* fails us on Megasthenes, and the notices in it about India reflect both tenth century biblical interests and the decline in knowledge of the East. For example, a particular area in India is referred to as, "the place from which the gold came to Solomon."[5] The important *testimonia* about Megasthenes have been assembled by Jacoby, though that scholar's lamented death appears to have postponed indefinitely the commentary that is so badly needed.[6] The *testimonia* tell us the following: that Megasthenes lived at the time of Seleucus Nicator (312–280 B.C.); that he spent some time with Sibyrtius the satrap of Arachosia; and also that, by his own report, he frequently visited Sandrocottus the Indian king.[7] Arrian amplifies this elsewhere, saying that Megasthenes did not see much of India, though he did travel beyond where Alexander had gone. A reference to Porus has crept into the text of Arrian which raises technical problems that need not be discussed here.[8] The fact that Megasthenes was ambassador to Sandrocottus (or Chandragupta) can be accepted as established. This took him through much of northern India, at least to Palimbothra (or modern Patna) on the Ganges River. But when did he go? It must have been during a period of good relations between Seleucus and Sandrocottus. Stein believes that Megasthenes made only one stay in India, but that a prolonged one, during which he had frequent audiences with the king, rather than that each meeting with the king represents a separate journey. As to the period, Stein suggests 303–292 B.C. The first date marks the probable end of hostilities between Seleucus and Sandrocottus, the latter year the date when Deimachus was sent out to Palimbothra to present his credentials to Sandrocottus' successor, King Allitrochades. Sandrocottus died somewhat earlier (297? 299?), but Stein thinks Megasthenes stayed on for some years until Seleucus finally had to replace him for reasons of health—because India does not agree with Europeans![9] But this goes far beyond the evidence. One further inference is permissible. Having spent some time (how much?) in Arachosia, a satrapy near the Indian border, Megasthenes probably knew something about India even before he went there as an ambassador. In fact, that is very likely what recommended him to Seleucus, who had every reason to regard this post as one of the greatest importance. Without the 480 Indian elephants he obtained, quite likely through negotiations handled by Megasthenes, Antigonus would have won the day.[10]

Generally speaking, Megasthenes seems to have enjoyed a good reputation as a historian—Arrian praises him and Pliny cites him—but Strabo feels differently: "For the most part, all writers on India have been liars, especially Deimachus, but Megasthenes is right behind him. . . ."[11] Strabo probably echoes Eratosthenes in this judgment. As a geographer Eratosthenes was annoyed at not finding the precise data on India he needed for his own work, and as a critical scholar he was suspicious of attempts to substantiate the old stories of heroes.[12] Megasthenes was interested in the stories connecting Dionysus and Heracles with India, but this does not mean he is not to be trusted to give an accurate account of what he had seen with his own eyes.

The *Indica* was originally published in four books, though the references we have do not permit us to determine the content of each.[13] It will be convenient to discuss the fragments topically, beginning with the geography of India.

Megasthenes thinks of India as a quadrilateral bounded on the eastern and southern sides by the sea, on the west by the Indus River, and on the north by the Emodus Mountains, which separate India from the Scythian country.[14] He also maintains that the length of India was from north to south, the width from east to west. This width, where it is narrowest, amounts to 16,000 stades. It is worth noting how he arrives at such a figure. There is supposed to have been a royal road from the Indus all the way to Sandro-cottus' capital on the Ganges at Palimbothra, which was accurately measured as amounting to exactly 10,000 stades.[15] Megasthenes accepted this figure from his written source, then added 6,000 stades more ". . . on the basis of the voyage up the Ganges to Palimbothra from the sea."

This means he obtained his information from some merchant shipman who had made the trip and who, no doubt, gave his estimate on the basis of the number of days it took to make the voyage.[16] And that was a reasonable procedure on the historian's part. But geographical data without reference points giving latitude and longitude are never satisfactory. Here the erroneous assumption was made that the Ganges ran more or less *due east* to the sea! Strabo seems to feel that Megasthenes (and his successor Deimachus) have a more conservative view of the size of India than Ctesias (who says it was as large as all the rest of Asia), or Onesicritus (India was one third of the inhabited world), or even Nearchus who said it took four months to cross the Indian plains.[17]

No one was in a position to make an accurate estimate of the size of India with the instruments at his command, but some details, such as the size of rivers, could have been calculated with better results. Megasthenes appears to have a special interest in Indian rivers, and he was probably the writer who first insisted on the superiority of the Ganges to the Indus. This is to be expected. The Alexander historians, when they saw the Indus, compared it favorably with the Nile, but they had not seen the Ganges and Megasthenes had. Many centuries later the Roman governor Arrian, himself the author of a work on the Black Sea, is still impressed by the writers on India. "There should be no doubt," he says, "about the Indus and the Ganges, nor are the Danube and the Nile to be compared with them."[18] But Megasthenes is more specific, he is reported as saying:

*Now where the Ganges is* narrowest *it is 100 stades* [at least 10 miles] *wide. In many places the river swells so that the shore cannot be seen on the other side—where the land is flat, that is, and not marked out by hills.*[19]

However Strabo, usually more accurate than Arrian, has Megasthenes give 100 stades as an *average* width and 20 fathoms as the minimum depth.[20] Although this is still too large, at least it is a recognizable distortion of the truth, assuming as we must, that the estimate was made during the flood season—as in fact Arrian's statement implies. Of course he also saw the Ganges when it was low, but he knew his readers would be interested only in its enormous size. One other writer speaks of 30 stades where the river is narrowest, and some true doubting Thomas reduces this to a mere 3 stades![21] Megasthenes makes other general remarks about Indian rivers, for example he says there were some fifty-eight navigable rivers flowing into the outer sea, not counting the Ganges and the Indus; but he also sanctions that old story about a river in which nothing will float.[22]

Like earlier Greek writers Megasthenes mistakenly pictures India as a land of plenty, where famine is unknown:

*There are two rainy seasons in India each year, one in the winter—the time for sowing wheat there as elsewhere—and the other at the time of the summer solstice, when they are accustomed to plant their barley, bosporum (an Indian cereal?), and also sesame and millet. Usually they reap both harvests in India, but even though both do not turn out satisfactorily they are sure to succeed with one of them.*[23]

The abundance of crops is matched by the superior size and strength of the animals that live there, man being no exception. But this does not complete the advantages of that favored land which also include quantities of silver, gold, copper, iron, and even tin.[24]

These blessings are also responsible for India's early development and history. No outside power invaded India successfully before Alexander, nor did the Indians campaign beyond their own borders.[25] This is how he describes their early history:

*In ancient days the Indians were nomads like the nonagricultural Scythians, who wander about on their wagons from one part of Scythia to another, neither living in cities, nor honoring the gods in temples. Likewise, the Indians had no cities and built no temples for their gods. But they dressed in the skins of animals and ate the bark of trees. These trees the Indians called Tala, and on them as on the tops of palm trees there grows something resembling a ball of wool. They also ate whatever animals they could catch, devouring them raw, until Dionysus came to India. For when Dionysus came and made himself master of India, he built cities and established laws for them, and he became the giver of wine, for the Indians as well as the Greeks, and he taught them to sow the land, furnishing them with seed.*[26]

The reference to the Scythians invites comparison with the Father of History. In writing about Scythia, Herodotus was in a less favorable position than Megasthenes in dealing with India, but he made excellent use of the opportunities he had for getting information by asking questions in Olbia and elsewhere in the Black Sea region[27] to supplement what Hecataeus and others had already written. In his theory of man's development, however, Megasthenes is influenced, perhaps indirectly, by Thucydides, who abandoned the Golden Age idea of the remote past so dear to Homer and to Hesiod in favor of man's gradual rise from original brutishness to civilized life.[28] The civilizing influence of Dionysus on India follows a familiar pattern, and the Alexander historians also, sought and found traces of the visits of Dionysus and Heracles to India. Megasthenes reacts against the idea expressed by other writers that they had come to India as military conquerors. In Hellenistic times there was considerable interest in victorious kings who civilized the peoples they defeated, for their own good. Alexander has been depicted in this way by Onesicritus.[29] One of Megasthenes' contemporaries was Hecataeus of Abdera who wrote an *Egyptiaca* (probably under Ptolemy Soter) in which Sesostris, the Egyptian conqueror, performs a similar role. He overruns much of the *oecumene*, spreading the benefits of the good life to his new subjects. Hecataeus anticipates, perhaps inspires, the famous Euhemerus of Messene, whose theory of gods who earned their godhood by the benefits they conferred on men played a considerable role in intellectual circles.[30] Megasthenes may or may not have read the *Egyptiaca*, but he has heard enough about Sesostris' exploits from some source to feel obliged to deny that that ruler reached India. Dionysus, however, while he did not subdue India by force of arms, left many indications of his presence there, which were duly attested by the historians of Alexander.[31]

Heracles likewise went to India according to the Greeks. Megasthenes makes use of this tradition to explain the Indian custom of child marriage, which evidently made a deep impression on him. Heracles had many sons but only one daughter, born when he was already near the end of his days. Fearing she would find no suitable husband after his death, he lay with her when she was a mere child of seven. This then became the custom in the part of India ruled over by her descendants.[32] Also connected with the tale of Heracles in India is the discovery of pearls. Heracles collected a large number of them to adorn his dear daughter. The historian adds the following account of pearl fishing:[33]

*Megasthenes says they fish for oysters with nets, for the oysters swarm together like bees, in one spot in the sea. Now these oysters have a king or a queen like the bees, and whoever manages to catch that one easily captures the rest of the oyster swarm. But if the king dodges them, then the others can no longer be taken. The fishermen wait for the meaty part to rot away, and then use the bone for an Ornament. In India a pearl is worth three times its weight in refined gold—for gold, too, is extracted from the soil of India.*

But Megasthenes cannot be blamed for his account of pearl fishing. He depended on oral testimony filtered through interpreters. The normal tendency of fishermen to tell tall stories is compounded here by the desire to keep a valuable trade secret. But Megasthenes had seen pearls and very likely gives a correct idea of their market value.

However, we may call Megasthenes to a stricter accounting when he speaks as an eye-witness. As the envoy of Seleucus and a frequent visitor at court he was in a better position than anyone else to describe Indian political and social institutions. We are fortunate in having his account of the class system in considerable detail, as preserved by three different writers: Diodorus Siculus, Arrian, and Strabo. In the time of Sandrocottus, when Megasthenes visited Palimbothra, he just may have met Kautilya, an important official at court who is supposed to have written the *Arthashastra*, which deals (among other matters) with the duties of a king. But there is no agreement among scholars when the *Arthashastra* (rediscovered in 1909) was written. The possibility is strong that our text has been so altered by later interpolations as to make it next to impossible to separate this extraneous material from the original. Therefore it is not safe at present to use this work as a check on the accuracy of Megasthenes. Even Megasthenes has suffered some distortion in transmission.[34]

According to Megasthenes, there are seven classes (not the four castes known to us later):[35]

    I. The Philosophers (small in number, great in honor)
    II. The Farmers (large in number)
    III. The Shepherds and Hunters
    IV. The Artisans
    V. The Warriors
    VI. The Supervisors
    VII. The Counsellors and Advisers of the King.

Of these, the "philosophers" include the Brahmans, some of whom evidently talked with Megasthenes. This may account for his rather abstract picture of Indian society—for example, the statement that the classes are completely sealed off from one another:

*It is not permissible to marry from a different class or vice versa. Nor is the same man allowed to follow two trades or even to change from one class to another, that is for a herdsman to become a farmer or for an artisan to become a herdsman.*[36]

All three Greek transmitters of Megasthenes note one duty of the philosophers, that of meeting with the king at the beginning of each year to make their predictions. Repeated false predictions were punished—in a way to impress any philosopher, Greek or Indian—by the imposition of silence for the rest of their lives. The ban on changing from one class to another was probably an ideal, not the practice. The Brahmans, for all their superiority and the high regard in which they were held, evidently could not count on being supported. That is why they alone (in Megasthenes) were permitted to follow any occupation they wished.[37] These Brahmans had a long and arduous period of training in seclusion for some thirty-seven years. After that they could return, and promptly marry

*. . . as many wives as possible in order to have many children . . . since they have no slaves the nearest equivalent is being waited on by their children. The Brahmans do not discuss philosophy with their wedded wives lest, if the women are of low character they repeat what it is a sacrilege to divulge to the profane, while if they are virtuous, lest they abandon them.*[38]

As B. C. J. Timmer has pointed out, women in India were usually barred from studying the Vedas.[39] What Megasthenes has added is a typically Greek rationalization—a practical reason for not having a learned wife. She will desert you! His insistence on there being no slavery in India (where he may have been misled by not recognizing in India slavery as he knew it at home) leads him to see a special reason for polygamy.[40]

There is no space here to examine the account of each of the seven classes, but a few scattered observations may be made. The Farmers are said to carry on their activities undisturbed, even when opposing armies are in the neighborhood, because neither army will molest those whom they look upon as common benefactors.[41] This is not true; but perhaps, with Derrett, we may attribute the error to a particular instance, known to the historian, where farming continued during a battle and from which he draws this sweeping conclusion, but it must be added, on very insufficient evidence.[42] The Warriors, it will be noted, do correspond to a real Indian caste, the Kshatriyas. So do the Farmers (Vaisyas), and of course the Brahmans. Megasthenes has no exact parallel for the Sudras (Laborers) or the outcasts, the Pariahs. His other classes are not accurately defined. He rightly recognizes the monopoly of high court offices by a small aristocracy (Class VII).

Megasthenes spent some time at court, and he also visited an Indian army camp. Therefore what he has to say about monarchy and about the military has particular value. He must have met the king in his capital city of Palimbothra. He was impressed by the size of the city, which he describes as protected by a deep trench and a wall with 64 gates and 570 towers. This city is quadrangular in shape (80 stades in length and 15 in width) with a wooden wall pierced with holes to permit archers to discharge their arrows from inside. The ditch was not only for defense; it also was used to dispose of sewage.[43]

As to the king who lived behind these walls, Strabo has a number of curious statements from Megasthenes crowded into a single chapter—as is his way. Unlike Arrian and Diodorus, our other chief sources on Megasthenes, Strabo is writing a geography. Therefore he excerpts passages from the historians whom he read, but when he starts writing his own work he goes back over his notes and fits these pieces into a very different context. When we read Arrian or Diodorus our problem is to recognize distortion caused by uneven abridgment having upset the original balanced treatment by a writer (say Megasthenes) whom they happen to be following. But with Strabo, there is not only distortion of this kind, but the order in which he presents details from Megasthenes is not based on the order in which Megasthenes originally presented them. Therefore we are often in danger of missing the point that was made in the *Indica*.[44] In one passage Strabo tells us that the king was attended exclusively by women, who had been purchased by the king from their fathers.[45] The regular guards stayed outside the palace gate. Even inside the king is not entirely safe: ". . . the king may not sleep in the daytime, and even at night he is forced to change his couch at intervals, for fear of plots." He must be careful to avoid alcoholic excesses: "A woman who kills a drunken king is rewarded by marrying his successor." These statements (except for the guards stationed outside the palace) all smack of some legal or religious source, they are not of a kind the ambassador could learn by personal observation. But we are also told that the king is in the habit of holding public audiences. On such occasions, when the usual hour for physical therapy comes around, the king has "rubbers" brought in, who massage him with ebony rods while the hearing continues without interruption. That does sound like an eye-witness report. We also learn that when the king goes hunting he is surrounded, once again, by female attendants, fully armed. All other persons are kept away by ropes, and anyone forcing his way in is subject to the death penalty. The king, himself, stands on a raised platform with drawn bow, waiting for the game to be driven within range. On hunts in the open country he shoots from the back of an elephant. Was Megasthenes present on such an occasion? It seems not at all unlikely. He does give us the best account we have in antiquity on the hunting and taming of elephants—a method not unlike that used in modern times. It is summarized quite fully by Arrian and briefly by Strabo.[46] Interest in the elephant was high. Alexander had learned to appreciate its value in war and the noble beast came west from India to join the armies of the Successors. Ptolemy succeeded in training African elephants and so did the Carthaginians. Did they learn how by reading Megasthenes? Perhaps that helped, but probably mahouts from India helped more. The elephant continues to play an important part in warfare until the time of Caesar. In Sandrocottus' kingdom the elephant cannot be owned by private persons, but only by the king, both the horse and the elephant being regarded as royal animals. There seems to have been one Indian republic ("beyond the Hypanis river") which was governed by a Council of Five Hundred men, "each of whom furnishes an elephant to the state."[47]

Megasthenes visited an army camp. He appears well informed on military matters. There was a special board in charge of the military, consisting of six five-man commissions. Among their responsibilities is that of furnishing oxcarts for the transport of food and equipment, including "food for man and beast"[48]—hay for the hundreds of elephants must have strained their resources. There were also servants of all kinds, including bell-ringers, grooms, and mechanics;[49] the last-named presumably repaired the rolling stock, for we do not expect a Macedonian-type engineering corps. Soldiers did not retain their weapons when off duty, but deposited them in a royal armory. Likewise the horses and elephants were kept in government stables cared for by grooms, not by the soldiers.[50] Each war elephant carries three bowmen in addition to the mahout.[51] Megasthenes praises the discipline maintained in camp. In the one he visited there were 40,000 men yet very little stealing. And he paints a favorable picture of Indian morality generally— houses did not need to be locked up when the owners were away, and so on. However, he does not approve of the Indians' habit of eating alone whenever they felt hungry. As a Greek who enjoyed table talk this horrified him.[52] This idyl of life in the army is also modified by two other random observations: that the camp was filled with unpleasant odors, and that government spies got their information from the camp prostitutes.[53]

There was a special department of government, another five-man commission, to look after foreigners who arrived in the kingdom. They were given a place to stay and servants were assigned to them. If a foreigner became ill they provided him with a doctor, and if he died they not only buried him but arranged to have his effects sent back to his family. However, they also kept close watch over his activities, and here no doubt the servants proved useful.[54]

The overall impression of Indian life in and near Palimbothra is one of considerable regimentation. No detail is too small for the attention of the government. Trade is strictly controlled, different types of merchandise requiring different stamps, with penalties for all violations. Taxation would seem to have been the moving consideration behind all these arrangements. A record of births and deaths was also kept for tax purposes. Does this mean a death tax? We are not told. But the tax dodger was called a "tax stealer" and if caught was liable to the death penalty.[55] A complicated tax system of this kind must have been hard to enforce, and the heavy penalties may reflect the despair rather than the brutality of the government. The ambassador was in no position to distinguish legal theory from practice.

Megasthenes' interest in Indian animals was not confined to the elephant. He has a good deal to say on the subject of the tiger, big snakes, Indian dogs, and monkeys. But his account, far from marking an improvement over his predecessors, is often even less accurate than theirs.[56] These just mentioned, though exaggerated, are at least real animals, but Megasthenes also believes much that he has read in Ctesias and elsewhere of fabulous animals—and people. He writes of winged snakes whose urine, dropped from above, causes immediate putrefaction of the flesh of the unwary; and of course he mentions the gold-digging ants.[57] The fabulous people include many old favorites: men whose feet were reversed; others with no mouths; still others with ears so long they slept inside them; and many more.[58] Even the story of the Pygmies and the Cranes turns up again in Megasthenes, but with significant additions. The Pygmies wage war against the cranes each year in an effort to destroy their eggs. Sometimes a wounded crane escapes with one of the Pygmies' bronze arrowheads embedded in him. This is evidently offered in an attempt to corroborate the story,[59] a need not felt by Homer, but characteristic in the Hellenistic Age of Reason.

A regrettable loss is the section of the *Indica* which summarized early Indian history. We have only the figures, and the text itself is not altogether reliable. Megasthenes says that the Indians counted 153 kings over a period of 6042 years, between Dionysus and Sandrocottus. During that whole time "freedom" (republican government?) occurred only three times—but the figures we have for the duration of each period are corrupt. Strangely, the same number of 153 Indian kings occurs elsewhere, but there the time span is from Dionysus to Alexander the Great, and the number of years 6451.[60] The other general statement he makes is that there are exactly 119 different Indian peoples. Arrian asks, not improperly, how he knows this, when he saw such a small part of India, and when the Indian peoples did not maintain relations with one another.[61]

Considered by itself only, and using professional standards, Megasthenes' *Indica* is not a particularly distinguished performance. One can think of quite a number of Greek historians who would have made better use of his opportunities than he did. On the other hand he was a professional diplomat, not a historian, conditioned by the very nature of his office to writing a favorable report. Relations between the Seleucids and India did not end immediately with him. He could not write exactly as he chose, not even to the extent that Ctesias was free to speak his mind on Persia when he returned to Cnidus. We would like to know how long Megasthenes spent in India, and when he decided to write a book about it. However, though his work is open to criticism it is the best we have. Knowledge about ancient India still depends to a large degree on what he wrote, and we have come a long way in leaving behind us the *martichora* of Ctesias with stingers in his tail, to reach the only partly exaggerated picture of the Bengal tiger in Megasthenes. Things have not improved but worsened when we open the pages of Philostratus' *Life of Apollonius,* written half a millennium later. So let us be grateful—within reason.

## II. Timaeus of Tauromenium

Timaeus is the best historian among the western Greeks,[62] though two Syracusans, Antiochus in the fifth century B.C. and Philistus in the fourth, might possibly challenge his position if we had more to judge them by. The major historians we have already considered are all easterners: two—Thucydides and Xenophon—from Athens; most of the others from Asiatic shores—Hecataeus, Hellanicus, Herodotus, Ctesias, Ephorus, and Theopompus—while some, like Megasthenes, are of unknown antecedents. Is there any particular reason why the West should have produced so little in the way of historical writing of high quality? This depends in part on how one restricts the term "historical writing." If we redefine it in the spirit of Thucydides as political history, intimately related to the Greek polis and the forces that tend both to motivate and to destroy it, then our answer is clear. The Greeks of Sicily and Magna Graecia lacked the centuries of political continuity that are found in Athens, where the citizens claimed to be autochthonous, or in the older Greek cities of Asia. Syracuse, for example, had frequently witnessed wholesale deportations and, with equal frequency, the assignment of citizen rights to large numbers of persons with no background in Syracusan affairs. Under these circumstances the flavor of politics in the West is very different. Despite internal bitterness and even revolutionary change the older Greek polis retains its identity. Athens is always threatened by internal strife but never in actual fact betrayed to an external foe; nor was Sparta. Thebes was, but Thebes is an exception to most rules. Syracuse, Croton, Acragas, Sybaris-Thurii—all have such experiences. This may in part explain why Philistus felt as he did, that strong-arm government was best.[63] But even though political history, in the Greek sense, loses much of its meaning when the citizen body is constantly changing, the Greeks in the west had more than their share of intellectual curiosity about the world around them. Famous names in philosophy like Empedocles and Parmenides demonstrate this sufficiently; while the success of Pythagoras in Italy, even though he comes originally from Samos, proves the same thing. And it is not inappropriate that Herodotus, the embodiment of historical curiosity, should have ended up as a citizen of Thurii. Timaeus belongs rather to the Herodotean than to the Thucydidean school of historical writing. He was not born a moment too soon if the western Greeks were to produce a major historian, because not long after he died his native Sicily became a Roman province as the result of the First Punic War—a war whose significance Timaeus appears to have been the first historian to grasp.[64]

But while Timaeus was a western Greek his formative years were spent elsewhere, specifically in Athens. His father Andromachus, a man of uncertain antecedents, enters the clear light of history as the founder of Tauromenium (358 B.C.), and its ruler. This strategically located city was colonized largely by refugees who had escaped the destruction of Naxos by the tyrant Dionysius, and of course Andromachus may have been one of them.[65] He welcomed Timoleon when he came out from Corinth on what seemed to many to be a fool's errand, to put an end to the tyranny of the younger Dionysius and restore constitutional government to Sicily.[66] Timaeus, who as a historian wrote most unfavorably of both Dionysiuses, may have met Timoleon as a boy in his father's house. And now we come to the best attested statement about the life of Timaeus, a statement presumably made by the historian himself, to the effect that he spent fifty years as an exile in Athens, and wrote his history there.[67] The question that needs to be answered is when his exile began, and I have argued and still believe that it began during the decade 339–329 B.C., to give time enough for fifty years to elapse before the death of his enemy Agathocles enabled him to return to Sicily. Others have argued, on the basis of Diodorus' statement that it was Agathocles who drove Timaeus into exile, for a much later date.[68] It would be tedious for the reader to repeat these arguments here.

There is a statement in the *Macrobioi* saying that Timaeus

(*The British Museum*)

COIN OF TAUROMENIUM
This coin comes from the time of Timoleon, the friend and ally of Timaeus' father Androsthenes. It belongs to the early period in the historian's life, when he was still living in Tauromenium.

lived to be ninety-six years old.[69] Even if this is correct it does not tell us exactly when he was born. We know that he brought his historical work down to the crossing of the Roman army into Sicily in 264 B.C.[70] He probably died not long afterwards, perhaps in the neighborhood of 260 B.C. Conjectural though this date is, it may serve to remind us of what one man might live through in that time of rapid change—to be born the same year as Alexander the Great, and to die with the sound of the Roman legions already coming down the pike![71]

If Timaeus came to Athens in the decade 339–329 B.C., the fifty years he spent there must have included the period from 329–289 B.C. The most likely explanation of his going to Athens in the first place was to complete his education, presumably preparing himself ultimately for a public career in Tauromenium, then ruled by his father. It was in Athens where he developed the rhetorical style so much admired by Cicero for its charm, though castigated by others for its artificiality.[72]

His teacher was Philiscus of Miletus, who made a considerable reputation as a flute player before he studied rhetoric under Isocrates. Presumably Philiscus was living in Athens.[73]

His early years of residence came during an exciting period. Intellectually the Academy was impressively if not brilliantly represented by Xenocrates of Chalcedon, who headed the school from the time Plato's nephew Speusippus died in 339 until his own death in 314. But Aristotle was also in Athens, until a wave of anti-Macedonian feeling forced him to leave after Alexander's death in 323, to be succeeded by Theophrastus, who remained in charge of the Lyceum until about 285 B.C. Politically, Athens must have been an interesting listening post. Callisthenes' early installments describing Alexander's campaign must have been sent off to Athens. But the Athenians, most of them, were far from being admirers of Alexander. Athenian citizens were among the mercenaries fighting on the Persian side who were made prisoners at the Granicus and then sent off to Macedonia to do hard labor. Later, when Alexander had gone east to India, many did not expect him to return. When he finally did come back, he requested divine honors as well as the restoration of political exiles to all the Greek city-states. This led to bitter resentment in Athens, as reflected in the Lamian War immediately after Alexander's death. Subsequently, a Macedonian garrison was installed by Antipater to insure obedience and oligarchical control of Athens. For some years the city was ruled by an Athenian governor, Demetrius of Phalerum, who acted in the Macedonian interest and who was also a learned member of the Peripatetic school. This regime was followed by the liberation of Athens by another Demetrius, Antigonus' son, and the restoration of the old democracy. And while these spectacular changes were taking place in Athens, a new strong man had appeared in the west, Agathocles of Syracuse, whose enmity towards Timaeus prevented any thought of a return to Sicily until the tyrant's death in 289 B.C.

Deprived of the possibility of a public career Timaeus turned to writing and decided to become a historian. He is credited with three separate historical works: An *Olympionicae*; the *Pyrrhic Wars*; and his *History* (perhaps called *Sicelica*) in thirty-eight books.[74] Other separate works are possible though such putative titles are more likely to refer to parts of his major history. The problem cannot be solved at present, because we do not have enough information about the internal organization of his *History*.[75] Before taking up the *History* a few words may be said about the minor works.

Not enough is left of the *Pyrrhic Wars* for discussion here. It falls within the time period of his general history, bridging the gap, as it were, between the death of Agathocles and the First Punic War, and conceivably Timaeus regarded it in that light. We cannot tell. The *Olympionicae*, on the other hand, was in all probability a preliminary work, a historical monograph in which the historian demonstrated his professional competence. We have already seen that the historian Callisthenes, along with Aristotle, was honored in a Delphian inscription for working up a list of victors in the Pythian Games,[76] and Aristotle himself had also written an *Olympionicae*.[77] Why, then, did it need to be done over again? As happens so often with Timaeus, we learn most about him from his bitterest critic, Polybius, who writes:

For this [i.e., Timaeus] is the man who made a tabulation from the beginning of the ephors and the kings in Lacedaemon, of the archons in Athens and the priestesses in Argos, setting them against the Olympic victors, and refuting the errors in the city records which amounted to more than three months. And Timaeus is also the one who discovered the stelae in the back of the building, as well as the proxeny inscriptions on the door jambs of the temple.[78]

Timaeus, then, was trying to work out a chronological pattern to which all historical events could be referred, and he was probably the first to make use of the Olympiads as a general basis for dating. This was a great service, and Eratosthenes later adopted it as his own. Whether Timaeus also regarded the first Olympic festival (776 B.C.) as the dividing line between history and prehistory we do not know, but it seems likely that he did. Eratosthenes probably accepted this also, though his most famous date, that for the Fall of Troy (1184 B.C.) was tacked on to the Olympic era by counting backwards by generations.[79] This Olympic era, invented by Timaeus, has a long history, and we have already encountered it frequently in the many citations about historians in Photius and the *Suda.* Unfortunately it remained only a scholar's device, never spreading to popular usage as modern eras such as the Christian or the Mohammedan have done, though we can be thankful that Polybius, and after him Diodorus Siculus did adopt it. Archon dating is much less satisfactory, because it presupposes a complete list of the eponymous archons, while the Olympic era deals in numbers. Polybius' comment makes it quite certain that Timaeus was not merely an armchair historian. He must have made trips away from Athens to obtain his data, trips that took him at the very least to Olympia, Argos, Sparta, and Locris. Perhaps he continued on further on the homeward track as far as Corcyra, in which he later shows a considerable interest.[80] Be that as it may, the *Olympionicae* establishes Timaeus' reputation as a meticulous scholar with a professional interest in documents and chronology. And now let us see how he made use of his technical skills in writing a general history.

Although we cannot begin to restore a Table of Contents for the *History,* there are a number of clues. According to Polybius, Timaeus wrote only about Italy, Sicily, and Africa; though Agatharchides is probably more accurate in calling him a historian of the West.[81] According to Dionysius of Halicarnassus, Timaeus was the first Greek to write about Roman history, except for Hieronymus of Cardia.[82] He included the history of colonization in the West as well as a great deal of legendary material. Jacoby believes all this served as a five-book introduction to the main work,[83] and there are also one or two specific references to later books that help. For example, Book X is cited for the events of 493/492 B.C.; Book XIII for 415 B.C.; and Book XXII for Dionysius the Younger. The history of Agathocles, according to Diodorus, falls in the last five books.[84] But Timaeus was given to digressing at any point and on any subject that happened to occur to him, which makes it virtually impossible to assign passages to a particular book on the basis of context alone. For example, the sixth century Pythagoras is discussed in Book X, while Timaeus refers to Socrates, who lived in the fifth century, in Book IX. His discursive style and avid interest in details led to his being called *graosyllektria,* or "Old Chatterbox."[85] If such an epithet were used of Herodotus we could refute it, but the extant passages from Timaeus are insufficient to prove anything. He did include details on an enormous number of subjects, but these details may have been related to a well thought out social and political history of the West. In contrast with Megasthenes, Timaeus brings us back to the normal Greek historical tradition in which the historian mentions earlier writers chiefly with a view to raking them over the coals. Herodotus had done this with Hecataeus, Thucydides with Hellanicus, Ctesias with Herodotus, and Theopompus with almost everyone. So effective was the historian from Tauromenium in this respect that he was often referred to as *epitimaeus,* a punning equivalent of "Fault-finder."[86] Nearly a hundred years later another scholar, Polemon the Periegete, wrote a twelve-book work attacking Timaeus; but save for one or two fragments this critique has been lost. Polybius, who began the western part of his own history where Timaeus left off, more than makes up for the lost treatise of Polemon. Polybius devotes almost all of Book XII, of which a good deal remains, to abusing Timaeus.[87] Polybius was constitutionally unable to appreciate Timaeus, whose approach to history was utterly different from his own. Like Thucydides, Polybius regarded political history as all-important, and even political history as unrewarding when it concerns a period before the historian's own time. He also had all the contempt some modern scholars have shown for the *Kultur Historiker*—the social and intellectual historian. He cannot forgive Timaeus for being a spectator rather than an actor. Any historian worthy of the name should have first-hand experience in the two things in life that really matter, public office and warfare. Timaeus had neither.[88]

We will turn now to some of the fragments from Timaeus that illustrate the breadth of his interests and something of his point of view. As a historian he could not very well neglect geography, and as a Sicilian he appears to have had a particular interest in islands, some of which is reflected in Diodorus' Fifth Book.[89] One of the islands that attracted him was Sardinia. The island was originally called "Sandaliotis" because of its shape, while in size it is comparable with Sicily.[90] Timaeus goes on to give the legendary history of the island. Sardinia was first colonized by a mixed population of Greeks and barbarians under the leadership of Ioläus, Heracles' nephew. The Greeks were called Thespiaeans, being the descendants of Heracles and the daughters of Thespius. Under orders from Heracles Ioläus, built cities there, complete with temples, gymnasiums, and the other amenities of civilized living; and he named the inhabitants Ioläeis after himself. An oracle predicted that they would always remain free. Presently Ioläus returned to Greece, and the other Greeks were subsequently driven out. They fled to Italy where they settled down near Cyme. But the oracle proved correct. Those colonists who remained occupied the rough interior of Sardinia. Even the Carthaginians who took over the island were unable to conquer them, thanks to their building their houses underground. Timaeus reports them as still independent, though thoroughly barbarized, and governed by leaders whom they have chosen from their own numbers.[91]

From this example we see how Timaeus brings his story down from legendary days to the present. There is no reason to believe he ever saw the underground houses he refers to, and it is possible they serve the double purpose of vindicating the oracle and explaining why the Carthaginians have not been able to subdue them. Diodorus adds as his own contribution, that the Romans also have not been able to conquer them. We have here a literary convention, by which an oracle must be fulfilled. Neither Timaeus nor Diodorus needed to go to Sardinia to write this account.

But there is something more in Timaeus than the fulfillment of an oracle. There is also a theory of progressive deterioration. The civilized Hellenic life with its temples and gymnasiums has gone, the Carthaginians have taken over, and the remnants of the older population have become brutalized. An example of this comes from another fragment, where we learn that the natives of Sardinia, when they decide their parents are too old to live any longer, take them away to a certain area, where they dig graves for them. Then each man clubs his own father and thrusts him into his grave. The old men, knowing what is coming, laugh, yet it is a laughter mixed with pain. From this practice arose the expression "Sardonic laughter."[92]

Timaeus' interest in the barbarians of the West takes him even further afield than Sardinia. One of the truly great discoverers of antiquity was Pytheas of Massilia, who sailed from his native city beyond Spain and through the Straits of Gibraltar all the way around to Britain and beyond. Because the Carthaginians tried to prevent others, particularly Greek sailors, from sailing westward, it has been argued that Pytheas must have made his voyage in the years 310–306 B.C., when Carthage was too busy dealing with Agathocles to police the approach to the Straits;[93] but this is not convincing. The ancients could never maintain a tight naval blockade. The fact is that few Greeks cared much for sea exploration. A determined man like Pytheas need not wait for Carthage to be at war. More important in dating him is that Aristotle does not refer to his famous voyage, while Aristotle's pupil Dicaearchus does.[94] Pytheas, then, was an older contemporary of Timaeus, and most Greek writers, including Dicaearchus and Polybius regarded him as a liar.[95] However, Timaeus did accept Pytheas' account of Britain, and in doing so finds himself in good company later with Eratosthenes and Posidonius.[96] But although he makes use of Pytheas he does not always accept his conclusions, preferring an explanation of his own for the ocean tides. Pytheas connected tides with the moon but Timaeus thought they were caused by the flow of rivers entering the Atlantic Ocean through the Celtic Mountains.[97]

Western colonization must have been treated at considerable length, both Greek and barbarian, with a distinction being made between heroic times and the historical period. Timaeus made a good deal of use of the epic tales, especially those describing the return of the heroes after the Fall of Troy, to explain the arrival of Greeks in Sicily and Magna Graecia. An example we still have concerns Diomedes, who returned to Argos to a hostile wife, Aegialeia. More fortunate than his comrade-in-arms Agamemnon, he managed to escape. He turned his ship's prow to the west until he reached Italy where, after numerous adventures, he died.[98] Timaeus also used the story of the Argonauts, whose return journey from Colchis lent itself to many different interpretations. Instead of coming back through the Dardanelles they sailed up the Tanais River (the Don?) to its source, then carried their ship overland to another river, down which they sailed to outer ocean. From there they continued on around to the west and then south, entering the Mediterranean by way of the Straits of Gibraltar. Various place names were pointed out by the historian as indicative of the presence of the Argonauts. They reached the island of Aethaleia (i.e., Elba) whose harbor they called Argous after their ship. Jason and Medea were married in Corcyra. In this version of the Medea story, as also in the localization of the Rape of Persephone on the island of Sicily,[99] there is evidence of patriotic feeling. This does not mean Timaeus was the first to give these versions, it does indicate that his choice among many varying accounts was motivated by his pride as a western Greek and his desire to show that the West shared fully in the common Hellenic heritage.

Coming down into the historical period it is interesting to find that Timaeus holds that Carthage and Rome were colonized the same year, and that this colonization took place in the thirty-eighth year before the first Olympiad, that is in 814/813 B.C.[100] This means that the famous story of Aeneas' visiting the newly founded city of Carthage becomes impossible. In fact the historian has a different version which presumably comes from a Phoenician source, the Tyrian history, which Polybius says he used.[101] Carthage was founded by Theiosso, which is the Phoenician equivalent of Elissa, according to Timaeus. When her husband was slain by her brother Pygmalion, the King of Tyre, she fled along with some other Tyrian citizens to find a new home. Arriving in Libya, where the natives called her "Deido" (presumably because of her long wanderings in "terror" of her brother), she built the city of Carthage. Later, to avoid marrying a Libyan king she threw herself from the window of her chamber on to a burning pyre which she had prepared. This date for Carthage is surprisingly late, and Timaeus must have felt that his Phoenician evidence was compelling. The synchronism with Rome he also accepted. Therefore Rome, too, must be founded later. The dean of Sicilian historians was Antiochus of Syracuse, a fifth century writer who belongs somewhere in the brief interlude between Herodotus and Thucydides. Antiochus had put the founding of Rome even before the arrival of Aeneas in Italy, according to Dionysius of Halicarnassus.[102] Evidently Timaeus does not mean the original settlement on the site of Rome, but the final colonization. He is a believer in Trojan colonization in the West, for he not only refers to Trojan pottery which was to be seen in the temple of Lavinium, but he describes a strange Roman custom of shooting down a warhorse each year in the Campus Martius, in commemoration of the betrayal of Troy by the wooden horse.[103]

For a Sicilian historian, the victory of Gelon over the Carthaginians at Himera in 480 B.C. was so glorious as to counteract the fact that this battle was won under the leadership of a tyrant. One of Timaeus' predecessors, Philistus, went even farther. In looking backwards he apparently decided that this was no accident, that tyranny was the form of government that might, in his own day, revive the greatness Syracuse once had under Gelon and Hieron. Accordingly Philistus became the historian of Sicily as well as the strong supporter of the tyranny of both Dionysiuses. Timaeus seems to have taken no dogmatic position on tyranny as an institution—after all his father had held a similar position in Tauromenium—but he wrote in glowing terms of the achievements of Gelon, with critical sharpness on both Dionysiuses, and with concentrated venom on Agathocles, the tyrant whose reign prolonged his own exile in Athens. Pindar, who spent some time in Sicily during the period of the early tyrants, likes to enhance his poems on the victors in the games with historical allusions. The scholiast on Pindar, writing when these allusions were no longer clear to his readers, attempts to explain them, and in doing so frequently has recourse to Timaeus' History. That is how we learn about Timaeus' favorable treatment of Gelon. One example is worth citing. Timaeus reported that Carthage actually acknowledged the overlordship of Gelon and agreed to pay tribute to Syracuse.[104] This makes it likely that Diodorus' account of the Carthaginian attack and defeat in 480 B.C. owes much to Timaeus, though it is also evident that he used other sources as well.[105] The chances are that Timaeus, Antiochus, and Philistus all presented Gelon in a favorable light.[106]

The next great moment for a Sicilian historian was the crushing defeat of the Athenian expedition against Syracuse. Thucydides' account, though that of an Athenian, was remarkably fair to Syracuse, so much so in fact that Philistus, an eyewitness of the events, is said to have based his own narrative entirely on that of Thucydides.[107] Timaeus, however, went his own way. He disagrees with Thucydides and Philistus on the fate of the captured Athenian generals Nicias and Demosthenes, for they both blamed the generals' deaths on the Syracusans (despite Gylippus' intervention in their behalf), while Timaeus has Hermocrates humanely provide them with the means of committing suicide.[108] Timaeus consistently belittles Gylippus for his low character. And of course Gylippus' later difficulties over attempted embezzlement support his judgment. However, there is every reason to believe that his military contribution to a Syracusan victory was a decisive one. It is strange under these circumstances that Timaeus should have written favorably of Alcibiades![109] Plutarch rightly upbraids him for what must be admitted to be a major fault in a historian, his descending to a play on words or to an obscure mythological allusion in the midst of important events. Timaeus made much of the fact that the *Hermocopidae*—those unknown rioters who mutilated the images of Hermes that stood before so many Athenian houses on the eve of the Syracusan expedition—are appropriately revenged by a Syracusan named after Hermes (Hermocrates). And he also sees Heracles as aiding Syracuse because Athens had come to the aid of Egesta, whose inhabitants were descendants of the ancient Trojans![110] If there was a great deal of this sort of thing, it is easy to see why Timaeus' thirty-eight books have not come down to us intact.

The feelings of patriotic pride aroused by the defeat of the Athenian naval expedition did not last very long. Party strife in Syracuse led to the exile of their great leader Hermocrates and the establishment of a radical democracy by his enemies. At the same time the feelings of good will that had united the other Siceliotes with Syracuse disappeared with the emergency that had created it. This time, finding no Greek city able and willing to help them Egesta appealed to Carthage for aid against her old enemy Selinus. The result was another large-scale Carthaginian attack on Greek Sicily which exacted an adequate though belated revenge for the Battle of Himera. One Greek city after another was taken and destroyed: Selinus, Himera, and most shocking of all the second city in Sicily, Acragas. One of the most illuminating passages we have from Timaeus comes from Book XV, where he describes Acragas in these words:

*In those days both the city and the countryside of the Acragantines were in a flourishing condition . . . most of the land was planted with olive trees; from these they harvested a plentiful crop which they used to sell in Carthage. . . . Many proofs of their wealth remain, and it will not be unprofitable to mention them briefly. 82 The sacred buildings, particularly the temple of Zeus, show the magnificence of the men of that time. Of the other buildings some were burned and others completely destroyed, because the city was frequently sacked. But the war prevented them from putting a roof over the Olympeium, and after the city was destroyed the Acragantines of later date were never able to finish the building. The temple has a length of 340 feet, a width of 60 feet and a height of 120 feet, not counting the foundation. It is the largest temple in Sicily, and one might reasonably compare it with temples elsewhere in terms of the magnitude of the undertaking. [A description follows—including the circumference of the columns as 20 feet, with room for a man to fit inside the fluting.]*

. . . .

*At that time there was an artificial lake outside the city, made nearly a mile around and 30 feet in depth. Introducing water into it, they also added a vast number of fish for the public festivals; swans lived there, too, and large numbers of other birds, such as to give great joy to those who beheld them. Their luxuriousness was also shown by the memorials they set up to their race horses, and others to the little birds kept by boys and girls in their houses . . . and in the preceding Olympics, the ninety-second (412 B.C.), in which Exaenetus of Acragas was victor, they brought him back to the city in a chariot, while, without counting the others, 300 pairs of white horses paraded with him, all belonging to the Acragantines. In general they began their luxurious living in childhood, wearing soft garments; and they wore much gold and even used scrapers and oil flasks of silver and gold.*[111]

The passage goes on to tell about the richest man in Acragas, one Gellias, who kept open house—once receiving a party of 500 horsemen who arrived during a storm. He not only entertained them but provided everyone with dry clothing. The very height of luxury, however, is associated with a certain Antisthenes, who celebrated the marriage of his daughter by feasting all of Acragas in the streets, providing lighting for the entire city and an escort of 800 carriages for the bride. He goes on to point a moral, however. All this luxury had so softened the fibre of the Acragantines that during the siege a drastic regulation was passed, limiting troops on garrison duty to one bolster, one fleece coverlet, and two pillows! Timaeus probably connects all this with the fall of the city, yet, as in his description of ancient Sybaris, we can detect a certain wistful feeling of regret for the departure of the good old days.[112]

The evil times came, nevertheless, and Timaeus attributes most of the blame to Dionysius, the hero of Timaeus' bête noir,

Philistus. There must have been a considerable literature on Dionysius and probably Timaeus had heard a good deal before he left Sicily is his youth. He tells us of a woman from Himera who dreamed she was transported to the homes of the gods, and that while she was there in heaven she noticed a large reddish man manacled beneath the throne of Zeus. When she asked who that might be her informant replied: "The scourge of Sicily and Italy, and if he is released he will destroy those lands." Later she met Dionysius escorted by his spear bearers, and recognized him as the man she had seen in her dream.[113] Timaeus was not the only one to tell this story, for we find it also in the writings of his contemporary, Heraclides Ponticus.[114] If either borrowed from the other, Heraclides probably did the borrowing. Philistus, obviously, would never have repeated such a story, because he was a loyal supporter of the tyrants, father and son. He finally died in the service of Dionysius the Younger, losing a naval battle to the rebellious Syracusans. Philistus' death is differently reported by Timonides of Leucas, by Diodorus Siculus, and by Timaeus and the differences are suggestive. Diodorus notes his bravery in battle. Afterwards, he committed suicide to avoid falling into the hands of the enemy, though his corpse was later dragged through the streets of Syracuse.[115] Timonides, a member of Plato's Academy and the friend of Dion, says that Philistus was captured alive. The Syracusans then stripped him, cut off his head, and turned his body over to boys (slaves?) with orders that it be dragged through the Achradina section of the city and thrown into the quarries.[116] Timaeus, also, says Philistus was taken alive, and then killed. His corpse was then dragged through the streets by his lame leg by young children. He adds that "all the Syracusans jeered at seeing the man who had told Dionysius he ought not to leave his tyranny on a fast horse, but only if dragged off by the leg, . . . himself dragged off by the leg."[117] This time Timaeus' prejudice blinded him to the facts, because we learn from Plutarch that Philistus mentions this drastic advice as having been given to Dionysius, not by himself but by someone else.[118]

Timaeus was, no doubt, sympathetic with Dion, not because Dion represented Plato's Academy (Timaeus accuses Plato of plagiarism[119]), but because he helped free Syracuse from the tyrant Dionysius. The one person we are certain that Timaeus approved of in every way is Timoleon. The authority of Timaeus' history in antiquity helps to explain the impossibly idealistic portrayal of Timoleon in our sources.[120]

Timaeus' delineation of the character of Dionysius the Younger is a masterpiece, as I have tried to show elsewhere.[121] His is a subtler touch than that of Theopompus in describing court life in Macedonia, there is more irony and less sarcasm. But when

COIN OF AGATHOCLES OF SYRACUSE, ca. 300 B.C.
The head on the obverse is that of Athena, while on the reverse is a winged thunderbolt with the inscription: "Of King Agathocles," whom most Greeks considered a tyrant. Until the king's death, at least, Timaeus did not dare return to Sicily.

he reaches the time of his arch enemy Agathocles, Timaeus loses all his scholarly detachment—as Polybius was quick to point out.[122] There is one excuse for him, but an insufficient one. He probably had less time to sift the evidence on Agathocles than he had in writing up Dionysius the Younger, but this does not explain the tone or the willingness to believe the worst without questioning his source of information.

Timaeus could discuss a historical question with coolness and logic, though even then he could not refrain from abusing his opponent. One such opponent was Aristotle. The dispute has to do with the Greek city of Locri in South Italy. Aristotle said Locri was founded originally by "runaway slaves, menials, adulterers and kidnappers," which Timaeus refutes by visiting the mother city in Greece, where he examined records on stone, and also by deductions he made from the institutions of the Italiot city. His research led him on to investigate the practice of sending out maidens from Greek Locris to act as priestesses of Athena in Ilium. This practice he finds as starting soon after the Fall of Troy and continuing on for 1000 years, until the end of the Phocian War (346 B.C.)—which means his own date for the Fall of Troy was an early one, about 1346 B.C. Included in his general argument against Aristotle is his view that in early days the Greeks had no purchased slaves. Right or wrong, his method is scholarly, and his points clearly made. He uses both documentary proof and arguments based on probability. As a clinching argument he maintains the Locrians could not have had a servile origin in a period before slavery was a recognized institution among the Greeks, and that is well put—provided we accept his premise.[123] His rather unpleasant remarks about Aristotle probably fit the period of Alexander's conquests. Aristotle was not liked in Athens, particularly during the years after Granicus before the Athenian prisoners-of-war were released. When Timaeus speaks of Aristotle as "a pedantic and detestable sophist just removed from his glorious surgery," and when he sneers at him for taking Hesiod's advice and living with one of the servant maids after his wife died, he probably reflects contemporary malicious gossip in Athens.[124]

With Timaeus, we reach the end of an era in Greek historiography. The second century historians are not less sharp in their criticism of other writers, but they are conditioned in what they say by a new wariness, to avoid giving offense to the powers that be. Timaeus was perhaps the last historian we know who wrote entirely to please himself. When the conditions that made that possible changed in the next century this also brought about a change in the Greek tradition of historical writing. There would be even more learned historians in the future than there had been in the past—men like Posidonius, Alexander Polyhistor, and Nicolaus of Damascus—but without complete freedom to write as the individual historian saw fit there would not be another Herodotus.

### Notes for Chapter Six

1. See E. Bevan, "Hellenistic Popular Philosophy," in *The Hellenistic Age*, by J. B. Bury et al. (London, 1925), 79–80.
2. For different views on Hieronymus, see: F. Jacoby, "Hieronymus" (10), *PW* viii. 1540–1561; W. W. Tarn, *Antigonos Gonatas*, 1912 (Chicago reprint, 1969), 246–247, 411; R. Schubert, *Quellen zur Geschichte der Diadochenzeit* (Leipzig, 1914), 659; T. S. Brown, in *Amer. Hist. Rev.* 52 (1947), 684 ff.
3. For Dicaearchus, see Wehrli, *Die Schule des Aristoteles*, No. 1: *Dikaiarchos* (Basel, 1944), fr. 1; for Duris references, see now M. von Albrecht, "Duris" (1), *Kl. Pauly* 1967, ii. 181 f.; on Aristoxenus see Wehrli, op. cit., no. 2: *Aristoxenos*, esp. frs. 10a–b, 71–89; for Phylarchus, T. W. Africa, *Phylarchus and the Spartan Revolution* (Los Angeles, 1961).
4. See W. W. Tarn, *The Greeks in Bactria and India*, 2nd ed. (London, 1951); cf. F. W. Walbank, *A Historical Commentary on Polybius* (Oxford, 1967), II, 313; also H. E. Schmitt, *Untersuchungen zur Geschichte Antiochos' des Grossen und seiner Zeit*, Einzelschrift No. 6 of *Historia*, Wiesbaden 1964, 64–86.
5. See *Suda* s.v. Θαρσεῖς (55).
6. See *FGrH* iii c, 2, no. 715. We still have E. A. Schwanbeck's *Megasthenes Indica*, 1846 (Chicago reprint, 1967), which has full discussion. Two solid studies on Megasthenes are B. C. J. Timmer, *Megasthenes en de Indische Maatschappij* (Amsterdam, 1930), which is confined to his account of Indian society and institutions, and not concerned with geography; and O. Stein, "Megasthenes," (2), *PW* xv. 230–326. See also my articles in *AJPhil.* 76 (1955), 18–33 and in *Phoenix* 1957, XI 12–24. The fragments of Megasthenes are most of them available in English translation in B. C. Majumdar, *The Classical Accounts of India* (Calcutta, 1960). However, Majumdar gives a translation of the extant writers; Megasthenes must be run down through the index. For a recent view see J. D. M. Derrett, "Megasthenes," *Kl. Pauly* 1969, iii, 1150–1154.
7. See *FGrH* 715. T 1 and T 2a.
8. No one argues that Megasthenes visited King Porus, who had died long before. The reference is a holdover from the Alexander historians. Porus had impressed Alexander, therefore he was important. See Timmer, *Megasth.*, 5 for discussion; also Schwanbeck, *Meg. Ind.*, 22. Jacoby accepts Schwanbeck's emendation, so does Roos in the Teubner ed. of Arrian.
9. See Stein, *PW* xv. 232, for dates of Sandrocottus; also A. K. Narain, "Sandracottus," in *OCD²*, 949 f.

10. See Diod. Sic. xx. 113. 4 for the elephants; also on their importance at Ipsus, see Plut. *Dem.* 29.
11. See Strabo ii. 1. 9 = *FGrH* 715. T 4. For Arrian and Pliny, see *FGrH* 715. T 6a–b and T 7a–c.
12. For his skepticism see Strabo (who disagrees) i. 2. 12–14.
13. Only four references give the book number, and one of these is corrupt (*FGrH* 715. F 1; see *ap. crit.*).
14. See *FGrH* 715. F 4 = Diod. Sic. ii. 35. 1; *FGrH* 715. F 6c = Strabo xv. 1.11.
15. The stade varies considerably—see J. O. Thomson, *History of Ancient Geography* (London, 1948), 161—so there is little point in trying to estimate this measurement in modern terms. On the source of the 10,000 stade measurement see Jacoby, *FGrH* ii d. 406–409, for discussion of the Bematists ("road measurers") in general, and ii b. (Baeton) 119. F 6, for this passage in particular.
16. See *Phoenix* (1957), 18–20 for discussion.
17. See *FGrH* 715. F 6b.
18. See Arr. *Ind.* 4. 13.
19. Arr. *Ind.* 4. 7 = *FGrH* 715. F 9a.
20. See Strabo xv. 1. 35 = *FGrH* 715. F 9b.
21. See Strabo xv. 1. 35. Jacoby attributes this to Pseudo-Craterus, an Alexander historian who wrote not long after Megasthenes (*FGrH* 153. F 2, and see *FGrH* ii d. 540 for his comment).
22. See *FGrH* 715. F 9a *ad fin.* for the 58 rivers; and F 10a for the Silas river in which nothing will float. Ctesias had such a view also, see Chapter 4, p. 82, n. 47. A growth in credulity rather than its diminution is shown by the fact that Democritus (who lived earlier than Ctesias) did not admit the possibility of such a river. Megasthenes, however, believes in it and Strabo (despite Aristotle's skepticism) clearly wants to accept it (see *FGrH* 715. F 10b, where Jacoby cites Democritus [Diels, *Vorsokratiker*[5], no. 68, fr. A 12]. Strabo should have known better as a professional geographer—but he argues that water might be too "thin" for anything to float, just as in some places the air is too light for a bird to fly.
23. See Diod. Sic. ii. 36 = *FGrH* 715. F 4; Strabo xv. 1. 20 = *FGrH* 715. F 8.
24. *FGrH* 715. F 4 (c. 36); as to Indian men, Porus was "over 5 cubits tall" (7½ feet)—see Arr. *Anab.* v. 19. 1.
25. See *FGrH* 715. F 11a–b.
26. *FGrH* 715. F 12 = Arr. *Ind.* 7. 2–4.
27. See Hdt. iv. i–144 for his account of Scythia; see also the discussion of this in the Budé edition of Herodotus by Ph.-E. Legrand (*Hérodote: Histoires IV,* 3rd ed. (Paris, 1960), 15–45).
28. See Thuc. i. 2–23 (*Archaeologia*) and Chapter 3 above, p. 51.
29. See Strabo xi. 11. 3 = *FGrH* (Onesicritus) 134. F 5; also the Indian sage's remark that it would be advantageous to have someone in authority who would persuade those who would listen and force those who would not, to behave properly—*FGrH* 134. F 17 = Strabo xv. 1. 64.
30. For the fragments of Hecataeus of Abdera see *FGrH* no. 264; and for Jacoby's comments, ibid., iii a, esp. 75–87 (on F 25). The general drift can still be seen in Diod. Sic. i. 10–98, though considerable extraneous material is also included. For Euhemerus see *FGrH* no. 63; see H. Dörrie, "Euhemeros," *Kl. Pauly* i. 414 f. for further references.
31. *FGrH* 715 F 12 (Arr. *Ind.* 7. 8–9)—where the use of drums and cymbals by Indian soldiers is traced back to Dionysus.
32. See *FGrH* 715. F 13a = Arr. *Ind.* 9.
33. See Arr. *Ind.* 8.
34. See Derrett, *Kl. Pauly* iii. 1151 for a charitable view on Megasthenes; on the *Arthashastra*, see Timmer, *Megasth.,* 51 f.
35. See *FGrH* 715. FF 4 (Diod. Sic. ii. 40), 19a (Arr. *Ind.* 11–12), 19b (Strabo xv. 1. 39–41, 46–49).
36. *FGrH* 715. F 19a = *Ind.* 12. 8.
37. See Timmer, *Megasth.,* 112–113; and on the different kinds of Indian philosophers in Megasthenes (the Brahmans with their 37-year period of training and the Garmanes) 84 ff. See *FGrH* 715. F 33.

38. See *FGrH* 715. F 33.
39. See Timmer, *Megasth.*, 92.
40. On slavery, see *FGrH* 715. F 16.
41. See *FGrH* 715. F 4 = Diod. Sic. ii. 40. 4.
42. See Derrett, *Kl. Pauly* iii. 1151.
43. See *FGrH* 715. FF 18a and 18b. Megasthenes notes that cities built beside rivers are made of wood, if they were of brick they would not survive the floods and heavy rains (F 17). The idea that bricks would not survive is disproved by their successful use in early Harappa on the Ravi River (see Stuart Piggott, *Prehistoric India* (Pelican Books, 1950), 158.
44. On this see Timmer, *Megasth.*, 32–34.
45. See *FGrH* 715. F 32 = Strabo xv. 1. 55.
46. See *FGrH* 715. F 20a = Arr. *Ind.* 13–14; F 20b = Strabo xv. 1. 42.
47. On Sandrocottus' kingdom where elephants are a royal monopoly, see *FGrH* 715. F 19a (c. 40–41), where we are also told all the land belongs to the king; on the aristocracy, see F 21a. The aristocracy is suspect, as it is mentioned along with the gold-digging ants and men who live to be 200 years old, but this is from Strabo and may not indicate its original context. The elephant is no problem in Caesar's day, see his *Bellum Africanum* 72.
48. See *FGrH* 715. F 31 (c. 52).
49. Ibid.
50. See *FGrH* 715. F 31 (c. 52); also see F 19 (c. 46–47), where we hear the soldiers lead a carefree life.
51. See *FGrH* 715. F 31.
52. See ibid., F 32.
53. For camp odors, see *FGrH* 715. F 27b (c. 57) and for the spies see F 19b (c. 48).
54. Ibid., F 31 (c. 51); and F 4 (c. 42. 3).
55. Ibid.
56. E.g., he speaks of snakes big enough to swallow deer or bulls whole! (F 22); of tigers twice as large as lions, and strong enough to outpull a mule (F 21a); of an Indian dog strong enough to hold a bull by the muzzle so tightly that the bull died (F 21a *ad fin.*).
57. See *FGrH* 715. F 21c and F 23a respectively.
58. Ibid., F 27a–b.
59. Ibid., F 27b (c. 56).
60. Cf. *FGrH* 715. F 14 (c. 7) with Pliny *NH* vi. 60, who cites Megasthenes a little earlier (vi. 58); the discrepancy in the number of years cannot be explained, except that Pliny used Megasthenes indirectly, through an unknown intermediary. See Timmer, *Megasth.* 16.
61. See *FGrH* 715. F 12 (c. 7).
62. For the fragments of Timaeus see *FGrH* iii b, no. 566; and Commentary, iii b (on nos. 297–607, 2 parts—*Text* and *Noten* resp. See also T. S. Brown, *Timaeus of Tauromenium* (Los Angeles, 1958); and G. L. Barber, "Timaeus" (2), in *OCD²*, 1074.
63. See Chapter 3, n. 61 above.
64. Philinus of Agrigentum (in Sicily) did write after Timaeus, but he is not a major historian. Vicenzo La Bua has tried to restore Philinus' history by analyzing the relevant passages from Polybius and Diodorus, but he exaggerates his contribution. See his *Filino-Polybio; Sileno-Diodoro, Il problema delle fonti dalla morte di Agatocle alla guerra mercenaria in Africa*, ΣΙΚΕΛΙΚΑ III, (Palermo, 1966); see also my review in *AJPhil.* 90 (1969), 379 f.
65. On this see *FGrH* 566. T 3a = Diod. Sic. xvi. 7. 1 and T 3b = Plut. *Timol.* 10. 6. In T 3a Diodorus speaks of Andromachus of Tauromenium as Timaeus' father, therefore his lone reference elsewhere to Timaeus the Syracusan (Diod. Sic. XXI. 16. 5) need not be accepted.
66. See *FGrH* 566. T 3b.
67. Ibid., T 4a–e.
68. See Brown, *Timaeus*, 1–7. Not everyone accepts this. G. L. Barber, e.g., in *OCD²*, 1074, says Timaeus "fled to Athens perhaps as late as 317, or when he [Agathocles] seized Tauromenium (312)." But see also P. Pédech, *Polybe: Histoires Livre XII* (Paris, 1961), 127; for a noncommittal view see Walbank,

*Hist. Commentary*, II, 388 (on Polyb. xii. 25d. 1). Jacoby suggests that Timaeus never returned to Sicily because he "fühlte sich offenbar an seinen athenischen sehreibtisch ganz behaglich. . . ." Yet Jacoby, himself a historian in exile (and for comparable reasons), *did* go back (*FGrH* iii b *Text*, 532).

69. See [Lucian] *Macrob*. 22 = *FGrH* 566. T 5.
70. See *FGrH* 566. T 6a.
71. This is neither more nor less credible than Plutarch's statement that Eunomus of Thria, who had heard Pericles speak, lived long enough to compare his powers as an orator with those of Demosthenes (Plut. *Demos*. 6).
72. For Cicero see *De orat*. 2. 55/8 = *FGrH* 566. T 20 and *Brut*. 325 = T 21; for an unfavorable comment see Anon. π. ὕψ. 4 = *FGrH* 566. T 23 and Dion. Hal. *De Din*. 8.
73. See *Suda*, s.v. Τίμαιος (602); and s.vv. Φιλίσκος, Μιλήσιος ῥήτωρ.
74. The *Suda* (s.v. Τίμαιος) gives only 8 books for an *Italica and Sicelica*, which was emended by Gutschmid from η' to read λη'—also accepted by Jacoby (566 T 1)—quite reasonably, since elsewhere the *Suda* s.vv. Ὧ τὸ ἱερὸν πῦρ οὐκ ἔξεστι φυσῆσαι (263)—where Timaeus' 38th book is cited; for *On Pyrrhus' Wars*, see Dion. Hal. *Ant. Rom.* i. 6. 1 = *FGrH* 566. T 9b.
75. See Jacoby's summation, *FGrH* iii b (*Text*). 546. 1-6.
76. See Chapter 5, p. 125, and n. 107.
77. See D.L. v. 1. 26; also, for fragments, see *FHG* ii. 182 f.
78. Polyb. xii. 11. 1-3. The translation is from Brown, *Timaeus*, 11.
79. Jacoby shows this by the fragments of Eratosthenes' *Olympionicae*, *FGrH* ii b. 241. FF 1-8; see his commentary, ibid., ii d. 708. 11-17.
80. See *FGrH* 566. FF 79, 80.
81. See Polyb. xxxix. 8. 4 = *FGrH* 566. T 6b; *cf.* Agath. *De mar. rubr.* 64 = *FGrH* 566. T 14.
82. See Dion. Hal. *Ant. Rom.* i. 6. 1 = *FGrH* 566. T 9b; see also T 9c.
83. See *FGrH* iii b (*Text*). 543—though Jacoby admits certainty is impossible.
84. See *FGrH* 566. FF 18, 23, and 32 resp.; and Diod. Sic. xxi. 17. 3 = T 8.
85. See the *Suda*, s.v. Τίμαιος—LSJ suggest "gossip-monger."
86. See ibid., also Strabo xiv. 1. 22 = *FGrH* 566. T 27.
87. For Polemon's work Τὰ πρὸς Τίμαιον, see L. Preller, *Polemonis Periegetae Fragmenta*, Leipzig 1838 (reprinted in Amsterdam, 1964) 69-84; see now the Budé ed. of Polybius by P. Pédech (*Polybe, Histoires Livre XII*, Paris 1961). There is no reason to think Polemon wrote in the same abusive fashion as Polybius. He was a very learned man, himself ridiculed for his obsession with epigraphical evidence and therefore given the nickname of στηλοκόπας ("Stone-chipper"). He uses gentle humor rather than vituperation. For example, he suggests that no one who read Eratosthenes' extraordinary statements about Athens would ever suspect he had actually lived there. See F. Susemihl, *Geschichte der griechischen Literatur in der Alexandrinerzeit* (Leipzig, 1891), I, 665-676 (esp. 670 f.).
88. See, e.g., Polyb. xii. 25g. 1-3.
89. The relevant passages are found in the *FGrH* under Timaeus (566) as F 164—an appendix to the named fragments. See Jacoby's explanation, ibid., iii b (*Text*). 593.
90. See *FGrH* 566. F 63 for shape, and F 164, c. 15 for the size. The two islands are comparable, and while Sicily is now held to be larger, E. A. Freeman (*History of Sicily*, Oxford 1891, I, 2) calls Sardinia the larger.
91. See *FGrH* 566. F 164, c. 15.
92. Ibid., F 64. There are other ancient attempts to explain the expression. See Brown, *Timaeus*, 42 for discussion and references.
93. See M. Cary and E. H. Warmington, *The Ancient Explorers* 1928 (Penguin reprint, 1963), 48.
94. See ibid., 47; also Wehrli (*Die Schule des Aristoteles*), fr. 111.
95. See Strabo ii. 4. 2.
96. On Eratosthenes see ibid.; on Posidonius see H. J. Mette, *Pytheas von Massalia* (Berlin, 1952), 13-14; and D. Stichtenoth, *Pytheas von Marseille, über das Weltmeer* (Cologne and Graz, 1954), 17-18.
97. See Mette, *Pytheas*, 38; also, for Timaeus, *FGrH* 566. F 73. It is not certain

exactly what Pytheas said because his remarks reach us very indirectly and in a corrupt form. However, he was an accurate observer and must have noted the number of tides each day. In the Mediterranean generally there is very little tide, but of course that changes once you reach the Atlantic, and spectacularly so as you go farther north. Timaeus apparently had no idea of the tide rhythm, though it is barely possible his explanation, if we had it in full, might associate the flow from the rivers with the moon.

98. See FGrH 566. F 53. Strabo has more, but to what extent he is following Timaeus is uncertain (see Strabo vi. 3. 9 f.).

99. See FGrH 566. F 85; F 87; and F 164 = Diod. Sic. v. 3. 1-3.

100. See FGrH 566. F 60 = Dion. Hal. *Ant. Rom.* i. 74. 1.

101. See FGrH 566. F 7 = Polyb. xii. 28a. 3; for Timaeus' account of the founding of Carthage, see F 82. For Jacoby's comments and further references see FGrH iii b (*Text*). 574.

102. See FGrH (Antiochus) 555. F 6.

103. See FGrH 566. F 59; and, on the horse, F 36.

104. See FGrH 566. F 20 = Schol. Pindar *Pyth.* 2. 2.

105. This is discussed in T. S. Brown, "Timaeus and Diodorus' Eleventh Book," *AJPhil.* 73 (1952), 337-355.

106. Timaeus speaks of Gelon's boyhood, mentioning his faithful dog, and also his being saved from death by a wolf (*FGrH* 566. F 95). Philistus tells us the faithful dog was named Pyrrhus (*FGrH* 556. F 48).

107. See Plut. *Nic.* 1. 5 = *FGrH* (Philistus) 556. F 54.

108. See FGrH 566. F 101 = Plut. *Nic.* 28. 5. For discussion see E. A. Freeman, *History of Sicily* (Oxford, 1892), III, 711-716.

109. See FGrH 566. F 99.

110. Ibid., F 102a-b.

111. FGrH (Timaeus) 566. F 26a = Diod. Sic. xiii. 81.

112. We read, for example, ". . . among the Sybarites vats were found where they lay to enjoy steam baths. They were the first to invent chamber pots, which they carried with them to drinking parties. They jeered at those who left their native land, and took pride in growing old on the bridges of their own rivers" (*FGrH* 566. F 50).

113. Ibid., F 29.

114. See Wehrli, *Die Schule des Aristoteles*, no. 7, *Heraklides Pontikos* (Basel, 1953), fr. 133, and comments, 99 f.

115. See Diod. Sic. xvi. 16. 3-4. He is evidently following Ephorus on the suicide (see FGrH 70. F 219. See the *Suda* for still another version (s.vv. Φιλίσκος ἢ Φίλιστος) (361), in which he dies in battle.

116. See FGrH 561. F 2.

117. See FGrH 566. F 115. Incidentally, the reddish color of Dionysius as well as his lameness (historically true or not) have a pejorative significance in the physiognomy of the period. There was once a considerable literature on this. We still have an example in the Pseudo-Aristotelian *Physiognomica*.

118. See Plut. *Dion.* 35. 6. Timaeus *may* have thought Philistus was concealing his identity.

119. See FGrH 566. F 14. The remark is incidental. Timaeus is telling how Pythagoras caught Empedocles stealing from others "like Plato"—assuming of course that the "like Plato" was not added by Diogenes Laertius (D.L. viii. 54).

120. This is admirably discussed by H. D. Westlake, see his *Timoleon and his Relations with Tyrants*, University of Manchester Faculty of Arts Pub., no. 5 (Manchester, 1952); also Brown, *Timaeus*, 83-87.

121. See Brown, *Timaeus*, 17-19, 80-83.

122. See FGrH 566. F 124a-d—the first three passages are from Polybius, the last from Diodorus, who reflects him.

123. There are a number of fragments (*FGrH* no. 566) from Timaeus on this matter: F 146a, b (on the maiden priestesses in Ilium); F 11a, b (the ancient Greeks had no purchased slaves); FF 12, 156 (a long discussion of Timaeus' views on Locri and his attack on Aristotle—from Polybius). For further discussion and references see Brown, *Timaeus*, 44-50.

124. See FGrH 566. FF 156, 157.

## I. Polybius

The two historians chosen here to represent the second century B.C., like their third century predecessors Megasthenes and Timaeus, are widely separated in their geographic emphasis; Agatharchides lived in Egypt and developed a special interest in the South, while Polybius, like Timaeus, tended to view world history from a Western or rather, Greek though he was, from a Roman standpoint.[1] As Mommsen says, this puts him in a class by himself, writing for the future rather than for his own time, because few Romans were intellectually ready for his conception of history, most of them no doubt dismissing him lightly as a foreigner; the Greeks, on the other hand, felt that he was disloyal to them.[2] There is a contrast between Timaeus' development as a historian and that of Polybius. Timaeus, forced to remain in Athens for fifty years as an exile, decided to write a history dealing primarily with his own part of the world—Sicily and the West—but Polybius, a political prisoner in Rome, reacted differently. He wrote a history centered around the enemy who had uprooted him and who, while he was still at work on that project, then added all of Greece to their rapidly growing empire. The obvious parallel for Polybius among the ancient historians is surely Josephus, like him a prisoner and like him endowed with the qualities needed to attract and hold the respect of his Roman masters. Josephus also took it upon himself to persuade his fellow countrymen of the hard necessity of accepting Roman authority. But there the parallel ends. Polybius may not have been quite as learned as his opposite number, but he completely outclasses him as a historian.

    The most reliable information about Polybius' life comes from statements in his *History*, but these alone do not tell us when he was born. However, a remark he makes about the Domitian Way, which was

POLYBIUS OF MEGALOPOLIS
Though badly marred, this plaster cast of a larger than life-sized relief sculpture
is probably as close as we can ever come to a portrait of the historian. Like his
History, Polybius survives in a fragmentary state.

constructed in 118 B.C.,[3] gives us a *terminus post quem* for his death.
The *Macrobioi,* so often cited for other historians, tells us that
Polybius died at the age of eighty-two as the result of injuries
sustained in a fall from his horse, which, if correct, gives us
200 B.C. as the earliest possible date for his birth.[4]

The notice in the *Suda* is rather brief, for a writer of Polybius' standing, and even that notice strangely calls his father Lycius, while Plutarch and others give his name as Lycortas.[5] Plutarch was right. We have an inscription from Olympia expressing the gratitude of the Elians to, "Polybius the son of Lycortas from Megalopolis."[6] Polybius' father held the office of General, equivalent to our President, of the Achaean League on more than one occasion. When the news came that Philopoemen had been poisoned to death in Messenia, it was Lycortas who was chosen to lead a punitive expedition against the Messenians. Polybius accompanied him and helped bring Philopoemen's body home for burial. Many years later Polybius used his influence to prevent the Roman soldiers from smashing the statues of Philopoemen found in Corinth when that city fell.[7]

Philopoemen was sufficiently realistic to avoid a direct challenge to Rome, but the years after the Second Macedonian War show how difficult it had become for the Achaean League to follow any policy not previously sanctioned by Rome. Philopoemen advocated a policy of strict observance of all treaty obligations to Rome, but also one of avoiding consultation on matters not specified in the treaty. To go further, from his viewpoint, was servility, but the Romans came to regard the mere failure to consult as insubordination. Philopoemen died before this issue was fairly faced, but apparently Lycortas continued to represent his point of view. By the time the Third Macedonian War broke out Polybius was old enough to be elected to the second highest office, that of Hipparch of the Achaean League, but his father was beaten in his contest for the generalship by Archon, who favored helping Rome in the war. All we know about these matters we read in Polybius, who would be less than human if he failed to present his own conduct in a favorable light. Even then, his actions seem so ambiguous that we are not surprised to find him selected as one of the 1000 hostages sent back to Italy by Aemilius Paulus.[8]

But Polybius was not destined, like his fellow hostages, to be hidden away in Etruria or some other out-of-the-way locality, for he succeeded in winning the lifelong regard of Scipio Aemilianus, whose teacher he became according to the *Suda*, though his own account indicates their relationship was a less formal one.[9] This young man had been adopted into the Scipio family, but his natural father, Aemilius Paulus, undoubtedly knew something about Polybius and was responsible for his being allowed to stay in Rome. This was a particularly happy circumstance for the future historian, because Paulus seems to have had literary interests. In fact he encouraged his sons to bring back from Macedonia any books from Perseus' library that might strike their fancy.[10] We would very much like to know what selection they made. The royal library should have been well stocked, perhaps from the days of

Philip and Alexander, and may have been built up systematically by Antigonus Gonatas, who had wide cultural interests. Among the books available to Paulus' sons were probably the *Philippica* of Theopompus; the *History* of Hieronymus of Cardia; and, considering his long association with Pella, the *Politics* of Aristotle. Polybius probably took a few of his own books with him into exile, including the *Hypomnemata* of Aratus—which would also have been in Perseus' library. Philistus' historical work would already have reached Rome, in all probability after the Fall of Syracuse in 211 B.C., if not before. One way and another, considerable library resources were available in Rome to any friend of the Scipios.

Like Ctesias, Polybius found himself in exile for some seventeen years before he was allowed to return home in 150 B.C., along with three hundred other surviving hostages. During these exile years his young friend Scipio Aemilianus began to make a reputation, beginning as a volunteer *legatus* under Lucullus in the unpopular Spanish war. Sent by his commander on a special mission to Masinissa for elephants, he was probably accompanied by Polybius.[11]

Another episode in which Polybius is known to have played a part during this period concerns the Seleucid prince, Demetrius, held in Rome as a hostage. He made his escape on the advice of Polybius and with the aid of a man recommended to him by the historian. All this is described in the *History*.[12] Von Fritz remarks that, "there can hardly be any doubt that Polybius acted with the knowledge and approval of his high ranking Roman friends,"[13] and this is true. Although the younger Scipio was not yet a member of the Senate, his father Aemilius Paulus was still alive, and obviously enjoyed enormous prestige. This suggests that Aemilius Paulus may have had a special interest in Polybius, even before the defeat of Perseus. Polybius' role during the Third Macedonian War is obscure. We do know he was caught between the rivalry of two Roman commanders,[14] and he may have come to Paulus' attention in consequence of his behavior on that occasion. Polybius was the last man in the world to engage in a quixotic enterprise. It is worth noting that when the actual day came around for Demetrius to make his escape, Polybius was too ill to leave his bed.[15]

Polybius, who had not been forced to stay on limits, like his fellow exiles, was free, as they were, to return home in 150 B.C.; but his expatriation was not yet ended. He joined Scipio during the Third Punic War and was present when Carthage fell. Shortly thereafter he undertook the delicate task of intermediary, to obtain what concessions he could for the Greeks after the Roman destruction of Corinth. His efforts were appreciated; and many Greek cities honored him, including Elis, whose inscription at Olympia has already been alluded to.[16] It was probably in this late period that Polybius visited—and disliked—Alexandria in Egypt, perhaps with Scipio, perhaps on his own.[17] Polybius also sailed beyond the Straits of Gibraltar and along the Atlantic coasts of Spain and Africa. He made other trips, though we do not know exactly where he went or at what times. For our purposes it is sufficient to establish that he became expert in practical geography with a Roman's eye for a suitable campsite, or for the topographical details necessary to understand current and past military operations. He also read on the subject, and was evidently familiar with the works of Strato of Lampsacus, and others.[18]

These are the external facts of Polybius' life, and while they show that he had unusual opportunities for gathering information for a history, they do not tell us when he decided to become a historian and what induced him to do so. In addition to the *History* Polybius is credited with three other works: a treatise on *Tactics*, a *Life of Philopoemen*, and a monograph *On the Habitability of the Tropics*,[19] but none of these survives, and they are of interest here merely as indicating the narrow range of Polybius' interests. The *Philopoemen* represents a rather emotional tie with the past, the hero of his youth, while the other two works are highly technical. They show that the author had mastered two important historical aids, geography and military science. Both play a major role in history as Polybius conceives it, but neither explains why the historian decided to write a work of monumental proportions on a period of just fifty-three years from 220 B.C. to 167 B.C., a period which was later extended to include a narrative of events through 146 B.C., when the Romans have assumed a direct responsibility for the government of Macedonia and Greece. The *History* contained forty books. Today we still have the first five pretty well complete, with excerpts of greatly varying size for the other books. Yet even so it is an impressive torso, much larger than the complete Herodotus or Thucydides, or than all the historical works of Xenophon.

Scholars will probably never agree on the details of composition, but there are certain fixed points. The idea that the entire *History* was written after 146 B.C. should be abandoned. Everything suggests an original plan to end with 167 B.C., and then a revised plan for going on to 146 B.C. Another established point is that the *History* was brought out in installments. This is a complicated matter which need not be argued again. One article by Maurice Holleaux will suffice as an illustration. Holleaux noted, as others had before him, that Polybius' digression in Book V on the Rhodian earthquake and the generosity of the kings and cities of that time in coming to the rescue, is out of context,[20] because the earthquake cannot have been later than 226 B.C., while Polybius is discussing the period of the Battle of Raphia, in 217 B.C. Nor does his narrative of the earlier period allude to the earthquake. Holleaux argues that Polybius has been angered by some recent example of niggardliness on the part of states in his time. Therefore he wishes to rebuke them by holding up this example of past generosity. The time to have made his point was while he was writing about Rhodes in Book IV. But it is now too late for that *because Book IV had already been published*—and *a fortiori* Books I–III. This means that the *History* came out in installments, some of them at least during the lifetime of the author. On the other hand, the work was not all published before his death because of the eulogy of the author in Book XXXIX. We still have no fixed dates. We do not know, for example, what incident of stinginess it was that aroused his anger and moved him to insert this *exemplum* on Rhodes, though Holleaux does provide us with examples of grudging generosity documented by inscriptions.[21] We do know that in the Preface to Book III in its present form Polybius refers to the revised 146 B.C. plan.

Considering Polybius' practical cast of mind the idea of writing a general history on the fifty-three years may have begun to germinate about the time of Pydna and the events that immediately ensued. His own political career, already well launched, was apparently at an end and he was obliged to adapt himself to a completely new existence as a hostage, and for an indefinite period.[22] This must have given a man of his ability and self-esteem a good deal to think about. From reflecting on what had happened to himself he may well have been led to consider the reasons for it, and as he continued to mull this over in his mind during the leisure that was momentarily his he may have rehearsed the details of Achaean policy, which undoubtedly were impressed on his memory. From Achaean policy it was only a step to the policies of her enemies, including Rome. The more Polybius learned about Rome from reading, and from what he saw in the circle of the influential politicians known to Aemilius Paulus, the more he seems to have been impressed, both by the power of Rome and by the effectiveness of her political institutions. This is reflected in the *History*, most obviously in Book VI. While we would like to know what influence the destruction of Corinth in 146 B.C. may have had on his thinking, there is no evidence, despite ingenious efforts of scholars to read between the lines. We do not even know when he decided to revise his original plan.

The first two books of the *History* are introductory, serving to provide his Greek readers with a background in Roman and Carthaginian history from the time the Romans first crossed over into Sicily (264 B.C.) where Timaeus breaks off, down to the 140th Olympiad (I. 5). Unlike the earliest historians Polybius does not name himself in the Preface, nor to the best of my knowledge is there any unambiguous allusion to himself in the first two books. By Book III this reticence begins to recede, for example when he speaks of his travels in Spain, Africa, and Gaul and his voyages along their outer coasts (III. 59), while still later he does mention himself by name. He tells us a very personal story of his early acquaintance with the Younger Scipio (XXXI. 23 f.); mentions how he came to know the Seleucid Demetrius because of a common love for boar hunting (XXXI. 14. 3); reports an encounter with Cato the Censor in which Cato sets him down rather neatly with a Homeric reference (XXXV. 6); and finally he apologizes for making so much use of his own name because he was the only person in his time who bore that name (XXXVI. 12). It looks as though the later Polybius had more self-confidence than the historian who speaks to us in the original Preface about the advantages of history to enable one to put up with the vicissitudes of life (I. 1. 2). This may be a commonplace, but that does not mean Polybius did not apply it to himself. In the very same breath as it were, he also expatiates on the practical advantages of the study of history for future statesmen. His eloquent argument for writing about the fifty-three years as a key period in history is well known and need not be repeated. It sets him apart from historians like Xenophon or Ctesias, and puts him on a line with Herodotus and Thucydides, for like them he has picked a subject with an organic unity of its own. He felt that in this period the histories of all the Mediterranean peoples merged into the history of Rome.

In Book I Polybius promises that at a suitable point he will interrupt the narrative in order to give an account of Rome's political institutions, which he regards as far too important to be treated merely in passing (I. 64. 2); the promise was made good in Book VI.

Another Polybian characteristic also meets us in the first book, and that is his habit of including a critical discussion of other writers. Later on the author frequently attacks historians whose works do not even overlap with his own, but his remarks about Philinus and Fabius Pictor in Book I are both more relevant and less acrimonious than the critique of Timaeus in Book XII. Polybius notes the prejudices of each, Philinus in favor of Carthage and Fabius in favor of Rome.[23]

The account of the First Punic War, though intended merely as an introduction, remains the most reliable account we have. However, it does not reveal Polybius at his best, because he is less interested in explaining events than in providing a launching platform for Book III where the *History* really begins. This is probably why Jacoby accuses him of combining his two chief sources in a rather mechanical fashion.[24] But even this first book offers examples of his ability to describe incidents so vividly that they leave a lasting impression. One of these is his account of the blockade runner at Lilybaeum.[25]

In Book II, which includes the period between the First and Second Punic Wars, he picks up the threads of Greek history, which furnishes him with a pretext for discussing two earlier historians, Phylarchus and Aratus of Sicyon. Aratus was the leading statesman of the Achaean League who made its influence felt throughout the Greek world, first as the enemy, then later as the ally of Macedon. It was Aratus who drove tyranny out of the Peloponnese, freeing one city-state after another, yet who in the end accepted Macedonian rule rather than submit to the ever more popular leadership of Cleomenes of Sparta. This about-face determined the future of the Achaean League, and of course Polybius was later elected Hipparch in that league. Aratus' *Memoirs* (*hypomnemata*) presumably covered the entire public career of the author, at least through the Cleomenic War. Phylarchus, on the other hand, described events from the point of view of King Cleomenes and his Spartan friends.[26] Here Polybius attempts no impartial evaluation, as he had with Philinus and Fabius Pictor: he praises Aratus without qualification and excoriates Phylarchus.[27] He seems to have forgotten what he said earlier about how it was the duty of a historian to praise his country's enemies, when the occasion calls for it, and to blame his most intimate friends.[28] It is difficult, in fact, to find an instance where he has put this sage advice into practice. There is one apparent exception. He tells us of his specially cordial feelings towards the Locrians of Italy. He had interceded for them and persuaded the Roman government to exempt them from the requirement of sending military aid, in gratitude for which he was publicly honored by Locri.[29] Nevertheless he finds it necessary to prove that Timaeus was wrong in denying the servile origins of Locri and that Aristotle was correct.[30] But this is not an example of the historian's impartiality. Far from it. His desire to discredit Timaeus is simply stronger than his sense of loyalty to his Italiot friends. Although no one has written more understandingly than Polybius about the high standards required of a historian, he fails to live up to them. The discrepancy is too great to be explained as hypocrisy. This was Polybius' blind side. He can be very perceptive in analyzing the motives of others; his own apparently eluded him.

In Book III Polybius reminds us that the introduction is now ended and the *History* proper is about to begin. He lists the high points down to the dissolution of the Macedonian kingdom, by which time the Romans clearly have made themselves the masters of the civilized world (III. 1–3). But then comes an unexpected addition. He has now decided not to stop as originally planned, but to continue the narrative on down to the "final defeat for all of Greece," that is to 146 B.C. (III. 4–5. 6). Polybius remarks that this new task will take time to complete, but that if he does not live to do so there will be others to finish it (III. 5. 8). More interesting than this announcement is Polybius' exposition of his views on causation. It is as though the historian has shifted his emphasis from explaining the conquest of the world by Rome in fifty-three years to the wider question of what makes history happen. He builds his explanation around three terms: "cause" (*aitia*), "pretext" (*prophasis*) and "beginning" (*archē*). And before applying his new theory to the Hannibalic War, Polybius gives us an example from another period to illustrate his terminology. He chooses the conquest of Persia by Macedonia. For this he finds two "causes": first, the inability of Persia to prevent Xenophon's 10,000 Greeks from getting away, which revealed her weakness; and second, the expedition of Agesilaus, abandoned because of troubles at home rather than Persian resistance, which confirmed the earlier impression. Philip of Macedon drew the proper conclusions, and in order to win Greek approval he made use of a "pretext"—the need to exact retribution from Persia for her injuries to the Greeks. Finally, the "beginning" occurs when Alexander crosses over into Asia (III. 6). After a brief reference to the War with Antiochus as having been caused by the anger of the Aetolians over their treatment by Rome at the end of the Second Macedonian War, he turns to Rome and Carthage.

The explanation of the Second Punic War is more elaborate, but worked out on the same principles as the others, more elaborate in that he posits no less than three "causes" (*aitiai*) which came about in the following order: (1) Hamilcar's feeling that he had not really been defeated by Rome but by circumstances, and therefore he need only wait for a more favorable opportunity to renew the war; (2) Hamilcar's anger (the most important "cause") over Rome's bullying tactics in regard to Sardinia; and (3) Carthaginian successes in Spain which provided her with the means for taking action. As to the "beginning," Polybius describes the Saguntine affair at some length, and he alludes to the many "pretexts" used by Hannibal in his determination to bring the war about.[31]

The rhetorical thinness of any such explanations of what happens in history needs no comment, though it is shocking when we compare it with Thucydides' ideas on the subject, with which Polybius must have been familiar. Worth keeping in mind, however, is Polybius' comparison between the statesman (who has read history) and the doctor, for this shows that wars, like diseases, can be prevented by competent diagnosis of the symptoms, before it is too late.[32] The author's views on the role of chance or fortune (*tyche*) in history reflect the period in which he lived, but they are not original with him and need not detain us here.[33]

After his rather elaborate introduction Polybius devotes the rest of Book III to a narrative of the Hannibalic War through the disaster of Cannae in 216 B.C. With Book IV he returns to the affairs of Greece, though not without a brief recapitulation and a restatement of his reasons for choosing the 140th Olympiad for the beginning of his *History*. This time he points to the coincidence of three kings dying at about the same time: Antigonus Doson, Seleucus III, and Ptolemy III.[34] And what is significant from this viewpoint is that the 140th Olympiad brought four rival leaders on the stage: Philip V in Macedon; Antiochus III in Syria; Ptolemy IV Philopator in Egypt; and—above all—Hannibal for Carthage. We may not unreasonably see these men as playing important roles preparing the way for Rome's conquest of the world. The Romans, according to Polybius, already have world conquest as their goal, while he later depicts Philip as influenced in a similar direction by his adviser Demetrius of Pharos.[35] Antiochus is not such a clear case, partly no doubt because we have to depend chiefly on fragments. One of these, however, is suggestive, i.e., where Antiochus, after his spectacular Eastern campaign, is spoken of as, "seeming to be worthy of the crown, not only to those who lived in Asia but to those in Europe as well."[36] However, when Polybius comes to describe the famous encounter with the Roman envoys in Lysimacheia, he presents Antiochus as denying any intention of interfering in Italian affairs;[37] but of course the king would not have revealed any such plans to the Romans even if the idea had occurred to him. The only king who acted out of character, from the historian's viewpoint, was Ptolemy Philopator. After defeating Antiochus convincingly at Raphia in 217 B.C. the Egyptian ruler failed to pursue his advantage. Instead, he soon concluded peace and retired contentedly to Alexandria. Polybius speaks of his easygoing disposition and the astonishment of his subjects at his victory.[38] One cannot help but think that Polybius was both puzzled and a little put out. Philopator just won't fit his rather limited pattern for the behavior of successful rulers. There must be something the matter with him.[39]

With the end of Book V the 140th Olympiad also comes to a close, and it is at this point that Polybius proposes to interrupt the narrative in order to discuss the Roman form of government. The moment is carefully chosen—when the Romans have just suffered their worst defeat of the entire war. To most observers at that time the Romans' position must have appeared to be all but hopeless, yet Polybius' readers would of course recognize it for what it was, a temporary setback on their march to world dominion. There must be some explanation as to how they were able to recover, and the historian finds this chiefly in the nature of Roman institutions.

Let us pause briefly to indicate the position of the rival leaders who had come into prominence in the Olympiad that was just ending. Hannibal stood at the peak of his career, astride the Italian peninsula with a victorious army. Revenge for the humiliations of the first war seemed imminent. Philip V, after quite a brilliant beginning, had succeeded in negotiating the Peace of Naupactus for himself and his allies with the Aetolian League, leaving him free to take a hand in the events in Italy. However, the real weakness of his position had been shown when a false report of the movement of Roman naval forces forced him into precipitate flight from Adriatic waters.[40] Antiochus III, despite Raphia, was able to turn his attention to his rebellious uncle Achaeus.[41] His recovery from a humiliating defeat is well under way, while Ptolemy now faces serious difficulties at home, where the part played by native troops in winning at Raphia led to the dream of revolution against the Macedonian regime in Egypt.[42] We have reached a time when the separate regions of the Mediterranean world begin to draw more closely together. Philip is increasingly concerned with Italy, and not only he but also the Aetolian statesman Agelaus is thinking in similar terms. The latter has already made his famous speech warning the Greeks to close ranks for fear of the cloud rising in the west.[43] Even Philopator found time to send envoys to Greece earlier, in an effort to mediate peace,[44] indicating that he saw Egypt's interests as affected by the situation in Europe. All this emerges from a careful reading of Polybius on the 140th Olympiad. Polybius' account of Roman government is probably the most widely read part of the entire *History*, and it has given rise to a scholarly literature sufficient to dismay anyone who approaches it for the first time. The problems are increased by our not having the complete text of Book VI, which leaves room for interpreters to speculate. One of the problems is to relate Polybius' theory on the history of government in general with the history of Rome. He has a cyclical theory which owes something to Plato,[45] where each form of constitution contains within it the seeds of its own destruction. No such government can be stable. The trouble with any cyclical theory is where to begin. Polybius starts with a disaster, such as has destroyed society in the past and may do so again. Out of this stage of anarchy emerges the strong man who rules by virtue of his physical strength as a bull dominates a herd. Growing refinement of manners transforms this "bull-man" rule into true monarchy. Eventually the hereditary monarchy degenerates into tyranny. This tyranny is then overthrown by leaders who set up an aristocracy. When in time the members of the ruling class become corrupt and selfish the aristocracy becomes an oligarchy. After the oligarchy has been overthrown in favor of a democracy, the democracy itself eventually worsens until mob rule takes its place. The resultant anarchy yields again to the control by a strong man.[46] However, Polybius also has a theory about the mixed constitution. If a government is set up in which all three elements (the one, the few, and the many) share the power then the decay that is sure to follow the supremacy of any one of them may be postponed.[47]

According to Polybius, Lycurgus was astute enough to see this. Therefore he devised a mixed constitution for Sparta which kept her free longer than any other state in history.[48] The difference between Sparta and Rome is that the Romans achieved their mixed constitution by a process of trial and error. Where Lycurgus solved the whole problem by his own genius, the Romans had to learn from experience. Unfortunately the account of the evolution of Roman government from Romulus on down has almost entirely disappeared from our text of Book VI. Pédech argues that it must have proceeded along the same lines as Aristotle attributes to Athens in his *Athenian Constitution,*[49] and this is certainly conceivable. For our purposes it is sufficient to point out that Polybius described Rome's government as a prime example of a mixed constitution, and that he assumes, and in fact documents, the first symptoms of decay in the Roman state.[50] But the historian's primary task is not to point this out, but rather to explain what there was about Rome's governmental institutions that will enable us to understand her phenomenal success in conquering the world in fifty-three years.[51] He adds the significant observation that Carthage, too, once had a thoroughly satisfactory government. Unfortunately for Carthage, Rome's high point so far as governmental institutions are concerned came precisely at the time of the Hannibalic War, when Carthage had already begun to decline.[52]

Book VI gives us an insight into Polybius' eminently practical views on morality and religion. He was impressed by the Roman custom, when a member of a prominent family died, of having a funeral procession in which his ancestors were represented by men wearing portrait masks and riding in chariots, each dressed in magisterial robes marking the highest office held by the deceased in life. He sees this as inspiring young men to emulate their forefathers.[53] But what particularly wins the historian's approval is the Roman belief in the gods. He applauds in them what elsewhere is often looked down on as mere superstition (*deisidaimonia*). Briefly stated, he praises the Romans for holding up the fear of the gods as a deterrent, to prevent the multitude from getting out of hand.[54] The purpose of religion is to insure high morality. That is why the Greeks, who have abandoned these views, have so much corruption in high places, while in Rome those who handle the public money almost never attempt to appropriate it for themselves. As Walbank points out, in a later book Polybius modifies this judgment.[55] Polybius' approach to religion and morality is not unlike that of Xenophon, but with one important difference. Xenophon, too, thought honoring the gods was advisable on purely practical grounds, because the gods punish those who neglect them, and the ruler needs their support. Polybius, on the other hand, sees danger to the state coming from within, therefore religion is a useful way to prevent deterioration. Yet Xenophon is no more idealistic at heart than Polybius. The difference is rather one between the fourth century and the second century B.C. way of looking at things. Added to this is the fact that Polybius' seventeen years in Rome opened his eyes to a new force in the world beyond anything encountered by Xenophon either in Asia or in the Peloponnese. And Polybius was a good enough historian to record what he saw and prepare the Greeks, unwilling as they were to accept it, for a bleak political future.

The emphasis in modern scholarship on Book VI may leave the impression that the Megalopolitan was as much a political scientist as he was a historian, but that would be a mistake. His importance for the study of Roman institutions depends on the accidents of survival. In actuality, Polybius' forte lies in his description of military and political events. He read widely, and showed great skill in combining a variety of sources into a clear narrative. An example of this, which commended itself to Rostovtzeff, is his account of the war of Rhodes against Byzantium, which was fought to force Byzantium to drop the toll she had imposed on all shipping to the Black Sea.[56] Polybius discusses the advantages of Byzantium's position for trade, along with her difficulties in coping with her Thracian neighbors. He includes a knowledgeable discussion of the Black Sea itself, and the likelihood of the rivers that empty into it turning it into a sweet water lake, similar to the Sea of Azov. And here Polybius is probably following the views of Strato of Lampsacus.[57] He then relates this to the political history of Byzantium and comes back to the particular crisis that provoked the war. Before the narrative ends we have been shown how this war ties in with Seleucid-Ptolemaic relations, the position of the growing Pergamene kingdom, the movements of the Gauls and also—and no doubt this attracted Rostovtzeff—he illuminates our understanding of maritime trade in the period.

I have dealt primarily with the parts of Polybius that are preserved best, but I may close with two references from the fragments that illustrate other aspects of this very versatile historian. One of these comes from Book X, and it gives us a detailed description of a signaling system used in the Roman army. Polybius speaks of earlier improvements made by Aeneas Tacticus,[58] and then goes on to the system devised by two men (otherwise unknown to us), Cleoxenus and Democlitus, which had been still further modified by the historian himself.[59] He ends this discussion with an enthusiastic statement on the advances in technology in his day.[60]

The other example is a short reference in Pliny to elephants' tusks. Polybius is reported as saying that in a remote part of Africa near the Ethiopian border tusks are used as doorposts, or serve as fence palings. He got his information from Gulussa, Masinissa's son.[61] This proves that on occasion Polybius still exhibits something of the old Ionian curiosity about the world and its denizens which delights us in the pages of Herodotus.

## II. Agatharchides

Agatharchides casts a long wavering shadow over Greek historiography.[62] His influence is suspected everywhere but can seldom be pinpointed, while to make matters worse he was a bookish historian living at a time when books on almost any imaginable subject had already been written, and in a place where virtually all that had been written would have been available to him. For Polybius we are reduced to speculation as to where he obtained his literary evidence, but for Agatharchides there is little doubt. He tells us himself that when he decided to give up a project he had long entertained of writing about the islands of the Erythraean Sea and their inhabitants, it was only partly because of the infirmities of age. The decisive reason was that the disorders in Egypt prevented him from making a careful examination of the records (hypomnemata).[63] But he did not get all his information from literary works. This was a period of southward exploration under the Ptolemies. The results were recorded in reports available in Alexandria, but Agatharchides may also have obtained firsthand accounts from returning members of such expeditions.[64]

We know then that as an old man he lived during disturbances in Egypt that prevented him from continuing his researches. The reference to these, however, is so vague that it is difficult to determine just what disturbances are meant. Rostovtzeff attributes them to a breakdown in communications during the reign of Euergetes II,[65] but other explanations are also possible. Let us leave this unsettled for the moment and examine Photius' statements about Agatharchides' early life and upbringing. He was a Cnidian by birth (like Ctesias) and he showed himself to be a grammarian by profession (perhaps a teacher?). He also acted as amanuensis and reader in the service of Heraclides Lembus, and he was brought up by Cineas.[66] Although Heraclides Lembus and Cineas were both advisers to Ptolemy VI Philometor (180–145 B.C.),[67] this gives us no precise dating for Agatharchides. However, if we assume with Jacoby that he had to leave Egypt during the confusion following the accession of Euergetes II in 145 B.C., and that (being as he tells us an old man) he was seventy years of age, then his birth took place in the neighborhood of 215 B.C. If, on the other hand, as I am inclined to believe, the disturbances referred to occurred in 132 B.C., at the time of the expulsion of Physcon (Euergetes II), he was born in about 202 B.C.[68]

Agatharchides is credited with quite a number of publications, including a collection of excerpts from various histories, a treatise dealing with remarkable winds, another in five books on the Troglodytes, a number of epitomes (one being an epitome of a work of his own),[69] and three clearly historical works: a *History of Asia* in ten books, a *History of Europe* in forty-nine books, and his work *On the Erythraean Sea* in five books.[70] The epitomes have a special interest ever since Bloch pointed out the resemblance between what Agatharchides was writing and the publications of his employer, Heraclides Lembus. He remarks: "Doubtless it was not a case of the secretary imitating his employer, but rather of the master taking his cue from a learned hireling."[71] But that is not altogether convincing. Heraclides was a highly important official, and he was presumably an intelligent man. If such a personage wished also to dabble in literature he did not need a suggestion from his employee to decide on writing epitomes of some of his favorite works. And if in fact, as Bloch and others maintain, Heraclides Lembus was the epitomizer of Aristotle's *Constitutions,* then he chose a subject on his own which seems quite distinct from the interests of Agatharchides, broad as they were.[72] Although Agatharchides is unlikely to have inspired Lembus' literary efforts, it would be surprising if his master had not made use of his services in composing his own work. Bloch suggests a fairly close parallel between Heraclides Lembus and Nicolaus of Damascus. And Jacoby has argued that Nicolaus' method was to mark the passages he wished to have excerpted, for his secretary to copy or summarize.[73] Presumably, if the parallel holds, the final touches would have been made by Heraclides. Nevertheless, in the process, his amanuensis would have learned a great deal which he later could put to use on his own account. Having a boss with literary aspirations probably kept Agatharchides too busy for much independent work. Therefore his own serious writing can best be attributed to the period after Heraclides ceased to monopolize him. Heraclides was an important official who took part in negotiating peace for Philometor with Antiochus IV, under very difficult circumstances. When Philometor died after tasting victory in 145 B.C. his successor and longtime rival, Physcon (Euergetes II),[74] could hardly overlook Heraclides when he divested himself of the leading members of the previous administration. But he did not need to strike at Agatharchides, who was probably a useful permanent official without the disadvantage of having been in a policy-making position.

Therefore he probably stayed on until events—perhaps those of 132 B.C.—made it impossible for him to consult the records in Alexandria. Accordingly he gave up his plan to write about the islands of the Erythraean Sea.

The only other information we have is indirect. We know that Artemidorus made extensive use of Agatharchides, while Marcianus of Heraclea, who in turn copied from Artemidorus, tells us that the latter flourished during the 169th Olympiad (104/101 B.C.).[75] And this fits in very well with the date suggested above for Agatharchides, though it does not easily accommodate itself with Dodwell's assumption that Agatharchides finished his work *On the Erythraean Sea* in 105 or 104 B.C.[76] Sufficient time must be allowed for Agatharchides' last publication to become well enough known generally before Artemidorus made up his mind to incorporate it into his own history.

We may tentatively assume that Agatharchides' period of greatest literary activity came between 145 and 132 B.C., a conclusion that might have pleased him as a Peripatetic, remembering those thirteen amazingly productive years spent by Aristotle in Athens while Alexander was conquering the world. And this certainly would be a flattering comparison, but as we shall see in looking at some of the fragments, Agatharchides was not entirely unworthy of his great heritage.

Let us begin where Jacoby's commentary still lends a feeling of security, with the ten-book *History of Asia*. Although there are only four named fragments remaining these are enough to show pretty conclusively that we have to do with a universal history, rather than one limited either to the Greeks or to modern times. The inference is based on two statements, one by Diodorus Siculus, who speaks of our historian as having written about Egypt and Ethiopia in Book II; the other taken from Agatharchides himself, who makes his well-known remark about the historian Hieronymus of Cardia as having survived his wounds to live to the ripe age of 104.[77] Schwartz goes so far as to attribute large sections of Diodorus' first three books to the *History of Asia*, some direct, others by way of an intermediary such as Artemidorus.[78] This can still be argued, but the question of Diodorus' sources is so complex that it is safer not to be too positive. It is sufficient here to emphasize that the *History of Asia* makes a major contribution to Diodorus' account, and that the *Historical Library* is the most extensive general history that has come down to us from antiquity. Even in its presently mutilated form, the Loeb edition of Diodorus requires twelve volumes, as compared with six for Polybius and only four for Herodotus. Therefore Agatharchides had much to do with shaping our tradition. The internal arrangement of the *History of Asia* cannot be reconstructed from four named fragments, particularly since

Agatharchides, perhaps influenced by Demetrius of Callatis, is guided by geographic considerations as much as by chronological ones. Despite this fact, it is worth noting that (judging on the basis of what we still have) he mentions Hieronymus only in Book IX, though the context in which he mentions him need not be, as Jacoby suggests, the very outset of the period of the Diadochi.[79] Perhaps the explanation is that he mentions Hieronymus not where he begins, but where he breaks off, just as Diodorus tells us something about Ephorus' *History* at the very point where it ends.[80] If that is so, then Agatharchides still had at least one more book in which to describe what happened in Asia from 272 B.C. down to his own day. However we look at it, the *History of Asia* is not a detailed account, for we find two references to Alexander in the previous book. These references in Book VIII both deal with Alexander and high living. As a philosopher, Agatharchides may be assumed to have taken a firm stand against luxury; but as a Peripatetic, his views on Alexander would be worth having.[81]

Stories about Alexander's companions and the luxury in Alexander's court must have been abundant, and wherever they were found they were grist for someone's mill. As a favorite topic this might be handled in a way favorable to Alexander, as for example in Plutarch, where the king rebukes his companions for their luxuriousness; or it might include criticism of the king himself, such as we find in Aelian's *Various History*; or magnificence might merely be depicted as a device used by Alexander to impress the barbarians.[82] The best source for life at court was Chares of Mytilene, Alexander's Master of Ceremonies (*eisangeleus*) and one of the first to bring out a book on Alexander. He is unlikely to have said anything critical of his employer. Duris of Samos, however, who made use of him, was quite capable of introducing his own interpretation into an unbiased account of events; this also applies to Phylarchus, who had the added advantage of being able to use not only Chares, but Duris as well. We do know that Duris and Phylarchus both dealt with luxury at Alexander's court, which means Agatharchides presumably had all three writers—Chares, Duris, and Phylarchus—available to him when he wrote. But despite inferences that have been drawn, we do not actually *know* how Duris represented Alexander, nor do the fragments serve to define Agatharchides' position.[83] However, the deeper we go into the Hellenistic period, the more luxury and magnificence must have come to be taken for granted, especially by a historian familiar with the court of the Ptolemies.

Turning now to the *History of Europe*, the first difference that strikes us is that there is much greater detail in this leisurely forty-nine–book account than in the niggardly ten books devoted to the *History of Asia*. The desperate suggestion that the figure 49 includes the 10 books of the *History of Asia* still leaves an imbalance between 10 books on Asia and 39 on Europe and ought to be rejected.[84] Perhaps Agatharchides wrote the *History of Asia* first, and it may represent a transitional stage between writing epitomes of the works of others and attempting an independent work of his own. We do have thirteen fragments specifically citing the *History of Europe* as compared with only four for *Asia*, but they all come from the same source, Athenaeus, who was always interested in sensational stories for their own sake and seldom concerned with the context in which he found them. There must have been a great deal to his liking scattered through the *History of Europe*, since he cites from twelve different books, and from only one of these, Book XXVII, twice. We have no direct evidence for the first five books or for anything later than Book XXXVIII.

The reference to Book VI is admittedly trivial, but worth mentioning as one of the rare instances where a Boeotian has the last word. Some stranger was curious about a Boeotian custom: whenever they caught a Copaic eel of great size, they crowned it with a garland, sprinkled it with barley, and then offered up the fish as a sacrifice to the gods. When the visitor asked why this was done, the Boeotian replied that old customs ought to be observed and never explained to outsiders.[85]

From Book XII there is a pejorative remark about the greed and quarrelsomeness of the Aetolians which, like the remark about Boeotia, does not suggest any particular period, though as Jacoby notes, their prominence as a great power stems from the Lamian War; however, they also played a very important role earlier, administering a stinging defeat on the Athenians in 426 B.C.[86] We cannot tell whether the present fragment belongs to the later or earlier period, but the next passage, which comes from Book XVI, is much more precise.[87] It describes the last days of Magas of Cyrene, who became so fat from over-indulgence that he could no longer breathe. Thanks to Justin,[88] we know he died about 250 B.C.; yet it is strange to find this in the *History of Europe*. Müller's explanation that the death of Magas is treated as a part of Macedonian history, because the Macedonian prince Demetrius the Fair goes out to Cyrene to marry the heiress, is reasonable in itself.[89] However, the very next passage, which comes from Book XIX, has an anecdote about Epaminondas,[90] who died in 362 B.C.! As Jacoby says, the relationship of this fragment to the *History of Europe* is "quite uncertain."[91] Incidentally, the anecdote has Epaminondas outwitting the Athenians—another example of Boeotian quick thinking, not enough to prove anything, but interesting nonetheless. But Epaminondas is often depicted as a well-educated man, even as a man trained in philosophy. His victory here, suggests erudition.[92]

In Book XXII we are back again in the third century.[93] The topic is a favorite one with Greek historians from Theopompus on down, that of a tyrant (or ruler) and his flatterers. This fragment refers to Aristomachus the tyrant of Argos. There were two, father and son, but Jacoby prefers the father, presumably on chronological grounds.[94] The flatterer, in this instance, is a pancratiast—a combination boxer and wrestler. There is a long Greek philosophical tradition of denigrating athletes. Xenophanes, for example, says that no city is any better off for having famous athletes, and he speaks with particular feeling of "that frightful competition they call the *pancration*."[95] When an athlete appears, as he does in our fragment, in the role of parasite we can be sure Agatharchides follows in the wake of Xenophanes, Plato, and Aristotle rather than Pindar and Xenophon.

The next four fragments deal with Sparta, and though they are not all from the same book, they may be considered here as a unit.[96] Spartan interest in physical fitness is mentioned, and with obvious approval. Agatharchides apparently applauds the training that builds good soldiers even though he does not have a high regard for athletes. He tells us how the ephors inspected every young Spartan at regular intervals to be sure he was not becoming flabby. Even an important man like Naucleides was threatened with losing his citizenship unless he got rid of his fat.[97] The reverse side of physical fitness is illustrated by an example borrowed from Xenophon, where Agesilaus shows his men some of the barbarian prisoners, whose muscles had not been hardened, like theirs, by strenuous exercise.[98] Not only physical fitness but also the morals of the young are a matter of concern. We hear of a Spartan called Gnosippus (otherwise unknown) whose behavior was notorious. He was forbidden to associate with the young men.[99] The last of this series refers to another undesirable Spartan, Aerisippus, with a reputation for playing up to rich men so long as their wealth lasted.[100] As usual, Athenaeus provides no context. He merely includes this tidbit in a whole series of examples culled from various authors about flatterers.

Fragment 14, from Book XXXI, gives us one of our few references to the island of Zacynthus, which is usually mentioned only as a way station to somewhere else. The Spartan King Demaratus fled there after being deposed, on his way to Persia, and the historian Herodotus visited the island, probably on his way to Thurii.[101] Unlike the citizens of Corcyra, the Zacynthians were not strong enough to exploit their position on the communications route west to Sicily and Magna Graecia. Instead they were subject to attacks and had their island devastated. During the Peloponnesian War, as allies of Athens, they were plundered by Spartan hoplites.[102] In the passage under consideration, Agatharchides says the Zacynthians were not ready for war because their wealth and prosperity had accustomed them to a luxurious existence. And that is all Athenaeus tells us. Polybius mentions Zacynthus twice, both times in connection with Philip V of Macedon. In 218 B.C. Philip experienced a humiliating setback in his effort to take Pale on the island of Cephallenia. However, he had seen that it was assailable from the Zacynthian side, that is from the south. Next year while waiting for the delegates to arrange peace with Aetolia to assemble, he suddenly swooped down on Zacynthus with his fleet and then sailed off, "after he had arranged matters in that island."[103] The circumstances fit our fragment very well as everyone from Müller on has recognized;[104] and if this is so, it tells us a little more about Agatharchides. Polybius' Book V is fully preserved, which means that he barely mentions the incident in passing, brushing the Zacynthians aside as of no importance. Yet generally he is highly critical of Philip. Why is he not outraged by this flagrant violation of international law—as he professes to be on other occasions? Agatharchides, however, is concerned. Although he blames the lack of resistance on the soft life they have led, he is unlikely to have condoned Philip's action. We will see other indications of his sympathy for the suffering of helpless persons in the face of overwhelming force.

The last three named fragments, from Books XXXIV, XXXV, and XXXVIII respectively, are desperately hard to fit into a historical framework.[105] The first has a suspicious etymological flavor, purporting to explain the name of the Phasis river (of Argonaut fame). Agatharchides writes: "multitudes of birds called 'pheasants' (*phasianoi*) congregate there because of the food found at the mouths of the river." Sometimes the same term (*phasian*) was used to describe a breed of horse. Connecting this passage with Philip's campaigning in the Hellespontine area is not only "very uncertain" but highly unlikely, considering how far he was from reaching the Caucasus.[106] The next fragment (F 16) looks more promising at first sight, because it refers to a Mithridates. The Arycandians of Lycia were so lazy and debauched in their ways that they ran into debt. Therefore they sided with Mithridates, hoping to obtain the cancellation of their debts as a reward. It is too early for the famous Mithridates, but finding a substitute is not easy and it is safer not to try. The example of Zacynthus warns us that Agatharchides is quite as apt to be concerned with small incidents as with episodes of great historical significance. This seems to be another example.[107] And finally, we have a fragment dealing with slavery among the Dardanians. The statement attributed to Agatharchides is strange and in fact quite unbelievable. He tells us individual Dardanians had as many as 1000 slaves, whom they used on their farms in time of peace, then led them off as a unit to fight in time of war.[108] The Dardanians were a tough warlike tribal people, a constant threat to their Macedonian neighbors. They had no historians. Presumably the blind obedience of clansmen to their chiefs has been distorted into a picture of slavery, blind obedience not being a Greek trait.[109]

In addition to these named passages from the Asiatic and European histories Jacoby has gathered together a number of statements citing Agatharchides without citing him by title. One or two of them deserve discussion, both on their own account and as a welcome relief from the snippets of Athenaeus. The most interesting of these is probably Agatharchides' incidental reference to the Jews, which so much impressed Josephus that he refers to it in his *Contra Apion* and then again, briefly, in his *Jewish Antiquities*.[110] The former puts his remarks into proper historical perspective. Agatharchides has been describing the adventures of Stratonice, the wife of Demetrius II of Macedonia who left him when he contracted another marriage. She came to Asia where, when her nephew Seleucus II refused her hand, the high-spirited queen stirred up the city of Antioch against him. After Antioch became unsafe she fled to the port of Seleuceia and might easily have gotten away by sea, but was deterred from doing so by a dream. As a result she was arrested and put to death. This rather romantic story needs to be examined critically to get at the real motivations of Stratonice, Demetrius II, and Seleucus II,[111] but our concern is not with the history of the period as such, but with the historian. Agatharchides rebukes Stratonice for her foolish *superstition* (*deisidaimonia*). This leads him to give another example and he finds it in the Jews. He tells us they live in Jerusalem, the most strongly fortified city imaginable, yet because of their custom of doing nothing at all on the seventh day, Ptolemy Lagus was able to take the city without opposition and the Jews fell into the hands of a cruel ruler. Experience has taught everyone except this people not to rely on dreams or legal interpretations that weaken their ability to reason like human beings.[112] Does this mean Agatharchides was an anti-Semite? There must have been some in his day, particularly in Egypt, where Jew and Greek rubbed elbows in the streets of Alexandria. But nothing that he says, nor anything that Josephus says about him justifies such a label. Rather, he regards the Jews in the light of their misfortunes. Like the Zacynthians and the Arycandians they have been handled roughly, and in each instance the blame lies with themselves. Agatharchides is a rationalist. He is capable of sympathy, as is shown in his portrayal of the adventures of Stratonice, but his chief concern is to find the root cause of a historical catastrophe so that intelligent people will avoid making the same kind of mistakes in the future. Like his contemporary Polybius he finds part of the remedy in better institutions.

In Agatharchides' case the emphasis is more on education than political theory. This is natural in a man who lived under an absolute monarch. But he is not one of that growing number who sought for an outlet in some mystery religion. Here again he is a credit to the founder of his school.

An entirely different side of Agatharchides meets us in Fragment 21. Here he is discussing a strange African people, the Psylli. They are almost extinct as the result of a war with their neighbors the Nasamones, though some managed to escape and moved to a different part of Africa.[113] Herodotus has little to say about the Psylli though he too makes them neighbors of the Nasamones.[114] It may be, as Jacoby hints, that the reference here comes from Agatharchides' account of Ophellas' march along the African coast from Cyrene on the way to his fatal rendezvous with Agathocles in 308 B.C.[115] The Psylli are like any other people except for their immunity to the bites of venomous creatures such as the snakes, spiders, and scorpions that abound in their country. Husbands test their children's legitimacy by exposing them to venomous snakes, as the snakes will attack anyone with impure blood. Considering the rationalism shown by Agatharchides elsewhere, we dare not impeach him here. The story he tells about the Psylli is obviously something he read in an earlier writer and his own version has been abstracted by Pliny and Aelian for their own purposes. Agatharchides probably indicated his disbelief in the validity of such a test of marital fidelity but he may have regarded it as a superstitious practice comparable to those of the Jews. Perhaps this helps to explain the near annihilation of the Psylli by the Nasamones. On the other hand, he may have had some notion about immunity to poison acquired by gradual exposure to it, then transmitted by heredity. The idea of inheriting acquired traits is as old as the fifth century Hippocratic *Airs, Waters and Places*.[116] His contemporary Attalus III of Pergamum was an expert on toxicology, and Nicander's poem on snakebites (*Theriaca*) is now thought to have been written about the same time, indicating a lively contemporary interest in such subjects.[117]

The last work by Agatharchides is his treatise *On the Erythraean Sea* in five books, our knowledge of which depends largely on Photius, who includes Book I and Book V in his *Bibliotheca*.[118] It is rather odd that he should have read only the first and last books, but this may indicate that the other three books had already disappeared, or at least that they were not obtainable in ninth century Constantinople. Photius' summaries of the remaining two are capricious. Some things interest him, others do not, with the result that we are unable to recover the original emphasis placed on them by Agatharchides. This is particularly true of Book I where we cannot check Photius by referring to Diodorus. Photius begins

THE RED SEA MOUNTAINS OF EGYPT FROM THE EAST
This is a part of the area described by Agatharchides. It has probably changed little.

with an account of how Ptolemy Philadelphus organized hunting, particularly the hunting of wild elephants, later to be trained for warfare. There was some question as to just what Philadelphus' contribution was, since elephants had already been used by Porus against Alexander and many others had used them in warfare before Philadelphus. We are left with the impression that he was the first Egyptian ruler to tame the African elephant. Agatharchides must have known that elephants decided the Battle of Ipsus in 301 B.C., but those were Indian elephants. Ptolemy I missed that battle, and nothing indicates that he had any elephants of his own. Taming the African elephant was apparently a first. Presumably this was initiated under Ptolemy II and it must have given him a new feeling of confidence in his relations with the Seleucids, who could easily tap the Indian supply.[119]

Photius' interest in elephant hunting soon flags, but he is evidently fascinated by the long and, to us, arid account of how the Erythraean Sea got its name. This well illustrates the limits of Agatharchides as a scientific geographer. Explanations were current in his day, based on the color (Erythraeus = red) of the soil, of the mountains reflecting the sun's rays in such a way as to resemble glowing coals, and so on. He rejects them, then turns to a popular Greek notion that the sea was named for a son of the hero Perseus (for whom Persia was named!), a certain Erythras. This also he rejects, in favor of the account given him by a Persian named Boxus, who left his own country to live in Athens. Boxus' story, which Photius gives at length, is that a Persian named Ery-thras gave his name to the Erythraean Sea. It was he who colonized the islands of that sea, islands which he reached by becoming the first man in those parts to build a boat. This should not lead us to infer that Agatharchides had met Boxus in Athens. The story has an artificial flavor about it that suggests the Library of Alex-andria rather than a stroll near the agora with this convenient Persian who had learned to speak Greek in Athens. Also, it seems to be a variant of the explanation already known to Nearchus, perhaps given to him by another Persian, Mazenes, who acted as his pilot on the last part of the voyage.[120] Agatharchides evidently felt the necessity of taking a stand on an old controversy. Similarly, though in which of his works is uncertain, he summarized the many views that had been held from Thales on down to his own day on the puzzle of the Nile flood. He himself associated the phenom-enon with the rain pattern in Ethiopia.[121] What characterizes Agatharchides here as elsewhere is his familiarity with the litera-ture. He makes no contribution of his own.

Quite a long abstract of a speech addressed by the guardian of a young ruling Ptolemy to his charge, pointing out the dangers of a war with the Ethiopians must have appealed to Photius' profes-sional interest in elevated discourse.[122] But we would like to know the historical setting. Bevan has suggested that the reference in the last chapter of Book I, where Ptolemy is said to have enlisted 500 picked cavalrymen for service in Ethiopia may refer to this same war. He argues plausibly that the war occurred while Ptolemy V Euergetes (210–180 B.C.) was still a boy ruler.[123] The only possible objection to this is that Book I seems a little early for Ptolemy V, but no argument based on Agatharchides' chronological ar-rangement of his material carries much weight. Worth noting is the historian's description of the clothing these cavalrymen wore for service in the tropics. They made use of a felted cloth which covered them completely, except for their eyes, and also covered their horses. The garments locally were called *kasas*.[124] Presumably this costume protected them from the intense heat of the sun, but it may also have helped man and beast against the assault of the African insects. Let us hope their clothing was not black, like that worn by the Portuguese Christovão de Gama when he led his expedition into Ethiopia in 1541.[125] With Agatharchides we are never quite sure whether details like this are borrowed from earlier accounts like those of Ctesias, or based on Ptolemaic government records, which he also consulted.

In the absence of the next three books of *On the Erythraean Sea* we turn finally to Photius' summary of Book V. The most celebrated passage we have is his description of the gold mines operated for the Ptolemies near the Red Sea coast on the borders of Egypt and Ethiopia.[126] The black gold mines are interspersed with dazzling white marble quarries. The gold is extracted by convicted felons and political prisoners under the direction of specially trained engineers. The miners wear lamps on their heads as they chop their way through the mining tunnels. Watching them carefully at their back-breaking work are barbarian guards, whose ignorance of the Greek tongue makes it impossible for them to be bribed. The process of breaking up the ore and smelting it is described in detail. In galleries too narrow to admit grown men, boys were used. The miners have a completely hopeless existence, working on until they drop dead. There can be no other release. We also learn that the early rulers of the region discovered the mines and that they had continued in operation ever since, except for periods when the Ethiopians overran Egypt. Mining was continued by the Persians and still went on in Agatharchides' day, the only change being the use of iron tools instead of bronze. He speaks of the incredible number of bones of dead workers to be found there. And he adds that the use of gold lies somewhere between pleasure and pain (a Stoic type remark).

The historian has given a detailed and seemingly accurate account of how these mines were operated. The circumstances still have the effect of horrifying us many centuries later, even though they reach us indirectly through Diodorus and Photius. There can be no doubt that Agatharchides was making a moral protest. This is unlike anything we read in his contemporary Polybius, because it is the inhumanity of the punishment of these men that concerns Agatharchides, not their guilt or innocence of the political crimes for which they are being punished.[127]

Although these mines are the best known part of Book V there are many other passages which sum up for us the knowledge of the East African area as it had been built up by Ptolemaic exploration. One of these pioneers is known to us by name. The historian tells us that Ptolemy III sent one Simmias out to make a careful examination of the coastal regions to the south of Egypt. Simmias must have written a report on the results of his investigations which Agatharchides then read in Alexandria.[128] Apparently Simmias, along with describing what he saw, includes some less credible details that he must have heard from others. The peoples referred to are the Ichthyophagi (fish eaters), already known to us from earlier writers like Nearchus. Simmias speaks of a particular group of them who are so far removed from all other peoples that they have not learned to fear anyone. Even the sight of a drawn sword makes no impression on them, and if invaders kill their women and children before their very eyes they look on with complete unconcern. They do not speak articulately, merely making signs and pointing. He adds that seals live with these people and share their way of life.[129] And it is likely that somehow the behavior of seals, which does fit the description, has been confused with that of a primitive people, which does not. The use of the ribs of whales for making houses has an authentic ring about it, as does the reference to a tepee-like dwelling constructed by fastening the tops of trees together.[130] But the most ingenious living arrangements are made by tribes who tunnel out spacious chambers for themselves in the compact mass of seaweed which has accumulated along the shore. Here they live happy and cool. When the tide comes in they rush out to seize the fish, then when it recedes they retire to their seaweed homes to eat their catch. When they die their bodies become food for the fish. So we have an ecological paradise, a balance in nature that delights Agatharchides.[131]

There is much here that reflects actual new discovery, but the historian gets his information in the library, and he tidies it up for purposes of his own. For example, he recognizes, as earlier writers seldom did, that in general there are two high tides each day. But the actual behavior of the tides is too irregular for him to accept, so he says that as a rule high tide comes at the ninth hour and again at the third hour.[132] One realistic touch is a reference to the swarms of insects—gnats and mosquitos. But even these have a part to play in nature's plan. They drive away the lions, which would otherwise make the land uninhabitable, and they do it not by their bites but because the noise they make is unbearable for the lions![133] One last example may be mentioned, his account of the ostrich. This huge bird uses its wings, but not for flight; he spreads them out like sails. And that is a good description. But Agatharchides adds an observation of his own. When the wind dies down the birds tire and are easily captured.[134]

As with Megasthenes on India, so with Agatharchides on Ethiopia and the southern regions generally, this was an excellent beginning. Unfortunately little that was written after them in classical times adds much to our knowledge of these areas in antiquity. The most important exception, to which the reader may be referred, is the *Periplus of the Erythraean Sea* written in early Roman days in Greek by an unknown Egyptian merchant. He was not, however, in any sense a historian.[135]

## Notes for Chapter 7

1. Out of the vast bibliography on Polybius the following may be mentioned as particularly helpful: K. Ziegler, "Polybios" (1), *PW* 1952. xxi. 1439–1578;

F. W. Walbank, *A Historical Commentary on Polybius* (Oxford, 1957-1967) vol. 1 (on Books I-VI), vol. 2 (on Books VII-XVIII); K. von Fritz, *The Theory of the Mixed Constitution in Antiquity* (New York, 1954); F. Susemihl, *Geschichte der griechischen Literatur in der Alexandrinerzeit* (Leipzig, 1892), II, 80-128; Paul Pédech, *La Méthode historique de Polybe* (Paris, 1964). Of these, Susemihl, while the oldest, has the very great merit of offering the most convenient reference to the ancient evidence. The standard text of Polybius is still the Teubner edition of T. Büttner-Wobst; however, the Budé edition of P. Pédech now appearing, may replace it. The standard English translation is that in the Loeb Library (W. R. Paton); see also a recent translation, though only of selected passages, by M. Chambers, *Polybius: the Historian* (New York, 1966), with an introduction by E. Badian.

2. See Theodor Mommsen, *Römische Geschichte*, 9th ed. (Berlin, 1903), II, 450-451.

3. See Polyb. III. 39. 8; and Walbank, *Commentary*, I, 1, n. 1; and 373.

4. See [Lucian] *Macrob.* 22. The reference to the manner of his death suggests that the author is following a circumstantial account in some history, which is at least better than his reference to Xenophon (ibid., 21) or Timaeus (ibid., 22). Unfortunately no authority is cited here as it is for Hieronymus of Cardia (ibid.) where he is following Agatharchides.

5. Cf. *Suda*, s.v. Πολύβιος (1941); Plut. *Phil.* 21; [Lucian] *Macrob.* 22.

6. See Dittenberger, *Sylloge Inscriptiomum Graecarum*[3] (Liepzig, 1915-1924), 686; also see 893 for Polybius' descendants, along with the editor's comments.

7. See Plut. *Phil.* 21.

8. For a thoughtful appraisal of the political scene see v. Fritz, *Mixed Const.*, 18-25.

9. Cf. the *Suda*, s.vv. Πολύβ. καθηγησάμενος Σκιπίωνος τοῦ Ἀφρικανοῦ; and Polyb. xxxi. 23 f. Aemilianus must have been about 18 when he met Polybius. See Diod. Sic. xxxi. 26. 5—where Polybius instructs him in philosophy!

10. See Plut. *Aem.P.* 28. The text reads: Μόνα τὰ βιβλία τοῦ βασιλέως φιλογραμμ·ατοῦσι τοῖς υἱέσιν ἐπέτρεψεν ἐξελέσθαι. Niese writes: "nur aus der Bibliothek des Perseus liess er seine Söhne auswählen" (*Geschichte der griechischen und makedonischen Staaten* 1903 Darmstadt reprint, 1963, III 186). This seems to me preferable to A. H. McDonald's statement that ". . . of the spoil he kept only Perseus' library" (see "Paullus (2) Macedonicus," in the *OCD*[2], 792. Walbank suggests that Polybius' acquaintance with Aemilianus may have started through books borrowed by the former from Perseus' library now in the possession of Paulus (Walbank, *Commentary*, I, 3, n. 5). This is pure fancy. Polybius will have brought along books of his own, and we are not told whether he was the borrower or the lender.

11. For Scipio's mission see App. *Pun.* 71; for Polybius' participation in it see Walbank, *Commentary*, I, 4, and Pédech, *La Méthode*, 556.

12. See Polyb. xxxi. 11-15. The prince ruled Syria as Demetrius I Soter, 162-150 B.C.

13. K. v. Fritz, *Mixed Const.*, 26.

14. See ibid., 23.

15. Polyb. xxxi. 13. 7—τὸν δὲ Πολύβιον συνέβαινεν κατά τὸν καιρὸν τοῦτον ἠσθεν-ηκότα μένειν κατὰ κλίνην.

16. See n. 6 above.

17. See Polyb. xxxiv. 14; Strabo xvii. 1. 12. For discussion and references see Walbank, *Commentary*, vol. I, p. 5 and n. 11.

18. For a thorough discussion of his interests in geography see Pédech, *La Méthode*, chap. 12; on the Bosporus see F. W. Walbank, "Polybius on the Pontus and the Bosphorus," in *Studies presented to David M. Robinson*, Vol. 1, ed. by G. E. Mylonas (Saint Louis, 1951), 469-479.

19. The *Philopoemen* work was probably the earliest and while lost as such, is the chief source for Plutarch's *Life* (see Walbank, *Commentary*, vol. I, p. 2 and n. 2). The *Tactics* is referred to by Polybius himself (ix. 20. 4) and various dates have been suggested for its composition—including one as early as 170 B.C. (see Walbank, *Commentary*, II, 148). The geographical work περὶ τῆς περὶ τὸν ἰσημερινὸν οἰκήσεως is cited by Geminus, a first century B.C. writer on astron-omy (for references see Walbank, I, 6). For conflicting views held in Polybius' time on whether or not the equatorial belt was too hot to sustain human life,

see Pédech, *La Méthode*, 588. The Stoic Panaetius held that it was habitable, Agatharchides that it was not.

20. See M. Holleaux, "Polybe et le tremblement de terre de Rhodes," in his *Études d'Épigraphie et d'Histoire grecques*, ed. by L. Robert (Paris, 1938), vol. I, chap. 32; Polyb. v. 88–90.

21. See *Études*, vol. 1, pp. 5, 458, n. 1.

22. Something of his unhappiness over this may still be seen. See Polyb. i. 1. 2; Pédech, *La Méthode*, 529. Walbank, however, regards this as a mere commonplace (*Commentary*, I, 39).

23. See Polyb. i. 14, also Walbank's comments (op. cit. 64 f.). For the text of Philinus see Jacoby, *FGrH* ii b, no. 174; and for his comments, ibid., ii d. 598. Since the appearance of Pédech's work (*La Méthode*) Vincenzo La Bua brought out his monograph, *Filino-Polibio; Sileno-Diodoro: Il problema delle fonti dalle morte di Agatocle alla guerra mercenaria in Africa*, ΣΙΚΕΛΙΚΑ III (Palermo, 1966), which attributes to Philinus much the same approach to history posited by Pédech for Polybius. La Bua's discussion is well worth reading, but it illustrates the dangers of approaching the fragments of a lost historian with a pattern already in mind. It is only too easy, on this basis, to assign long passages in Polybius to Philinus (see my review, *AJPhil.* 90 (1969) 379 ff.) Fabius Pictor is a Roman senatorial analyst who fought in the Hannibalic War. He was the earliest Roman historian and he wrote in Greek. For the fragments see *FGrH* iii c, no. 809.

24. See *FGrH* ii d. 598. La Bua demonstrates this in detail by a careful analysis of Polyb. i. 10–64—comparing this account with Diod. Sic. xxiii–xxiv; see his *Filino* op. cit., pt. 1.

25. See Polyb. i. 46. 4 to 47. 10. Perhaps here the vividness comes from his source, Philinus, who may have been an eye-witness. See Walbank, *Commentary*, I, 110.

26. On Aratus' *Memoirs* see Susemihl, *Gesch. griech. Lit. Alex.* (Hildesheim reprint, 1965), I, 284–299; also *FGrH* no. 231; on his life, see F. W. Walbank, *Aratos of Sicyon* (London, 1933). For Phylarchus, see T. W. Africa, *Phylarchus and the Spartan Revolution* (Los Angeles, 1961); also *FGrH* no. 81.

27. See esp. Polyb. ii. 56–63. This is discussed in Africa's *Phylarchus*, 29–34; see also T. S. Brown, *Timaeus of Tauromenium* (Los Angeles, 1958), 94–99.

28. See Polyb. i. 14.5.

29. Polyb. xii. 5. 1–3.

30. See p. 168 n. 123, above.

31. Polyb. iii. 9. 6 to 10. 6, and 12. 7–15. See Pédech, *La Méthode*, esp. 75–98 for full discussion of Polybius' theory on "causes," by which Polybius means primarily causes of wars.

32. See Polyb. iii. 7. 4–7.

33. On this see K. v. Fritz, *Mixed Const.*, 388–397; Pédech, *La Méthode*, 336–354; Walbank, *Commentary* (on Pédech), II, 493.

34. See Polyb. iv. 1. 9.

35. See Polyb. i. 3. 6; also 63. 9; and v. 101. 10.

36. Polyb. xi. 39. 16—ἄξιος ἐφάνη τῆς βασιλείας οὐ μόνον τοῖς κατὰ τὴν Ἀσίαν ἀλλὰ καὶ τοῖς κατὰ τὴν Εὐρώπην.

37. Polyb. xviii. 51.

38. Polyb. v. 87. 3–7.

39. See T. S. Brown, "Polybius' account of Antiochus III," *Phoenix* 18 (1964), 124–136.

40. See Polyb. v. 110.

41. Ibid., 107. 4.

42. Ibid., 107. 3.

43. For his eloquent speech see Polyb. v. 103. 9 to 104. 11. See also Walbank's *Commentary* (on v. 103. 9), I, 629, where he suggests this speech, "is likely to be based on a contemporary record."

44. See Polyb. v. 100. 9.

45. As Polybius admits (vi. 5. 1).

46. Polyb. vi. 5. 4 to 9. 9.

47. See on this C. O. Brink and F. W. Walbank, "The Constitution of the Sixth

Book of Polybius," *CQ* 1954, 4, 97–122, esp. 116 where they say: "It appears to be the function of the μικτή to act as a brake. . . ."

48. Polyb. vi. 10.
49. See Pédech, *La Méthode*, 305, n. 13.
50. For discussion see Brink and Walbank, *CQ* 1954, 105 f.
51. See ibid., 107.
52. See Polyb. vi. 51.
53. See Polyb. vi. 53. 1 to 54. 3.
54. Polyb. vi. 56. 6–11.
55. See Polyb. 56. 6–15, and Walbank, *Commentary*, I, 741. Walbank cites xviii. 35— where Polybius notes a falling off in public morality (ἐν τοῖς νῦν καιροῖς). Polybius goes on to cite two examples of the kind of morality he so much admires: viz. L. Aemilius Paulus, the conqueror of Macedon who died in very modest circumstances; and the Younger Scipio, Polybius' friend, who did not take any treasures from Carthage for himself.
56. See M. Rostovtzeff, *Social and Economic History of the Hellenistic World* (Oxford, 1941), II, 679, referring to Polybius' "detailed and lucid account." See Polyb. iv. 37. 8 to 52. 9.
57. See n. 18 above, and also Walbank's *Commentary* (on iv. 38. 1–45. 8), I, 486.
58. See Polyb. x. 44. 1; for the reference to Aeneas see Walbank's *Commentary*, vol. II, on this passage.
59. See Polyb. x. 45. 6. When Polybius did this is unknown. Walbank (*Commentary*, II, 260) rejects Schulten's idea of connecting it with the Numantine War, where Appian (*Hisp.* 90) does mention something of this sort (see *CAH* 8, 322), because this would be too late (in Walbank's view) for Polybius to have described it in Book X. However, the system devised earlier might still have been in use in the Numantine War even though the historian was not present.
60. See Polyb. x. 47. 12.
61. Polyb. xxxiv. 16. 1; also the Budé Pliny (*Histoire naturelle, Livre VIII*), Commentary on viii. 31, by A. Ernout.
62. For the fragments of Agatharchides see Jacoby, *FGrH* ii a. no. 86. However, it is regrettable that on "raumtechnischen gründen" the editor does not include the Περὶ τῆς Ἐρυθρᾶς Θαλάσσης, but sets it aside for Part 5 (*FGrH* ii c. 151). Therefore for this work we must rely on C. Müllerus, *Geographi Graeci Minores* (*GGM*) 1855 (Hildesheim reprint, 1965), I, 111–195. Müller also divided Agatharchides in the same way. For his edition of the other fragments see the *FHG* iii. 190–197. For Müller's discussion of Agatharchides' life see, however, *GGM* I, liv–lix. For his work *On the Erythraean Sea* see also: E. H. Bunbury, *A History of Ancient Geography*[2] 1883 (New York reprint, 1959), II, 50–61; W. W. Hyde, *Ancient Greek Mariners* (New York, 1947), 196–200.
63. See *GGM* I Agath. 110 for the disturbances (ἀποστάσεις) and the ὑπομνήματα. These *hypomnemata* are further defined in a passage in Diodorus based on Agatharchides; see Diod. Sic. iii. 38. 1, where he says, speaking of the Arabian Gulf of which he will give an account: τὰ μὲν ἐκ τῶν ἐν Ἀλεξανδρείᾳ Βασιλικῶν ὑπομνημάτων ἐξειληφότες.
64. See preceding note. The passage cited there from Diodorus continues: τὰ δὲ παρὰ τῶν αὐτοπτῶν πεπυσμένοι.
65. M. Rostovtzeff, *Hellenistic World*, II, 925. This was a long reign (145–116 B.C.), and the disturbances (ἀποστάσεις) may mean something quite different. Apparently Euergetes II reacted against some of the intellectuals dear to his brother Philometor (Ptolemy VI) and drove them out of Egypt (see E. R. Bevan, *The House of Ptolemy; A History of Egypt under the Ptolemaic Dynasty* 1927 (Chicago reprint, 1968), 308). Jacoby thinks this happened at the beginning of the reign (145 B.C.) and that Agatharchides was one of those who left Egypt (*FGrH* ii c. T 3. 151 f.); while Susemihl suggests a later date right after Physcon (Euergetes II) was temporarily driven out of Egypt in 132 B.C.—see Susemihl, *Gesch. gr. Lit. Alex.* I, 687 f. There is no consensus.
66. See *FGrH* Agath. T 1 = Phot. *Bibl.* 213; ἦν δὲ καὶ Θρεπτὸς Κινέου—(presumably Jacoby's τρεπτὸς is a typographical error). Henry, the Budé editor of Photius' *Bibl.* (vol. 3, 1962) translates: "Il fut aussi l'esclave de Cinéas"—a possible meaning for Θρεπτός (see LSJ) but highly unlikely here. Müller speaks of:

*Cineas vero, qui educavit A* (GGM I, liv); the edition of 1653 by Hoeschel translates: *fuit et alumnus Cinnaei;* and Rostovtzeff speaks of Agatharchides "as a member of Cineas' household," and as, "certainly not unknown to the rulers of his time" (*Hellenistic World* II, 925). Incidentally, Jacoby accepts Müller's suggestion of κινέου as the correct reading rather than the κινναίου of the codd. This enables Jacoby to identify him with the Cineas mentioned by Polybius as a member of Euergetes' special council in 170 B.C.—provided, that is, we also accept Ursinus' emendation of the text of Polybius xxviii. 19. 1 from κιναίαν to κινέαν! See *ap. crit,* in Jacoby; also *GGM* I, liv.

67. For Cineas see preceding note; for Heraclides Lembus, see Susemihl, *Gesch. gr. Lit. Alex.* I, 501–505; and esp. H. Bloch, in *TAPA* 71 (1940), 27–39.

68. For the disturbances of 145 B.C. see E. R. Bevan, *House of Ptolemy,* 307–308—[Euergetes] "hand was especially heavy on the *intelligentzia* of Alexandria"); on the rebellion of 132/131 B.C., see ibid., 311 f. Jacoby argues for 145 B.C. as better suited to Agatharchides' post under Heraclides, and therefore suggests 200 B.C. for his birth, a man "wer a.145 in höherem alter steht" (*FGrH* ii c. 152)—but 55 is too young an age for Agatharchides when he lays down his pen. Other things being equal I prefer 132 B.C. on the strength of the very argument Jacoby uses against it.

69. See *FGrH* (Agatharch.) 86. T 2. Jacoby is sure this latter epitome is by a later writer. The five books on the Troglodytes probably refer to his treatise *On the Erythraean Sea.*

70. See *FGrH* 86. T 2.

71. Bloch, *TAPA* 71 (1940), 38.

72. The idea that Lembus is the author of the epitome of Aristotle's *Constitutions* had long been held, although, according to Bloch, for the wrong reasons (ibid., 31 f. and esp. n. 17).

73. See ibid., 38; Jacoby, *FGrH* ii c. 233. 29–36. It may be added that both Nicolaus and Agatharchides are called Peripatetics. See the *Suda* s.vv. Νικόλαος Δαμασκηνός; and Strabo xiv. 2. 15. On Nicolaus see further B. Z. Wacholder, *Nicolaus of Damascus* (Los Angeles, 1962), 17–21.

74. See Susemihl, *Gesch. gr. Lit. Alex.* I, 501, n. 53; also Bloch, *TAPA,* 71, 33—with further evidence.

75. See Susemihl, *Gesch. gr. Lit. Alex.* I, 695, for Artemidorus' use of Agatharchides; see Müller, *GGM* I, 566, 31–33 for Artemidorus' *floruit;* see Bunbury, *Hist. Anc. Geog.* II, 660 f., for Marcianus, a very late Greek geographer.

76. See *GGM* I, liv—citing Dodwell's *Dissertatio.* It may be mentioned in passing that Agatharchides was once believed to be the guardian of a Ptolemaic prince. This is based on *De Mari Erythr.* 17 (*GGM* I, 118). Müller thinks the passage refers to Agatharchides himself, but this view had already been rejected by Niebuhr and is no longer held by anyone.

77. See Diod. Sic. iii. 11 = *FGrH* 86. F 1; and Phlegon *Macrob.* 2 + [Luc.] *Macrob.* 22 = F 4a–b; and *FGrH* ii c. 150.

78. See E. Schwartz, "Agatharchides von Knidos," *PW* i. 1739.

79. On all this see *FGrH* ii c. 150 f.

80. See Diod. Sic. xvi. 76. 5; a modern example might be Gibbon, who pauses to take leave of Ammianus Marcellinus (in chap. 26 of the *Decline and Fall*).

81. The death of Callisthenes, Aristotle's kinsman, at Alexander's hands has led many scholars to believe that the Peripatetic School thereafter wrote unfavorably about Alexander. See esp. W. W. Tarn, *Alexander the Great,* Vol. 2 (*Sources and Studies*) (London, 1948), 69 and n. 1; but this view has been challenged. See E. Badian, *CQ* n.s., vol. 8, 1958, 144 ff.); also J. R. Hamilton, *Plutarch: Alexander, A Commentary* (Oxford, 1969), lx–lxi; E. Mensching, *Historia* 12 (1963), 274–282; and A. B. Bosworth, *Historia* 19 (1970), 407–413.

82. See Plut. *Alex.* 40; *V.H.* ix. 3; and Polyaenus, *Strat.* iv. 3. 24.

83. For references see Hamilton, *Plut. Alex. Comm.,* 106 (on Plut. *Alex.* 40. 1). Of Duris, we know he refused to accept the story about Alexander and the Amazon queen (*FGrH* 76. F 46); and also that he contrasts the thrifty Philip, who was so proud of having a golden drinking cup that he kept it under his pillow, with Alexander's companions (ibid., F 37 a–b). Neither passage reflects on Alexander. Duris also was a Peripatetic. As for Phylarchus, the problem

is to decide whether the tone is his own or derived from Duris. The bald statement that Alexander sent off for purple cloth for the Companions might even go back to Chares.

84. Jacoby is half-hearted in his suggestion—*FGrH* ii c. 151.

85. See *FGrH* 86. F 5. Agatharchides' contemporary, Heraclides Criticus, who wrote an account of his travels in Greece, closes his description of Boeotia with a line from the fifth century comic poet Pherecrates: "If you have any sense stay out of Boeotia!" [Text ed. by F. Pfister, *S.B.* Vienna, vol. 227, monograph on *Die Reisebilder des Heraklides* (Vienna, 1951), 84 (i. 25).

86. See *FGrH* 86. F 6 and Jacoby's comments (ii c. 152); for the Aetolians' role in the Peloponnesian War see Thuc. iii. 94–98.

87. *FGrH* 86. F 7.

88. *Epit.* xxvi. 3.

89. See Müller, *FHG* iii. 192.

90. *FGrH* 86. F 8.

91. See *FGrH* ii c. 152.

92. Plutarch's *Life* of Epaminondas is lost, but his *De genio Socratis* (8–16 = *Moralia* 579 D to 585 D) treats him as a man steeped in Pythagoreanism. See also Diod. Sic. x. 11. 2. Polybius pays him the compliment of comparing him with Aristides and Aemilius Paulus (Polyb. xxxi. 22). Even Xenophon, his enemy, speaks well of Epaminondas (Xen. *Hell.* vii. 5. 8)—discussed on p. 97 above.

93. See *FGrH* 86. F 9.

94. See *FGrH* ii c. 152; Müller rightly refuses to conjecture: *quemnam Noster intellexerit, non liquet* (*FHG* iii. 193).

95. See H. Diels, *Die Fragmente der Vorsokratiker*[8], vol. 1, 128 f., no. 21, F 2—τι δεινὸν ἄεθλον ὅ παγκράτιον καλέουσιν.

96. *FGrH* 86. FF 10 & 11 are from Book XXVI, F 12 from XXVIII, and F 13 from XXX. The only clues as to date are the names Naucleides (mentioned by Xenophon as an ephor, *Hell.* ii. 4. 36), Lysander and Agesilaus (which occur also in F 16). The assumption that we have to do with an elaborate account of the reforms of Agis and Cleomenes in the third century, with a background in earlier Spartan history has much to recommend it (see Müller, *FHG* iii. 193; Jacoby, *FGrH* ii c. 152.

97. This is in *FGrH* 86. FF 10 and 11. There is a somewhat more detailed account in Aelian's *Varia Historia* xiv. 7, obviously from the same source. Whether this is because Aelian excerpts Agatharchides more fully, or because both he and Agatharchides made use of Phylarchus independently is uncertain, but Phylarchus is likely to be the ultimate source when the context concerns Agis and Cleomenes (see T. W. Africa, *Phylarchus*).

98. See *FGrH* 86. F 11 and Xen. *Hell.* iii. 4. 19.

99. See *FGrH* 86. F 12.

100. See *FGrH* 86. F 13.

101. For Demaratus see Hdt. vi. 70; for the historian's visit, and his interest in their method of obtaining pitch see Hdt. iv. 195 and chap. 2 above, p. 41.

102. See Thuc. ii. 66.

103. See Polyb. v. 4. 2 (218 B.C.) and 102. 3 (217 B.C.).

104. See *FHG* iii. 194. F 9.

105. *FGrH* 86. FF 15, 16, 17.

106. See LSJ for the meanings of φασιανός; also *FHG* iii. 194. F 10 for Müller's conjecture, and *FGrH* ii c. 153 (on F 15) for Jacoby's cautious demurrer. The puzzle is, why mention the Phasis in a European history? But some analogy with a European river is always possible.

107. On this see: E. Meyer, *Geschichte des Koenigreichs Pontos* 1879 (Chicago reprint, 1968), 53, n. 1; Jacoby, *FGrH* ii c. 153 (on F 16); D. Magie, *Roman Rule in Asia Minor* (Princeton, 1950), II, 1384 f., n. 41; H. H. Schmitt, *Untersuchungen zur Geschichte Antiochos' des Grossen und seiner Zeit* (Wiesbaden, 1964), 286 f.

108. See *FGrH* 86. F 17.

109. Nor had it ever been. Herodotus gives us a fictional example among the Persians (Hdt. viii. 117) and Xenophon a real one (Xen. *Anab.* i. 5. 8).

110. See *FGrH* 86. F 20 a–b.

111. See E. Will, *Histoire politique du monde hellénistique* (Nancy, 1966), I, 269 for discussion and references.

112. The key words here are: τοῖς ἀνθρωπίνοις λογισμοῖς . . . ἐξασθενήσωσιν, also used by Diodorus Siculus in explaining what happened to Agathocles (Diod. Sic. xx. 78. 1): ἐξησθένησε τοῖς λογισμοῖς. As to when Ptolemy I took Jerusalem, that is anyone's guess. P. Jouguet may well be right when he points to 312 B.C. after Ptolemy's victory over Demetrius at Gaza (P. Jouguet, *L'Impérialisme macédonien et l'héllenisation de l'orient* (Paris, 1926), 174.

113. This statement of their moving away from the Nasamonians is in *FGrH* 86. F 20 a = Pliny *HN* vii. 14; Aelian says nothing about the Nasamonians (F 20 b = Ael. *NA* xvi. 27).

114. Hdt. iv. 173.

115. See *FGrH* ii c. 154; iii b. (Callias) 564. F 3; also his comments on Callias F 3. Diodorus does not mention the Psylli by name (Diod. Sic. xx. 42). Jacoby thinks Duris is Diodorus' source, but offers no evidence.

116. See Hippoc. *Airs, Waters and Places* 14.

117. For Nicander, see A. Lesky, *Geschichte der griechischen Literatur*, 2nd ed. (Bern and Munich, 1963), 804–807, who maintains Nicander's contribution was purely literary, and that the scientific content goes back to Apollodorus of Alexandria who lived in the early part of the third century B.C. For a harsh judgment on Nicander's poetry, see Susemihl, *Gesch. gr. Lit. Alex.* I, 304 f. (refuting Cic. *de Orat.* i. 16). For Attalus III see D. Magie, *Roman Rule* II, 779, n. 89 (see also I, 31).

118. References to the text will all be to Müller's edition (see n. 62 above) in vol. I of the *GGM*. Müller divides the text into chapters, Book I containing chapters 1–20, and Book V, 21–111. He has added a separate section of *Fragmenta sedis incertae*, which contains chapters 112–114 (derived from Diodorus Siculus, Plutarch, Aelian, and Pliny—in that order). Further, he has printed the text of Diodorus where it exactly parallels the text given by Photius and printed it below that text, with the same chapter divisions. This begins on page 123 with Chapter 23 and continues through virtually all the rest of Book V. The Diodorus passage comes from Diod. Sic. iii. 12–48.

119. See Agath. (1) in Phot. *Bibl.* cod. 250. On the war elephants of the Ptolemies see Rostovtzeff, *Hellenistic World* I, 383 f. We also have an inscription dealing with elephants from the Aethiopian and Troglodytic land, "which his father and he (i.e., Ptolemy III Euergetes—246–221 B.C.) were the first to hunt in those countries, and which they brought back to Egypt to train them for use in warfare." (Dittenberger *OGI* 54).

120. See Arr. *Ind.* 37. 2.

121. See Diod. Sic. i. 38–41; see also H. Diels, *Doxographi Graeci* 1879, 3rd ed. (Berlin reprint, 1958) 226–227. The same problem continues to interest Posidonius in the first century B.C.; see Hyde, *Greek Mariners*, 275.

122. At one time this was thought to be Agatharchides' own admonition to Ptolemy. See above n. 76.

123. See Bevan, *House of Ptolemy*, 260.

124. On the word, see κασῆς in LSJ, where the Hebrew *kasah* = covered is cited. Also use of horse coverings, see Xen. *Cyr.* viii. 3. 8. Diodorus describes a special garment designed by Semiramis which came to be the usual Median and Persian costume, in a passage based on Ctesias (Diod. Sic. ii. 6. 6). Explaining native costumes seems to have been a well-known τόπος long before Agatharchides.

125. See Basil Davidson, *The Lost Cities of Africa* (Boston and Toronto, 1959), 215.

126. See *GGM* I, Agath. 23–29.

127. See Rostovtzeff, *Hellenistic World* I, 382, who refers to Agatharchides' "wonderful description"; Hyde, *Greek Mariners*, 197–198 and n. 34, who compares this with the passage about mining in *Job* (2. 8. 1–11); and L. A. Tregenza, *The Red Sea Mountains of Egypt* (London, 1955), 43, who saw this area on foot.

128. These are the *hypomnemata* referred to in n. 63 above.

129. For Nearchus on the Ichthyophagi, see Arr. *Ind.* 26. 2 to 29. 8; for Simmias and his account, see *GGM* I Agath. 41–42.

130. See *GGM* I Agath. 43.

131. See ibid., 44–45.
132. See ibid., 32.
133. See ibid., 50.
134. See ibid., 57 (only in the Diodorus version, i.e., Diod. Sic. iii. 28. 3–4.
135. The account does make fascinating reading. It can be read in translation in R. C. Majumdar's *The Classical Accounts of India* (Calcutta, 1960), 288–309. For the Greek text, see Müller's *GGM* I, 257–305.

# SELECTIVE BIBLIOGRAPHY

Classical authors are cited by title where more than one work is known, otherwise merely by name or recognizable abbreviation (Hdt., Thuc., etc.) The numbered references are usually self-explanatory, the Roman numeral standing for a book and the Arabic numerals for subdivisions. When an added number is given in parentheses it refers to the pagination of the *editio princeps; e.g.*, Plut. *De Stoic. repugn.* 20, 6 (1043 D). The 1043 D refers to the fourth part of p. 1043 in the first standard printed edition of Plutarch's *Moralia* (the *Moralia* being a general title to embrace everything Plutarch wrote except the *Lives*, and *De Stoicorum Repugnantibus* being one of the essays included in the *Moralia*). Similar double references are given for Strabo, Athenaeus, Aristotle and others, in the notes. In general the abbreviations are those found in the *Oxford Classical Dictionary* of 1970.

## Source Materials

ADLER, A. *Suidae Lexicon* (Leipzig, 1928–1938). Cited by title of article in Greek. *E.g.* Suda sv. Ἡρόδοτος. Abbreviation: *Suda.*

DIELS, H. *Doxographi Graeci* (1879; Berlin reprint 1958). Abbreviation: Diels, *Dox. Graec.*

———. *Die Fragmente der Vorsokratiker*, 8th ed. by W. Kranz, 3 volumes (Berlin, 1956). Cited by volume, author's number (with or without his name), and number of fragment. *E.g.* Diels, *Vorsokr.*, I, 12 (Anaximander) A 1. The "A" fragments are distinguished from the "B" by Diels, the latter being closer to the author's own words; the former, remarks about him or his work made by others—much like the "F" and "T" designations used by Jacoby (see below).

DITTENBERGER, W. *Sylloge Inscriptionum Graecarum* (Leipzig, 1921–1924; reprinted as 4th ed. in Hildesheim, 1960). As no changes were made, cited here as *SIG³.*

———. *Orientis Graeci Inscriptiones Selectae* (Leipzig, 1903–1905; also reprinted in Hildesheim 1960). Cited as *OGI.*

HERCHER, R. *Epistolographi Graeci* (Paris, 1873). These letters are arranged alphabetically under the names of the letter writers. Cited by the name of the epistolographer and the number of his letter. *E.g.,* Hercher, *Epistolog. Graec.,* Julian, *Epist.* 21.

JACOBY, F. *Die Fragmente der griechischen Historiker*, edited with a German commentary (Berlin and later Leiden, 1923–    ). Cited by volume, with or without the name of the historian, by his number and the number of the fragment (F) or *testimonium* (T). The *testimonia* give what other ancient writers have to say about the historian or his writings, while the fragments proper (F) purport to be what he actually said, as given in later writers. In the notes such a fragment might be cited as: *FGrH* II A, 76 F 40 = Plut. *Alex.* 15. This would mean the fortieth fragment of Duris of Samos, found in volume II A of Jacoby's work, and derived from chapter fifteen of Plutarch's "Life" of Alexander. When Jacoby's commentary is cited, the appropriate volume and page is given. Abbreviation: *FGrH* (with or without Jacoby).

MAJUMDAR, B. C. *The Classical Accounts of India* (Calcutta, 1960). An English translation of classical writers on India, reprinting those of J. W. McCrindle and others. Materials not otherwise available in one volume.

MÜLLER, C. and T. *Fragmenta Historicorum Graecorum*, edited along with a translation and commentary in Latin, in 5 volumes (Paris, 1841–1870). Usually cited by volume and page, sometimes by number of fragment. Abbreviation: *FHG* (with or without the Müller).

MÜLLER, C. *Scriptores Rerum Alexandri Magni*, bound up with Dübner's edition of Arrian (Paris, 1846).

MÜLLERUS, C. *Geographici Graeci Minores* (1855; Hildesheim, Germany reprinting 1965). Cited as *GGM*.

TOD, M. N. *Greek Historical Inscriptions*, vol. I, 2nd ed. (Oxford, 1946); vol. II (Oxford, 1948). Cited as *GHI* I² and *GHI* II.

## Commentaries

Commentaries may be cited by the page in the commentary, or by the passage in the author commented on.

BRUCE, I. A. F. *An Historical Commentary on the Hellenica Oxyrhynchia* (London, 1967).

GOMME, A. W., and others. *A Historical Commentary on Thucydides* (London, 1945–    ).

HAMILTON, J. R. *Plutarch: Alexander, A Commentary* (Oxford, 1969).

HOW, W. W., and WELLS, J. *A Commentary on Herodotus*, 2 volumes, I (Oxford, 1912), II, revised (Oxford, 1928).

WALBANK, F. W. *A Historical Commentary on T Polybius* (Oxford, 1957–    ).

## Secondary Works

ADCOCK, SIR FRANK E. *Thucydides and his History* (London, 1963).

AFRICA, T. W. *Phylarchus and the Spartan Revolution* (Los Angeles, 1961).

BELOCH, K. J. *Griechische Geschichte*, 2nd ed. (1912–1927, Strassburg, then Berlin and Leipzig), 4 volumes, each appearing as two separate parts, part 1, text; and part 2, a discussion of special topics within the period for that volume. Cited as Beloch, *Griech. Gesch.* I, 1² etc.

BENGTSON, H. *Griechische Geschichte*, 2nd ed. (Munich, 1960).

BERVE, H. *Die Tyrannis bei der Griechen*, (Munich, 1963). This work is published in two volumes, the first containing the text and the second the notes; the pages are continuously numbered.

BEVAN, E. R. *The House of Ptolemy: History of Egypt under the Ptolemaic Dynasty* (1927; Chicago reprint 1968).

Brown, T. S. *Onesicritus, A Study in Hellenistic Historiography* (Los Angeles, 1949).

―――. *Timaeus of Tauromenium* (Los Angeles, 1958).

Bunbury, E. H. *A History of Ancient Geography* (1883; new reprint 1959).

Bury, J. B., and others. *Cambridge Ancient History*, 12 volumes (London, 1923-1939). Cited as *CAH*[1], to distinguish it from the revised edition now beginning to appear under the editorship of N. G. L. Hammond and others.

Cary, M., and Warmington, E. H. *The Ancient Explorers* (1928; Penguin reprint).

Christ, W. von. *Geschichte d. griechischen Litteratur*, revised by W. Schmid and O. Stählin, part II, 1 (Munich, 1920); II, 2 (1924). Cited as Christ-Schmid-Stählin II, 1[6] and II, 2[6].

Connor, W. R. *Theopompus and Fifth-Century Athens* (Washington, D.C., 1968).

de Romilly, Jacqueline. *Thucydide et l'Impérialisme Athénien* (Paris, 1947).

Diller, A. *Tradition of the Minor Greek Geographers*, American Philological Association publication (Lancaster, Pa., 1952).

Finley, J. H., Jr. *Thucydides* (Cambridge, Mass., 1947).

Guthrie, W. K. C. *A History of Greek Philosophy* (London, 1962–      ).

Hammond, N. G. L. *History of Greece to 322 B.C.*, 1st ed. (Oxford, 1959).

Henry, W. P. *Greek Historical Writing* (Chicago, 1967).

Hignett, C. *A History of the Athenian Constitution* (Oxford, 1952).

Jacoby, F. *Atthis: The Local Chronicles of Ancient Athens* (Oxford, 1949).

Kirk, G. S. and Raven, J. E. *The Presocratic Philosophers* (London, 1957).

La Bua, Vincenzo. *Filino-Polibio; Sileno-Diodoro; il problema delle fonti dalle morte di Agatocle alla guerra mercenaria in Africa*, ΣΙΚΕΛΙΚΑ III (Palermo, 1966).

Lesky, A. *Geschichte der griechischen Literatur*, 2nd ed. (Munich, 1963).

Murray, G. *Greek Studies* (Oxford, 1946).

Myres, J. L. *Herodotus: Father of History* (Oxford, 1953).

Olmstead, A. T. *History of the Persian Empire*, (Phoenix Books, 1948).

*Oxford Classical Dictionary*, 1st ed. (Oxford, 1949), cited as *OCD*[1]; 2nd ed. (Oxford, 1970), cited as *OCD*[2].

Pauly, Wissowa, Kroll and others. *Real-Encyclopädie d. classischen Altertumswissenschaft*, 1893–      . Cited as *PW*, along with author of article, title and the volume and column. There is also a smaller work under the same auspices entitled *Der Kleine Pauly* (Stuttgart, 1964–      ), cited as *Kl Pauly*.

Pearson, L. *Early Ionian Historians*, (Oxford, 1939).

―――. *The Lost Histories of Alexander the Great*, American Philological Association publication (New York, 1960).

Pédech, P. *La Méthode historique de Polybe* (Paris, 1964).

Rose, H. J. *Handbook of Greek Mythology*, 5th ed. (London, 1953).

Rostovtzeff, M. *Social and Economic History of the Hellenistic World*, 3 volumes (Oxford, 1941).

Sandys, Sir John E. *A History of Classical Scholarship*, vol. I, 3rd ed. (London, 1921).

Schmid, W., and Stählin, O. *Geschichte der griechischien Literatur*, (Munich,

1929–1948): I, 1 (1929); I, 2 (1934); I, 3 (1940); I, 4 (1946); I, 5 (1948).
Cited as Schmid-Stählin, I, 1⁷; I, 2⁷, etc.

SCHMITT, H. H. *Untersuchungen zur Geschichte Antiochos' des Grossen und seiner Zeit* (Wiesbaden, 1964).

SUSEMIHL, F. *Geschichte der griechischen Literatur in der Alexandrinerzeit*, 2 volumes (Leipzig, 1891).

TARN, W. W. *Alexander the Great*, volume II, *Sources and Studies* (London, 1948).

———. *Antigonos Gonatas* (Oxford, 1913).

———. *The Greeks in Bactria*, 2nd ed. (London, 1951).

THOMSON, J. O. *History of Ancient Geography* (London, 1948).

TIMMER, B. C. J. *Megasthenes en de Indische Maatschappij* (Amsterdam, 1930).

VON FRITZ, KURT. *Die griechische Geschichtsschreibung* (Berlin, 1967–     ). Cited as GG I (Text) and GG I A (Anmerkungen).

———. *The Theory of the Mixed Constitution in Antiquity* (New York, 1954).

WACHOLDER, B. Z. *Nicolaus of Damascus* (Los Angeles, 1962).

WADE-GERY, H. T. *Essays in Greek History* (Oxford, 1958).

WESTLAKE, H. D. *Essays on the Greek Historians and Greek History* (New York, 1969).

# INDEX

*A selected list of references to the historians and other literary figures*

Eratosthenes of Cyrene, universal scholar, 5, 8, 9, 16, 18, 139, 142, 158
Eudoxus of Cnidus, geographer, 22 n.44
Euhemerus of Messene, 145, 165 n.30
Euripides, 15, 63, 73 n.63
exiles and writing of history, 35

Fabius Pictor, Roman annalist, 175–176

Genealogies, by Hecataeus of Miletus, 11, 22 n.49
Gryllus, name of a son, a grandson and the father of Xenophon, 87, 90
Gymnosophists, Indian wise men, 127

Hecataeus of Abdera, 11, 22 n.48, 145, 165 n.30
Hecataeus of Miletus, 4, 5, 6–12, 16, 50, 81, 91, 145
Hellanicus of Lesbos, 12, 14–18, 23 n.77, 55, 133 n.38
Hellenica (Hellenic History). See Antipater, Callisthenes, Ephorus, Oxyrhynchus, Theopompus
Heraclides Lembus, historian, 181, 183
Heraclides Ponticus, historian, 162
Heraclitus of Ephesus, 7, 33
Herodotus, Father of History, 2, 4, 7, 9, 10, 13, 18, 25–42, 47, 49, 50, 51, 53, 57, 62, 71, 78, 84, 85, 86, 91, 94, 95, 114, 128, 145
Hesiod, and Hesiodic writers, 3, 16, 19 n.9, 71 n.7
Hieronymus of Cardia, Hellenistic historian, 140, 155, 172, 184, 185
Hippocrates, Airs Waters Places, 22 n.52, 190; Ancient Medicine, 56
Hippodamus of Miletus, 44 n.26
historical writing before the Greeks, 1ff.
Homer, 3, 6, 7, 20 n.15, 71 n.7, 175

Indica, by Ctesias, 81–82
Indica, by Megasthenes, 143
Ion of Chios, historian, 5, 57
Isocrates of Apollonia, 116
Isocrates of Athens, 87, 108, 115, 123

Josephus, compared with Polybius, 169; refers to Agatharchides, 189
Julian the Apostate, 26, 77
Justin, epitomizer of Trogus Pompeius, 128

Kautilya, author of Arthashastra, 146

Lesbiaca, by Hellanicus, 17
logographers, general term for early Greek prose writers, 25

Lucian of Samosata, 82
Ps. Lucian, see Macrobioi
Lycortas, father of Polybius, 171
Lycurgus, Spartan lawgiver, 4, 180
Lydiaca, by Xanthus, 13
Lysias, Attic orator, 94

Macrobioi, falsely attributed to Lucian, 15, 23 n.71, 87, 129, 152, 170
Macrobius, 112
Marcellinus, biographer of Thucydides, 48
Megasthenes, author of an Indica, 83, 141–151
Memorabilia, by Xenophon, 90
Menedemus, Academic philosopher, 110

Naucrates of Erythrae, 116, 117
Nearchus "the Cretan," historian and friend of Alexander, 126, 127, 136 n.122, 143
Nicolaus of Damascus, historian, 14, 164, 183

Old Oligarch, name for author of Athenian Constitution which is falsely attributed to Xenophon, 66, 74 n.79
Olorus, father of historian Thucydides, 47
Onesicritus of Astypalaea, Alexander historian, 126–127
Oxyrhynchus historian, wrote an Hellenica, 96, 115

Panyassis, Greek epic poet, 3, 26, 27
Patrocles, explorer, 131
Pausanias, author of Description of Greece, 48
Periegesis, by Hecataeus of Miletus, 9, 81
Persica by Dionysius of Miletus, 13
Persica by Ctesias, 77, 81, 100
Pherecydes of Athens, early prose writer, 22 n.53
Philinus of Agrigentum, historian, 166 n.64, 175, 176
Philippica, see Theopompus
Philistus, historian of Sicily, 35, 62, 117, 134 n.61, 151, 152, 159, 160, 162
Philostratus, Life of Apollonius, 151
Phoronis, work by Hellanicus, 17
Photius, ninth century archbishop and epitomizer, 80, 82, 111, 116, 117, 121
Phylarchus, historian of Spartan revolution, 141, 176, 185
Plato, 3, 6, 90, 99, 111, 123, 162
Pliny, author of Natural History, 127
Plutarch, 26, 31, 35, 64, 77, 80, 109, 114, 128, 132, 140, 160, 162, 171

Polemon the Periegete, 156, 167 n.87
Polybius, 35, 97, 111, 112, 124, 154, 156, 157, 163, 169–182
Polycritus of Mende, historian of Sicily, 80
Porphyry, 22 n.45, 39
Posidonius, historian, 112, 158, 164
Ptolemy I Soter, Alexander's friend and biographer, 129–131, 132
Pythagoras of Samos, 7, 155
Pytheas of Massilia, explorer, 157–158, 167 n.97

Scylax, explorer and author of a *Periplus*, 9, 81
Ps. Scylax, author of a fourth century *Periplus*, 7, 11
Socrates, 88, 99, 155
Sophaenetus of Stymphalus, historian, 104 n.92
Sophocles, 15, 31, 44 n.53
Speusippus, Plato's successor, 117
Stephanus of Byzantine, 7
Strabo, geographer, 3, 11, 107, 112, 113, 142, 143, 144, 148

Strato of Lampsacus, Peripatetic philosopher, 173
*Suda*, tenth century Byzantine lexicon, 7, 14, 20 n.23, 27, 87, 107, 115, 141, 170, 171

Themistogenes of Syracuse (historian?), 91
Theopompus of Chios, 35, 39, 51, 107, 108, 111, 115–124, 125, 162
Thucydides, 2, 4, 25, 35, 38, 47–71, 86, 92, 94, 99, 109, 112, 114, 145, 160
Timaeus of Tauromenium, 4, 35, 67, 71, 125, 151–164, 174, 175, 176
Timonides of Leucas, 162
*Troica*, by Hellanicus, 17

Xanthus of Lydia, early historian, 12–14, 22 n.59
Xenocrates, Academic philosopher, 110, 153
Xenophon, 35, 51, 71, 80, 87–101, 181, 187
Ps. Xenophon. *See* Old Oligarch

Zoroaster, 122

1 2 3 4 5 6 7 8 9 10